Global Englishes in Asian Contexts

Also by Kumiko Murata

A CROSS-CULTURAL APPROACH TO THE ANALYSIS OF CONVERSATION AND ITS IMPLICATIONS FOR LANGUAGE PEDAGOGY (*1994*)

APPLIED LINGUISTICS AND LANGUAGE TEACHING IN JAPAN – A WIDDOWSONIAN PERSPECTIVE: Explorations into the Notion of Communicative Capacity (*co-edited with T. Harada, 2008, in Japanese – Komyunikeishon nouryoku ikusei saikou. Henry Widdowson to nihon no ouyougengo-gaku · gengo kyouiku*)

Also by Jennifer Jenkins

THE PHONOLOGY OF ENGLISH AS AN INTERNATIONAL LANGUAGE (2000)

ENGLISH AS A LINGUA FRANCA: Attitude and Identity (2007)

WORLD ENGLISHES (*2nd edition, 2009*)

Global Englishes in Asian Contexts

Current and Future Debates

Edited by

Kumiko Murata
Waseda University, Japan

and

Jennifer Jenkins
University of Southampton, UK

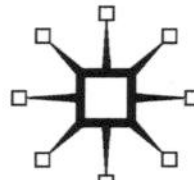

First published 2009 by
PALGRAVE MACMILLAN

Palgrave Macmillan in the UK is an imprint of Macmillan Publishers Limited, registered in England, company number 785998, of Houndmills, Basingstoke, Hampshire RG21 6XS.

Palgrave Macmillan in the US is a division of St Martin's Press LLC, 175 Fifth Avenue, New York, NY 10010.

Palgrave Macmillan is the global academic imprint of the above companies and has companies and representatives throughout the world.

Palgrave® and Macmillan® are registered trademarks in the United States, the United Kingdom, Europe and other countries.

ISBN-13: 978–0–230–22102–4 hardback
ISBN-10: 0-230-22102-5 hardback
ISBN:13: 978–0–230–22103–1 paperback
ISBN-10: 0-230-22103-3 paperback

This book is printed on paper suitable for recycling and made from fully managed and sustained forest sources. Logging, pulping and manufacturing processes are expected to conform to the environmental regulations of the country of origin.

A catalogue record for this book is available from the British Library.

A catalog record for this book is available from the Library of Congress.

Printed and bound in Great Britain by
CPI Antony Rowe, Chippenham and Eastbourne

To Professor Yasukata Yano for his major contribution to the debates on the varieties of English from an Asian perspective

Contents

Acknowledgements

We would like to thank the following institutions for allowing us to publish part of the materials which had originally been published with them:

Korea University Press for Kyung-Ja Park's article in Chapter 7
Waseda University Press for Yasukata Yano's article in Chapter 13

We would also like to thank Pathak Priyanka, Melanie Blair and Vidhya Jayaprakash of Palgrave Macmillan for their professional help, patience and understanding in preparing the volume for the publication; research assistants Charosporn Chalermtiarana and Takuro Harada for helping us with adjusting and preparing the computer environment ready for compiling and processing the information in preparation for the delivery; and last but not least, Barbara Seidlhofer and Henry Widdowson for their encouragement and advice on our pursuit of this project.

This book is dedicated by all its contributors to Yasukata Yano on the occasion of his retirement, in recognition of his major contribution to World Englishes in general and Asian Englishes in particular.

List of Contributors

Tej K. Bhatia is Professor in the Linguistics and Cognitive Sciences Program at Syracuse University, New York, USA.

Saran Gill is Professor of Sociolinguistics and Intercultural Communication in the School of Language Studies and Linguistics, Faculty of Social Sciences and Humanities, Universiti Kebangsaan Malaysia.

Tony T. N. Hung is a Professor in the Language Centre, Hong Kong Baptist University.

Jennifer Jenkins is Professor of English Language at the University of Southampton, UK.

Braj B. Kachru is Center for the Advanced Study Professor of Linguistics and Jubilee Professor of Liberal Arts and Sciences Emeritus, University of Illinois at Urbana-Champaign, Illinois, USA.

Yamuna Kachru is Professor Emerita, Department of Linguistics, University of Illinois at Urbana-Champaign, USA.

Morizumi Mamoru is Professor of English and English Language Teaching at the Graduate School of International Relations, Obirin University, Japan.

Kumiko Murata is Professor of English and Applied Linguistics at Waseda University, Japan.

Kyung-Ja Park is Professor Emeritus of Korea University, Korea.

Alastair Pennycook is Professor of Language Studies at the University of Technology Sydney.

Barbara Seidlhofer is Professor of English and Applied Linguistics at the University of Vienna.

Larry E. Smith is Executive Director of the International Association for World Englishes (IAWE), Inc. Smith's background of experience includes more than two decades as a researcher and administrator at the East-West Center in Honolulu, Hawaii. He is the co-founding editor of the professional journal *World Englishes* with Braj B. Kachru.

Henry Widdowson is Emeritus Professor of Education, University of London and Honorary Professor at the University of Vienna.

Yasukata Yano is Professor of Applied Linguistics at Waseda University, Japan.

1

Introduction: Global Englishes from Global Perspectives

Kumiko Murata and Jennifer Jenkins

The spread of English and its influence are unprecedented compared with other languages in that the diffusion is far-reaching globally. This volume explores the spread of English in the world or global Englishes, and English as a lingua franca (ELF), also known as English as an international language (EIL) from varying perspectives, focusing specifically, but not exclusively, on Asian Englishes as used in their local contexts. The volume is unique mainly in two accounts: first, its overarching theme seen, in particular, from Asian perspectives; and second, its divergent contributors across languages and cultures mostly from Asia but also from other parts of the world. Although there are now a number of books which specifically focus on Englishes in Asian contexts, a volume which satisfies both of the above-mentioned points is a rarity.

The book, accordingly, is of multi-perspective, and offers an invaluable opportunity for language practitioners, scholars and students with differing perspectives and points of view on this issue to exchange opinions, participating in the discussions directly or indirectly, reflecting on differing views and contributing to enrich and deepen the discussions in the field. But first, we shall elaborate on these two perspectives in more detail.

The use of English in Asian contexts

We first need to discuss what is meant by 'Asia'; the concept of Asia is ever-expanding, as Pennycook (this volume) points out, so that it sometimes includes the countries of the Middle East, and even Australia and New Zealand (see also Y. Kachru and Nelson 2006). Even if we limit the region to the traditional, geographical Asian countries, it includes East Asia, which consists of countries such as China, Korea and Japan, and

South East Asia, which comprises countries such as Indonesia, Singapore and Malaysia, and then South Asian countries such as Bangladesh, India and Pakistan (see also Y. Kachru and Nelson 2006; Yano, this volume). These wide-ranging regions with their different social, historical, religious, cultural and language backgrounds have adapted and adopted English in various spheres of their lives for intra- and international communication. They form currently one of the most exciting regions of the world, one in which we can witness dynamic uses of English for various practical reasons, including social, cultural, economic and political ones, and they can also be said to be one of the most prominent regions in which the future of Englishes resides.

Accordingly, Englishes in Asia have recently attracted much attention and been the focus of a number of publications, including some by contributors to the current volume (see B. Kachru 2005; Y. Kachru and Nelson 2006, among others) and also some that deal with specific varieties of English in Asian contexts such as China English, Hong Kong English and Japanese English (see Adamson 2004; Bolton (ed.) 2002; and Stanlaw 2004, for example). There is also an academic journal dedicated to studies of Asian Englishes.[1] Thus, the question might arise: Why now another volume on Englishes in Asia? Answering this question leads us to the second of our unique features, namely, the participation of the contributors from differing 'camps' in the field of global Englishes, which we shall now discuss in more detail.

Global English(es), world English(es), EIL and ELF

As briefly touched upon in the preceding section, varying uses of English worldwide have been discussed under differing nomenclatures, such as global Englishes (Pennycook 2007), global language (Crystal 1997; Gnutzmann (ed.) 1999), world English(es) (WE) (Brutt-Griffler 2002; Jenkins 2003/2009; B. Kachru 1985, 1990, 1992, 1995, 2005, this volume; B. Kachru and Nelson 1996; Kirkpatrick 2007; Smith (ed.) 1987; Smith and Forman (eds) 1997; Strevens 1982), English as an international language (EIL) (Jenkins 2000; Smith (ed.) 1983; Strevens 1992) or international English (Trudgill and Hannah 1985) and English as a lingua franca (ELF) (House 2003; Jenkins 1998, 2000, 2002, 2007; B. Kachru 1996; Seidlhofer 2001, 2003, 2004, among others).

The proponents of WE are most notably represented by B. Kachru, who, together with L. Smith, launched one of the most influential academic journals in the field, *World Englishes*, in 1982, and whose classification of the English-speaking world into the three concentric circles of the Inner, the Outer and the Expanding (see B. Kachru, this volume; and Y. Kachru, this volume) is most influential in the history of the development of the field and widely quoted in numerous academic publications. It also plays an important role in this volume, being referred to directly or indirectly by most of the contributors to the volume (see Bhatia, Gill, Jenkins, Y. Kachru, Morizumi, Pennycook, Seidlhofer and Widdowson, Smith, and Yano, this volume). With the rapidly changing picture of the English-speaking world and the complex nature of social, economic, political and cultural dynamics of people all over the world, however, there have recently been suggestions of the need for modification or expansion of this classification (see Pennycook 2007 and this volume; Yano 2001 and this volume, for examples). It is, however, without any doubt that the notion has immensely influenced the development of the academic field and promoted the establishment of the legitimacy of world Englishes, their users and accompanying identities connected to respective Englishes, in both local contexts and international and intercultural settings, where people use their own varieties of English as an international lingua franca. Thus, the notion of WE is closely connected to that of ELF. Both world Englishes and ELF are by nature more centrifugal and diversifying, since they are not constrained by native-speaker (NS) English norms. The same is true for the notions of EIL and ELF although ELF is sometimes (mis)interpreted as being centripetal by virtue of the fact that it enables people with differing mother tongues and Englishes to communicate internationally and interculturally through English.

There are occasionally two seemingly contradictory notions associated with the global spread of English: first, one that sounds almost triumphant because of its focus on the influence and currency of English in its worldwide diffusion as a means of communication at wide-ranging levels of culture, economy, education, politics, science and personal and that assumes the ownership of English by the Inner Circle 'native' speakers of English who are the main beneficiaries and executors of this power (see Crystal 1997, among others); and second, a notion which is closely associated with English used in international and intercultural settings as a means of communication both in the interactions between 'native' speakers (NSs) and 'non-native' speakers (NNSs) of the language, but increasingly in those among NNSs from varying language and cultural backgrounds (see Jenkins 1998, 2000, 2002, 2007; Seidlhofer 2001, 2003, 2004; Widdowson 1997). In the latter case, the acronym ELF has recently been used to describe this characteristic, to which we shall now turn.

The term ELF is used, particularly by Anglo-European scholars in the field, in describing communicative interactions among mainly, but not exclusively, NNSs of English who use English as their chosen tool for communication in international and intercultural settings. Often in these interactions, no 'native' speakers of English are involved or, if they are, they are in the minority among the interactants (see House 2003; Jenkins 2007, this volume; Seidlhofer 2001 for the definitions of ELF). Increasingly, these days, most of the English communication in international and intercultural settings is likely to be ELF or EIL communication, where interactants who do not share a language cannot help using a language of their 'choice' as a means of communication, and in current international communicative situations it is most likely to be English with its global spread (see Graddol 2006, for example). In this situation, intelligibility (see Nelson 1982; Smith 1992, and this volume; Smith and Nelson 1985) among the users of ELF or EIL is essential, and extensive research has been conducted specifically focusing on it (see, e.g., Jenkins 2000, 2002; Seidlhofer 2003, among others). Here, to achieve intelligibility, a certain degree of convergence seems to be inevitable among diversifying users of English. The issue, then, is to what extent? For this purpose, large-scaled empirical research such as the Vienna Oxford International Corpus of English (VOICE) project is promising (see Seidlhofer and Widdowson, this volume), together with Jenkins's empirical research on the Lingua Franca Core (see Jenkins 1998, 2000, 2002, and this volume). It is also essential to achieve, in particular, what Smith (this volume) terms 'comprehensibility' and 'interpretability', which are particularly important in achieving cultural understanding, and thus, they receive special attention in the chapters by Y. Kachru (Chapter 8), Morizumi (Chapter 6) and Park (Chapter 7) as well as in Smith (Chapter 2) in this volume.

On the other hand, there is also another move which tries to reconcile the two tendencies of centrifugal and centripetal forces of English. Pennycook (this volume), for example, argues that a term 'plurilithic' English should be used to avoid, on the one hand, the region-based reproduction of the authority or the power of 'native speakers' and, on the other, the lack of integrity and comprehensibility. This, Pennycook further states, also encompasses Yano's (2001, 2008, and this volume) conceptualization of regional standard varieties of English, where Yano claims that English could converge into several regional standard Englishes such as Asian, European and Arabic Englishes, which represent regional acrolectal Englishes and yet also be intelligible to communicators outside the regions in international settings. Yano's paradigm is insightful; however, it has also been pointed out that in certain genres of English (for example, in youth culture) people are also communicating or expressing their views inter-regionally and internationally at meso- and basilectal levels, not necessarily always at acrolectal level (see Jenkins 2003/2009 and this volume; Pennycook 2007 and this volume, for examples).

Many of these terms are, on the face of it, different, but in reality they are used to describe the same phenomenon of the spread of English from slightly different perspectives, and with different foci and emphases. In this volume, we will use the term 'global Englishes', which covers all the above-mentioned notions and is of inclusive nature. It represents the diversifying nature of Englishes used worldwide, and yet simultaneously describes people's efforts to be intelligible in intercultural settings, negotiating meanings and enjoying creativity while retaining their own identities. Thus, we believe the term encompasses both centrifugal and centripetal natures of WE, EIL or ELF simultaneously.

We shall now turn to yet another perspective included in the volume, that is, the varying views from different cultural and language traditions of the different contributors.

Global Englishes from global perspectives

This volume also brings in perspectives from the Kachuruvian 'Expanding' Circle, as well as the 'Inner' and 'Outer' Circles at the level of contributors to the volume. This is significant since most of the discussions at the international level in the field so far are mainly lead by scholars from the Inner and the Outer Circles as well as the European Expanding Circle. By contrast, the volume also includes contributors from the Asian Expanding Circle, such as Japanese and Korean contributors. In order to reflect this diversity maximally, the volume fully respects each contributor's descriptions and views on the issue as well as their discourse and writing styles. Thus, no 'native speaker' English norms are prescriptively applied in terms of the lexico-grammatical features either. Furthermore, the contributors present differing views on the role and future of English, and naturally their views do not necessarily coincide with those of each other or the editors. In fact, they quite often have diversifying views; some regard language and culture as more fluid entities, while others regard them as more culture specific. We believe, however, that it is essential to include these differing views and voices in this volume. They are, in fact, all closely related to the extent that all of them are deeply concerned with the influence of the spread and diffusion of English at global as well as local levels. We shall now introduce each of these contributions in more detail.

The structure of the volume

The volume is divided into four main parts. Part I (Chapters 2–4) introduces the notions of WE, EIL and ELF, which are all related and have emerged together with the global spread of English. It also examines their communicative potentials and intelligibility in international, intranational and intercultural situations, illustrating, for example, how ELF users produce their own communities of practice and identity in its creative use, accommodating to each other. The three chapters in Part II (Chapters 5–7) focus on the issues of identity, ideology and attitudes in the use of varying Asian Englishes in their local contexts, referring also to language policies. Part III (Chapters 8–10) explores the actual use of the varieties of English in Asian academic and business contexts on the basis of the contributors' (Y. Kachru, Gill and Bhatia) research on both spoken and written discourses in advertising, school and workplace settings. Finally, Part IV (Chapters 11–13) concludes with discussions on the future of Englishes with a possible paradigm shift in mind. In the following, we shall elaborate on each part in a more detailed manner.

Part I comprises three chapters by Smith (Chapter 2), Seidlhofer and Widdowson (Chapter 3) and Jenkins (Chapter 4). Smith deals with cross-cultural understanding from the perspective of the three dimensions of intelligibility, comprehensibility and interpretability, starting with an explication of the terms. He then moves on to definitions of culture and what is meant by 'cross-cultural' with elaborations on the four stages of culture learning and understanding. He further elaborates on definitions of communication and illustrates them with various examples of meaning in different cultural and language contexts, particularly focusing on 'interpretability'. Smith concludes the chapter with some practical suggestions for better understanding in WE communication. The chapter thus consists of some theoretical underpinning with useful definitions and illustrations based on Smith's long-standing and wide-ranging experiences in dealing with actual cross-cultural communication.

Based on Sinclair's (1991) idiom principle, Seidlhofer and Widdowson (Chapter 3) demonstrate how this can be applied to ELF communication. Using the data from the VOICE Project, they illustrate how the interactants from varying language and cultural backgrounds exploit and modify the principle, co-constructing ELF-specific expressions for communicative purposes, creating and enjoying new ELF idiomaticity. This is a promising and foreseeable future scenario where people whose native tongue is not English use (and own) English (Widdowson 1994) as a lingua franca of their own free will and in their style, introducing their creativity and originality into the communities of practice (Wenger 1998). It opens up all sorts of possibilities in future ELF communication, which is not constrained by NS English norms.

In her article, Jenkins (Chapter 4), like Seidlhofer and Widdowson (Chapter 3), focuses on English in the Expanding Circle, and especially on the use of ELF among its Expanding Circle Asian users. Given that ELF is a relatively new and often poorly understood concept, she begins by clarifying how ELF is defined by the majority of its researchers, and in particular, she explains ELF's essential differences from traditional English as a foreign language (EFL). She goes on to describe some of the features that have been identified in ELF corpora as potential features of ELF use, pointing out how these features bear both similarities to and differences from developments in native English. She then turns to two types of strategies that characterize ELF speakers' use of English: accommodation and code-switching, and demonstrates how speakers accommodate and code-switch, making use of their multilingual resources, in order to signal group membership and solidarity and to enhance intelligibility, rather than – as is so often assumed in the EFL literature – to compensate for gaps in knowledge. Jenkins focuses in the final part of her article on responses to ELF, and on the implications of ELF for English speakers in the Asian Expanding Circle, stating that ELF may offer them more relevant and meaningful linguistic opportunities.

Part II starts with Hung (Chapter 5), who focuses specifically on Singapore English. Being inspired by Shaw's *Pygmalion* (hereafter *P&M* after Hung) and transferring the context to the current Singaporean situation, Hung satirically describes the use of English in Singapore, where the Cockney equivalent of Singlish is widely used among Singaporeans in informal intra-national communication and also as a lingua franca with the speakers of other languages. Its use, however, is stigmatized, in particular, due to the government's language policy, which promotes the use of acrolectal standard Singapore English in public. Illustrating the use of Singlish and its characteristics in the framework of *P&M*, Hung tactfully criticizes the government's language policy on the promotion of 'standard' Singapore English, which ignores the communicative and practical use of English by Singaporeans and could jeopardize their identity.

Just like Hung, Morizumi (Chapter 6) deals with the issue of language, culture, identity and power with specific reference to English used in Japan. Intentionally using the term EIAL (English as one of the international auxiliary languages) (see Smith 1976 as well) to avoid the power associated with other terms (Morizumi, this volume), he also argues that a polymodel stance should be taken in discussing the use of English, particularly in consideration with its connection with culture and language. Although Morizumi's description of the characteristics of Japanese English is largely based on and in comparison with 'native-speaker' models, he insists that culture-specific features and creativity in the use of English in its local context should be considered. He concludes the chapter by suggesting that the current global trends in the varying use of the varieties of English should be taught at school level and that this could be dealt with, for example, by introducing the issue into the hugely influential MEXT- (the Japanese Ministry of Education, Sports, Science and Technology) approved school textbooks at secondary level in Japan. Although the suggestion may sound very much locally oriented, it has implications for similar situations in differing cultural and language contexts.

Just like Hung and Morizumi, Park (Chapter 7) writes from the culture-specific perspective of Korea English (KE). She asserts that it is only a matter of time before Korea English becomes a recognized variety of English – what she terms a glocalized variety. Herein, she characterizes KE, focusing particularly on the influences from Korean cultural values, which heavily reflect Confucianism. Park concludes her chapter by emphasizing the importance of teaching this variety of English with its cultural specificities to Korean English learners as well as overseas business people who are likely to interact with Korean counterparts.

There are then some similarities between the characteristics of Japanese English presented by Morizumi (Chapter 6) and those of Korea English listed by Park (Chapter 7), particularly in their cultural traits, perhaps partly because Japanese culture and communication styles are also indirectly influenced by Confucianism. The younger generations, however, are rapidly changing their cultural assumptions and values, and thus, this tendency is worth further investigating in the future.

Part III focuses on Englishes used in academic and business contexts in Asia. Chapter 8, by Y. Kachru, focuses mainly on the use of English in academic contexts in India. It explores scientific writing across disciplines as well as across languages and cultures. In particular, Y. Kachru emphasizes the importance of recognizing the cultural conventions and values reflected in the seemingly generic structures of scientific writing, and urges us to investigate more into the field, not assuming that they are universal. On the basis of a study on Indian high school students' scientific writing, Y. Kachru also states that teaching its generic features as well as investigating the possibility of culture specificity is essential. The message here is that in considering localized varieties of English in various genres we should simultaneously seek for the reconciliation between genre and culture specificities in order to keep global intelligibility and local identity.

The next two chapters by Gill (Chapter 9) and Bhatia (Chapter 10) focus mainly on business and commercial discourses in Asian contexts. Gill (Chapter 9), starting with the historical background to the use of English in Malaysia together with its language policy, moves on to the discussion of the sub-varieties of formal Malaysian English on the basis of the results from her own survey on their perception and acceptability by gatekeepers in Malaysian business industries. It is interesting to see here that the Malaysian business executives who participated in Gill's study judged the acceptability of the varieties on the basis of the assumed interactants, accommodating to the interactant types. They are reported to employ the exonormative NS English standards when the assumed interactants are NSs, while in ELF communication less prescriptive norms are employed. Here we could observe the reality and dynamics of people's attitudes towards and perceptions of the use of sub-varieties of English and the perceptions of ordinary language users on this issue. Gill persuasively demonstrates it in her study.

Bhatia in Chapter 10 specifically explores advertising in Asian contexts and describes how advertisers or business industries utilize the power of English in its local context, using code-mixing and in its process also creatively using their own localized variety of English to make advertisement more powerful and persuasive. Thus, Bhatia deals with the issue of globalization and localization simultaneously in this specific field and demonstrates the positive effects of widespread code-mixing in Asian advertising. At the same time, he also illustrates how blurring of the boundaries among the three different Kachruvian concentric circles, particularly between the Outer and the Expanding Circles, is occurring. This is partly demonstrated by examples of advertising from both the Outer and the Expanding Circles. Bhatia's study is insightful in that it illustrates how the users of varieties of English in local contexts actually own the language and feel free to utilize it creatively and freely, changing it and adjusting it to produce maximum effects and originality, just as Seidlhofer and Widdowson's (this volume) ELF users are observed to be using ELF creatively. Here, the varieties of English users are described actively and positively as the owners of their own variety, not being constrained by the exonormative Inner Circle English standards. Bhatia vividly illustrates what is currently happening in the use of English in Asian contexts and predicts what will perhaps happen in various parts of the world in the future. This leads us to Part IV, which discusses the future of English.

Part IV comprises three chapters by B. Kachru (Chapter 11), Pennycook (Chapter 12) and Yano (Chapter 13), who all discuss the frameworks for the future of Englishes, referring to each other's theoretical frameworks.

B. Kachru in Chapter 11, with the comprehensive explication of and elaboration on the field, promotes multilingual perspectives in dealing with world Englishes. The chapter covers wide-ranging issues related to the field such as the ideology of English, multilingualism, creativity, pluralism, globalization and multi-canons, all in relation to the use of Englishes, in particular Asian Englishes. As one of the prominent founders of the field of WE, B. Kachru's discussion is, in terms of both its coverage and depth, very comprehensive and thorough, referring also to literary creativity. Furthermore, it is also written from the perspective of teaching world Englishes in their cross-cultural contexts, and thus, his discussion is balanced also with implications for language teaching and cross-cultural communication. The chapter persuasively claims the necessity of a paradigm shift in order to accommodate to the current situation.

Pennycook (Chapter 12), starting with Yano's (2001) framework, moves on to critically review both the Kachruvian concentric circle model of WE and the ELF model and proposes a more fluid one, which, according to him, incorporates language users and specific contexts of use. The differences in the models he refers to, however, seem to be largely terminological, as we discussed earlier, seen from slightly different perspectives and with different emphasis. Further development of the discussion on Pennycook's model, however, is much desired as it seems to be showing another way of interpreting the future development of the field. We shall now turn to Yano (Chapter 13), whose framework has been much discussed in Pennycook.

Yano's scenario for the future of English is the emergence of regional standard Englishes (RSEes), which are used by people within the wider regions of, for example, Asia, Africa and Europe (intra-RSEes) and show the characteristics of respective regions but also are intelligible to other regional standard English users. Starting with discussion on how change in the use of English is inevitable with time and its expansion in various parts of the world, Yano presents some illustrative examples of its use from various parts of Asia.

Along with the region-based model of English, Yano introduces standards on the basis of the genre-specific proficiency model, where the achievement of ESP (English for specific purposes) proficiency is placed above the EGP (English for general purposes) one. This dual framework is useful, including two different dimensions of regional differences and genre-specific proficiency in its discussion. Although it could be too complex, particularly with the inclusion of the three Kachruvian concentric models also in the framework, an attempt to combine the three influential models in one framework is ambitious. It will be interesting to see whether these regional standard Englishes develop and people in these wider regions communicate with each other with their own varieties of English, owning and using English in their own styles, which simultaneously makes it possible to communicate with people inter-regionally. This, then, could also be one of the promising future scenarios.

To conclude, the volume takes multi-perspectives, just as there are varieties of English (WE) and varying ways of approaching communicative situations where English is used as an international lingua franca (ELF). The future scenario by the contributors to this volume may not necessarily converge into one framework, paradigm or terminology, but it is closely connected with one consistent and recurrent message, that is, all contributors, although they may be using slightly different terminologies and frameworks, believe in multilingualism, multiculturalism, the creativity of the varieties of English users and their accompanying identities, while paying attention also to intelligibility of ELF or EIL communication.

Note

1. See *Asian Englishes* published by ALC Press, Tokyo.

References

Adamson, B. 2004. *China's English*. Hong Kong: Hong Kong University Press.

Bolton, K. (ed.) 2002. *Hong Kong English: Autonomy and Creativity*. Hong Kong: Hong Kong University Press.

Brutt-Griffler, J. 2002. *World English: A study of its development*. Clevedon: Multilingual Matters.

Crystal, D. 1997. *English as a Global Language*. Cambridge: Cambridge University Press.

Gnutzmann, C. (ed.) 1999. *Teaching and Learning English as a Global Language.* Tubingen: Stauffenburg-Verl.

Graddol, D. 2006. *English Next.* London: British Council.

House, J. 2003. 'English as a lingua franca: A threat to multilingualism?' *Journal of Sociolinguistics,* 7, 556–78.

Jenkins, J. 1998. 'Which pronunciation norms and models for English as an International Language?' *ELT Journal* 52(2), 119–26.

——. 2000. *Phonology of English as an International Language.* Oxford: Oxford University Press.

——. 2002. 'A sociolinguistically based, empirically researched pronunciation syllabus for English as an International Language.' *Applied Linguistics* 23(1), 83–103.

——. 2003. *World Englishes.* London: Routledge.

——. 2007. *English as a Lingua Franca: Attitude and Identity.* Oxford: Oxford University Press.

——. 2009. *World Englishes.* 2nd ed. London: Routledge.

Kachru, B. B. (ed.) 1982. *The Other Tongue: English across Cultures.* Urbana, IL: University of Illinois Press.

——. 1985. 'Standards, codification, and sociolinguistic realism: the English language in the outer circle.' In R. Quirk and H. G. Widdowson (eds) *English in the world.* Cambridge: Cambridge University Press.

——. 1990. 'World Englishes and applied linguistics.' *World Englishes,* 9(1), 3–20.

——. (ed.) 1992. *The Other Tongue: English across Cultures.* 2nd ed. Urbana, IL: University of Illinois Press.

——. 1995. 'Transcultural creativity in World Englishes and literary canons.' In G. Cook and B. Seidlhofer (eds) *Principle and Practice in Applied Linguistics.* Oxford: Oxford University Press. pp. 271–87.

——. 1996. 'English as lingua franca.' In H. Goebl, P. H. Nelde, I. Stary and W. Wölck (eds) *Contact Linguistics: An International Handbook of Contemporary Research.* Berlin: Walter de Gruyter.

——. 2005. *Asian Englishes beyond the Canon.* Hong Kong: Hong Kong University Press.

——. and C. L. Nelson 1996. 'World Englishes.' In McKay. S. L. and N. H. Hornberger (eds) *Sociolinguistics in Language Teaching.* Cambridge: Cambridge Unviersity Press, pp. 71–102.

Kachru, Y. and C. L. Nelson 2006. *World Englishes in Asian Contexts.* Hong Kong: Hong Kong University Press.

Kirkpatrick, A. 2007. *World Englishes.* Cambridge: Cambridge University Press.

Nelson, C. L. 1982. Intelligibility and non-native varieties of English. In B. B. Kachru (ed.) *The Other Tongue: English across cultures.* Urbana: University of Illinois Press, pp. 58–73.

Pennycook, A. 2007. *Global Englishes and Transcultural Flows.* London: Routledge.

Rubdy, R. and M. Saraceni 2006. 'Introduction.' In R. Rubdy and M. Saraceni (eds) *English in the World: Global Rules, Global Roles.* London: Continuum, pp. 5–16.

Seidlhofer, B. 2001. 'Closing a conceptual gap: the case for a description of English as a lingua franca.' *International Journal of Applied Linguistics,* 11, 133–58.

——. 2003. *A Concept of International English and Related Issues: From 'Real English' to 'Realistic English'?* Strasbourg: Council of Europe.

——. 2004. 'Research perspectives on teaching English as a lingua franca.' *Annual Review of Applied Linguistics,* 24, 209–39.

Sinclair, J. M. 1991. *Corpus, concordance, collocation.* Oxford: Oxford University Press.

Smith, L. E. 1976. 'English as an international auxiliary language.' *RELC Journal,* 7(2), 38–42.

——. (ed.) 1983. *Readings in English as an International Language.* Oxford: Pergamon.

——. 1992. 'Spread of English and issues of intelligibility.' In B. B. Kachru (ed.) *The Other Tongue: English across cultures,* 2nd ed. Urbana, IL: University of Illinois Press, pp. 75–90.

——. and Nelson, C. L. 1985. 'International intelligibility of English: Directions and resources.' *World Englishes,* 4, 333–42.

Stanlaw, J. 2004. *Japanese English: Language and Culture Contact.* Hong Kong: Hong Kong University Press.

Strevens, P. 1982. 'World English and the world's English – or, whose language is it anyway?' *Journal of the Royal Society of Arts,* 120, 418–31.

——. 1992. 'English as an international language: Directions in the 1990s.' In B. B. Kachru (ed.) *The Other Tongue: English across cultures,* 2nd ed. Urbana, IL: University of Illinois Press, pp. 27–47.

Trudgill, P. and J. Hannah 1985. *International English: A Guide to Varieties of Standard English.* London: Edward Arnold.

Wenger, E. 1998. *Communities of practice.* Cambridge: Cambridge University Press.

Widdowson, H. G. 1994. 'The ownership of English?' *TESOL Quarterly* 28(2), 377–89.

——. 1997. 'EIL, ESL, EFL: Global issues and local interests.' *World Englishes,* 16, 135–46.

Yano, Y. 2001. 'World Englishes in 2000 and beyond.' *World Englishes,* 20, 119–31.

——. 2008. 'Kokusai-go toshiteno eigo – kako • genzai • mirai (English as an international language – past, present, and future).' In K. Murata and T. Harada (eds) *Komyunikeishon nouryoku ikusei saikou. Henry Widdowson to nihon no ouyougengo-gaku • gengo kyouiku (Applied Linguistics and Language Teaching in Japan – A Widdowsonian Perspective: Explorations into the Notion of Communicative Capacity).* Tokyo: Hitsuji Shobo, pp. 205–27.

Part I

Understanding Englishes and English as a Lingua Franca (ELF) in Asia

2
Dimensions of Understanding in Cross-Cultural Communication

Larry E. Smith

Introduction

Although we may never be able to totally understand another's feelings or perspective in a cross-cultural situation (B. Kachru 1992, 2005; Y. Kachru and Smith 2008; Nelson 1995), we can attempt to increase our likelihood of understanding or at least decrease the possibility of our misunderstanding by developing a greater awareness of three of the dimensions of understanding (intelligibility, comprehensibility and interpretability).

We frequently hear people say, 'I don't understand him.' When we ask, 'Why?' sometimes the answer is, 'He garbles his words and never speaks clearly.' Sometimes, 'He speaks with such ambiguity that I don't know what he means.' Sometimes, 'His speech is clear and his words are simple, but I'm never clear about his intentions.'

Three dimensions of understanding

The above demonstrates that understanding has at least three dimensions (Smith and Nelson 2006). They are:

1. Intelligibility: the degree to which one is able to recognize a word or utterance spoken by another;
2. Comprehensibility: the degree to which one is able to ascertain a meaning from another's word or utterance; and
3. Interpretability: the degree to which one is able to perceive the intention behind another's word or utterance.

To illustrate these dimensions, let me use two examples. One is from the American poet, e e cummings and his poem, 'Anyone lived in a pretty how town'. If I were to say a few lines of the poem aloud at conversational speed with proper pausing and there was no disturbing outside noise, you would most likely be able to repeat it easily.

anyone lived// in a pretty how town//
(with up so floating// many bells down)//
spring summer autumn winter//
he sang his didn't// he danced his did//

If you were able to correctly repeat the lines after me, I would say that your intelligibility of my speech was high. I could also check your intelligibility of my speaking by asking you to write down, line by line, what I said.

children guessed (but only a few)
and down they forgot as up they grew

No doubt you could also do that without error, if you were interested and there was no outside noise to interfere.

If, however, we talk about comprehensibility, i.e. a possible meaning of these lines, you may not have much confidence that your comprehension is similar to anyone else's. If we ask about the intentionality, i.e. the interpretability, of the author when writing these lines, you may have no clue as to what it is.

The second example is from a Thai sentence, spoken by a male and written here in a (Mary Haas) phonemic alphabet.

'Khun kamlang ca pai nai khrab?'

This sentence is often shortened, among friends, to *'Pai nai?'* If I asked you how many syllables are in the last utterance, you could answer, 'Two', easily. If I requested that you repeat the utterance or write it using the English alphabet, you probably could do that without much trouble. If so, that would demonstrate that your intelligibility of the sentence was high.

If I told you that if we translate the elements of the sentence into English, we would learn that *pai* means go and *nai* means where. You would then have a comprehension of these two parts of the sentence. If I required you to guess a possible meaning of the utterance, you might say, 'Where are you going?' If so, your comprehension would be high.

If I asked you what the speaker's purpose was, you might say, 'The speaker wants to know where I am going.' In fact, that is not correct and would show that your interpretability is low. This Thai sentence is used as a greeting. In the same way that Americans say, 'How are you?' Thai males say, *'Khun kamlang ca pai nai khrab?'* or just *'Pai nai'* (Where are you going?). It is what linguists call 'phatic communion'. It is just to show politeness and is not a real question at all. The appropriate response is, 'To the market' or, 'On business'. It is formulaic and most cultures have greetings like this in common use. Once you realize this is a greeting, then your interpretability would be high.

These examples and our own life experience make it clear that we can have high intelligibility with low comprehensibility; and high comprehensibility with little or no interpretability. These are three dimensions of understanding. They are not elements which build on each other. They do not always follow the same learning sequence with intelligibility being first and interpretability being last. Intelligibility usually, but not always, refers to perceptions of speech, whereas comprehensibility commonly refers to what is spoken or printed.

So, those are the dimensions of understanding mentioned in the title of this chapter. Perhaps we should also offer an operational definition of the other terms used there.

Definition of terms

The meaning of 'cross-cultural'

'Cross' in the title means 'across' or 'between/among'. *Cross* is connected to *cultural* and the root word in 'cultural' is culture. I define culture as shared ways of behaviour which are *learned* that *groups* of people use to understand and interpret the world. These include customs, beliefs, values and conventions of communication. (Contrast this with *Human Nature* which is *inherited* and shared by *all* humanity; e.g. the emotions of fear, love, anger and lust, vs. *Personality* which is both *inherited* and *learned* and is *individual*.)

The meaning of 'culture'

There are several levels of culture within each of us:

National: e.g. Japanese; French; Chinese
Regional: e.g. Southern US; Pacific; Russian Far East
Ethnic: e.g. Hawaiian; Ilokano; Polish

Gender:	Male; Female (this doesn't refer to biology but to the socialization process that each culture agrees is the appropriate behaviour for males and females)
Generation:	e.g. What decade is most important to you? Generation X; Y; Z
Social:	e.g. White collar vs. blue collar
Religious:	e.g. Hindu; Moslem; Christian; Jewish
Corporate:	e.g. Sony is different from Fujitsu
University:	e.g. Graduate school vs. undergraduate

For some people, ethnic cultural identity is a key to understanding who they are, while others have little awareness or appreciation of it. Events that occur during the particular period of time in which people are raised often shape their lives and give identity to their generation. Television and computers have greatly affected baby boomers. Some specific events are so impressive that they need no further explanation or description. For example, '9/11' or 'the death of Princess Diana'. Certain influences are so pervasive that the majority of people's lives have been touched by them, such as the global marketplace with Yahoo! and Google, the spread of AIDS, the changing role of women in the workplace and in the family, and demographic changes in the world. If we are to understand others, we will have to know something about the levels of culture from which they draw their primary identity.

Four stages of culture learning and understanding

There are four stages of culture learning and understanding in cross-cultural situations (see Table 2.1). From my experience, I've chosen three references: Bruce Tuckman, Gregory Trifonovitch, and M. Scott Peck. Each describes the four stages with different names but very similar meanings.

In Stage 1, all interaction is pleasant as we get to know one another. We hear ourselves saying things like, 'This is a BEAUTIFUL place.' In this stage, there is a pretence of equality among everyone. At Stage 2, things are

Table 2.1 Four stages of culture learning and understanding (based on Tuckman 1965, Trifonovitch 1972 and Peck 1987)

1. FORMING	Honeymoon	Pseudocommunity
2. STORMING	Hostility	Chaos
3. NORMING	Humour	Emptiness
4. PERFORMING	Home	Community

different. We recognize some serious problems. The situation is disturbing and we feel a need to change things and make them 'right'. At Stage 3, we recognize that the way things are done here may be appropriate for these circumstances and people here. We understand how it works and we can laugh at our 'out-of-place' (inappropriate) behaviour. We decide that we don't have to do it 'our way'. At Stage 4, we can operate successfully. This can be a comfortable place to be. We are not afraid of difference or disagreement. We can express happiness when we are happy but we can also admit to being afraid or lonely when those are our feelings.

It has been my experience that these stages don't happen to everyone the same way and don't always move in the same order. You may get stuck in one or another may become your default position. You may find yourself at the 'Home' stage at some point but then return to the 'Hostility' stage as a result of an event or behaviour of a colleague or friend.

Perhaps that is enough for now about the term 'cross-cultural' from the title and we can move to 'communication'.

Various meanings of communication

For me, to communicate is to *share meaning/value/emotion*. This can be done in all kinds of ways but it is usually through a system of symbols, often in language. Communication is not just an exchange of information. Machines are able to exchange information, e.g. in data processing, but machines do not share meaning. Honeybees move their bodies (dance?) to transmit information but as far as we can tell, they do not share meaning/value/emotion.

According to Ogden and Richards in their book, *The Meaning of Meaning* (1923), meaning 'resides in the recipient as well as the originator of the thought'. In other words there must be a 'negotiation of meaning' between the sender and the receiver, the speaker and the listener.

Miscellaneous examples

Because English is the linguistic code most frequently used in international cross-cultural communication, the examples which follow are all in English. Because my experience has been primarily in Asia and the Pacific, I am going to draw my examples from that region. We all recognize that contemporary English vocabulary is being enriched by different national culture groups in Asia but that sometimes we don't understand what is being said. It may be a problem with intelligibility or comprehensibility or interpretability.

In India or in Indian writing, we are likely to hear the term *prepone* and it is unlikely that anyone would find it unintelligible. That is they could repeat it or write it down. The problem would be that there would be little, if any, comprehensibility. We need be taught that 'prepone' is used as the opposite of 'postpone' so that when something is 'preponed', it is brought forward on our calendar in the same way that when something is 'postponed', it is delayed. Once we learn that, the term is clear in comprehensibility.

From Thailand the term *minor wife* may be easily intelligible and we may guess (our comprehension) that the wife being spoken about is not the most important one, or not major. This comprehension is partly correct but the interpretation will be insufficient until someone explains that a minor wife is a woman with an important position with a man and may be the mother of some of his children but that she is often not a legal wife or the wife of official status. She is however more than a mistress and certainly not a prostitute.

In China the term *barefoot doctor* is surely intelligible to non-Chinese and those people may comprehend it as a physician without shoes, but it in fact refers to a poorly trained person who does health-related work in rural areas.

In Singapore if a person is called a *mountain turtle*, s/he will have no trouble with the intelligibility of the term and depending upon his/her feelings toward turtles, may feel complimented or insulted, but s/he is unlikely to interpret it correctly as a person from the countryside who is unfamiliar with urban customs and situations.

If a person in Japan identifies her/himself as a *paper driver*, no non-Japanese is likely to find the intelligibility of the term difficult at all, but probably most non-Japanese will have no idea of the comprehensibility or the interpretability of the term. Almost all non-Japanese need to be taught that a paper driver is one who holds a legal driver's license but does not consider her/himself competent as a driver and usually uses the license only as a means of identification when legally necessary.

Forms of address, politeness, irony and understatement

Different forms of address (Gaudart 1999) can also be sources of difficulty at each of the three dimensions of understanding. Thais use a title plus given name, as in 'Khun John', but it should not be misunderstood that Thais are on a 'first name basis' with others immediately. It doesn't mean that at all. It means that family names have been in use for fewer than 100 years, and Thais remember given names more easily than they do family names. Filipinos often use position title plus family name, e.g. Attorney Acosta, but that does not mean they are more concerned with occupation or status than non-Filipinos. Nicknames are commonly given to themselves and others in Australia and Thailand but that doesn't mean that they are more or less hospitable than other national/cultural groups.

Showing politeness is important in every culture but it is done differently in different varieties of English. A Japanese may say, 'That will be difficult' or 'I will consider it'. A non-Japanese will find these responses intelligible and comprehensible but usually will misinterpret them. These are polite ways of saying 'no', and a very strong 'no' at that.

A Lao speaker may nod his head, and say 'yes' to show politeness while you are speaking. It does not mean he agrees with you. It doesn't even mean he understands you. It just means he is being polite and his nodding his head means, 'I'm listening and doing the best I can to understand you.'

A Korean may say, 'I'm sorry', but it doesn't mean s/he is accepting responsibility or guilt for an event. It may only mean that s/he regrets the current situation and wishes it had not occurred.

Levels of irony and understatement are frequently not correctly comprehended or interpreted when speakers come from different cultures even when their English is fluent. Jokes intended to lubricate conversations are often causes of offence and hurt feelings across cultures.

Five senses in cross-cultural interaction

What can be done to help us prepare for cross-cultural interactions? I believe there are '5 senses' to keep in mind as we improve our probability for successful cross-cultural communication and understanding.

The five senses

1. The sense of Self: (From which levels of culture am I taking my primary identity?)
2. The sense of the Other: (From which levels of culture am I identifying the Other?)
3. The sense of the Relationship between Self and Other: (Do I consider us friends? Colleagues? Host/guest? Strangers? Adversaries?)
4. The sense of the Social Situation: (Office? Restaurant? Place of worship? Shopping centre? International Conference?)

5. The sense of the Goal: (Develop/maintain friendship? Borrow money? Get information? Sell a product? Get the job?)

It is also helpful to get exposure to the varieties of English one is likely to encounter on a regular basis. The more varieties one is exposed to, the more one learns in the areas of intelligibility, comprehensibility and interpretability.

Authenticity

One needs authentic language material from these varieties of English. There are creative works that are very useful from most countries. For example, I suggest you read Ha Jin's *The Bridegroom* to learn more about China; *Mass* by F. Sionil Jose to learn about the Philippines; *A Painter of Signs* by R. K. Narayan to discover more about India; and *People of Esarn* by Pira Sudham to learn more about Thailand.

Examples of speech and speech acts can be obtained from the Internet and cable network news in addition to international radio programmes and commercial audio/video tapes.

Three things to remember

In our search for understanding, it is important to remember three things:

1. Understanding is not common in human interaction. Misunderstanding is the norm. It may be caused by a lack of intelligibility, comprehensibility or interpretability, or a combination of these. It may be caused by a lack of a desire to understand.
2. For whatever reason, there will be times when you misunderstand others and others misunderstand you. Learn how to recognize these misunderstandings and how to repair them.
3. Understanding does NOT mean agreement. I can understand you completely and be in total opposition.

To help us understand others, Hawaiians say that we must learn to listen. We must listen with our ears as well as our eyes and our heart. If we do learn to listen with ears, eyes and heart, I believe we are likely to find the three dimensions of understanding more easily obtainable.

References

Gaudart, H. 1999. *The Trouble with Names: Forms of Address in Asia*. Singapore: SNP Editions Pte. Ltd.

Kachru, B. B. (ed.) 1992. *The Other Tongue: English across Cultures* (2nd edition). Urbana, IL: University of Illinois Press.

——. 2005. *Asian Englishes: Beyond the Canon*. Hong Kong: Hong Kong University Press.

Kachru, Y. and L. E. Smith. 2008. *Cultures, Contexts, and World Englishes*. New York and London: Routledge.

Nelson, C. 1995. 'Intelligibility and world Englishes in the classroom.' *World Englishes*, 14(2), 273–9.

Ogden, C. K. and I. A. Richards. 1923. *The Meaning of Meaning*,1989, Orlando, FL: Harcourt Brace Jovanovich.

Peck, M. S. 1987. *The Different Drum, Community Making and Peace*. New York: Touchstone, Simon and Schuster.

Smith, L. E. and C. Nelson. 2006. 'World Englishes and Issues of Intelligibility.' In B. B. Kachru, Y. Kachru and C. Nelson (eds) *The Handbook of World Englishes*. Oxford: Blackwell Publishing, pp. 428–45.

Trifonovitch, G. 1972. 'The Four Hs of Culture Learning.' A presentation during the August orientation for new participants at the Culture Learning Institute, East-West Center, Honolulu, Hawaii.

Tuckman, B. W. 1965. 'Developmental Sequence in Small Groups.' *Psychological Bulletin* 63(6), 384–9. American Psychological Association.

3
Accommodation and the Idiom Principle in English as a Lingua Franca

Barbara Seidlhofer and Henry Widdowson

Introduction

Although it is acknowledged that English is now being appropriated as a lingua franca by users all over the world, and being put to effective communicative use without needing to conform to native speaker norms of 'correctness', there remains an entrenched reluctance to grant the same kind of legitimacy to this 'Expanding Circle' variation that is now generally accorded to 'Outer Circle' varieties (Kachru 1985; Seidlhofer and Jenkins 2003). The non-conformity of English as a lingua franca (ELF) still tends to be stigmatized as an aberration. Our purpose in this paper is to argue, and demonstrate, that the very non-conformity of its formal features is symptomatic of processes that characterize any natural use of language.

The imperatives for language variation and change

Like any other language, English is a dynamic process, and naturally varies and changes as it spreads into different domains of use and communities of users. Though the extent of spread in the case of English is unlike that of any other language, there is nothing at all unusual about the processes of variation and change that are activated by it. But it is not that languages just vary and change proactively under their own steam, so to speak, but reactively in response to certain social forces. We would suggest that there are two main forces at work, and in this paper we want to explore how they operate in the use of English as a lingua franca (henceforth ELF).

We will call these forces the 'cooperative and territorial imperatives'. On the one hand, language change is brought about by the cooperative imperative: we need to continually modify our language in order to communicate with other people. On the other hand, we adjust our language in compliance with the territorial imperative to secure and protect our own space and sustain our separate social and individual identity. One imperative urges us to lower our defences and reduce our differences in the interests of wider communication with other people, the other urges us to close ranks and enhance our differences to keep others out (cf. Widdowson 1983: 47, 1990: 109–10).

The cooperative function would seem to be related to what John Sinclair calls 'the idiom principle':

> The principle of idiom is that a language user has available to him or her a large number of semi-preconstructed phrases that constitute single choices, even though they might appear to be analysable into segments. To some extent, this may reflect the recurrence of similar situations in human affairs; it may illustrate a natural tendency to economy of effort; or it may be motivated in part by the exigencies of real-time conversation. (Sinclair 1991: 110)

So one likely motivation for the idiom principle is that it makes for effective communication – you cooperate with your interlocutors by using conventionally pre-constructed phrases both of you are familiar with, and you do not have to construct meanings by what Sinclair calls the 'open-choice principle'. If both first and second person parties in communication have access to these patterns as part of their competence in the language, then this clearly makes both production and processing of text easier for them – a matter of assembling pre-fabricated formulae rather than making sense of each linguistic component bit by bit. In some cases indeed, particularly where these formulaic patterns take the form of proverbial sayings, it is not even necessary to produce the whole phrase. The first person needs only to cue the second person into it, and just the beginning will suffice to do that. 'Where ignorance is bliss...' the former might say, leaving the other to provide the completion... 'tis folly to be wise.'

So the idiom principle would seem to relate to the least effort principle in that it reduces the language user's on-line processing load and so facilitates communication. In other words, the idiom principle can be said to be motivated by the cooperative imperative. But if this is so, then although the principle can be adduced from its established realizations, these are only symptomatic of it as an underlying process. The principle does not stop working but continues to operate in the ongoing use of language to yield new realizations. The idiomatic patterning that typifies current usage is simply a snapshot of a continuing process.

The idiom principle can be seen as a means whereby users of a language accommodate to each other by conforming to shared conventions of established phraseology. But what if there is no knowledge of such shared conventions – as in the case of users of English as a lingua franca who are unfamiliar with these recurrent idiomatic features of native speaker usage. If the idiom principle is a natural feature of language use, it cannot be in abeyance. It must be expressed in other ways. It cannot simply involve the manifestation of previously established patterns of usage, the 'semi-preconstructed phrases' that Sinclair refers to. It must also involve the dynamic on-line application of the principle and we would expect this to result in changes in wording, and the use of local idiomatic coinages devised to meet an immediate communicative need. And this is indeed what we find in ELF usage, as we shall demonstrate later.

Meanwhile, what of the territorial imperative? Although the idiom principle would seem to be motivated by the cooperative imperative, the particular idiomatic wordings that the principle gives rise to in the usage of particular languages take on a territorial function when they become established as a conventional resource for communication, as 'pre-constructions', within a community of language users.

These patterns of usage are internalized by native speakers of a language by the natural process of acquisition and become unconsciously habitual as the customary idiom of their community. They are territorial markers of social identity and group membership and many are so deeply embedded in intuitive behaviour that only with the arrival of the computer have they become observable by analysis and a matter of declarative knowledge. Procedural knowledge of them is a part of communicative competence as described by Hymes – a knowledge of the degree to which an expression is actually performed by a community of users. (Hymes 1972: 281).

As with other aspects of socio-cultural behaviour, these idiomatic patterns represent accepted norms which community members are expected to adhere to. If you fail to conform, you reveal that you do not belong. Any departure from the accepted wording of an idiomatic turn of phrase, no matter how slight, is likely to mark you as an outsider. For example, a native speaker of English might say of something with a successful person that *s/he brings home the bacon*. But someone coming out with a variant wording such as *s/he brings the bacon home* would be noticed as non-native and, likely as not, be ridiculed (this variant has actually been attested, and its occurrence occasioned some native speaker merriment).

'Real' English?

Learners of English are encouraged to think that the closer they get to native speaker idiomatic behaviour the better, and now that corpus linguistics can provide a detailed description of this behaviour, teachers have been urged to teach this 'authentic' or 'real' English in their classrooms:

> Only by accepting the discipline of using authentic language are we likely to come anywhere near presenting the learner with a sample of language which is typical of real English. (Willis 1990: 127)
>
> The language of the corpus is above all, real, and what is it that all language learners want, other than 'real' contact with the target language. (McCarthy 2001: 128)

It needs to be borne in mind, however, that the more distinctively native-like the idiom that learners strive for, the greater the likelihood of ridicule if they fail to get it right, for the very attempt to make use of such an idiom would constitute an attempted territorial encroachment, an invalid claim to community membership, with its failure revealing the speaker as an impostor. Non-conformities with patterns of usage less marked for native-speaker community membership might simply sound oddly un-idiomatic ('I get what you mean but we just don't say that'). But even oddity could well diminish the status of the speaker and result in a devaluation of what is said, no matter how clear its communicative intent.

Nor is it only a matter of producing the accepted textual form of the idiom. It is a matter too of knowing the contexts in which it is appropriate to use such forms. Some kinds of recurrent patterning are of very general occurrence in native-speaker usage, but others are quite restrictive in range. Since the idiom principle is pragmatically motivated, its formal realizations in a particular language are naturally acquired by native speakers in association with the contexts in which it is appropriate to use them. The linguistic forms of idiomatic usage are acquired along with the contextual conditions of their use as part of the process of acculturation into a community. This process is not confined to first language acquirers, of course. Other people can acquire idiomatic competence of this kind by long exposure or experience within a particular community. And if it is their aim to be adopted, or at least accepted, as members, then it would make sense for them to do so in order to meet the conditions of membership.

But not everybody learns a language with this aim in mind, and certainly not English. In the quotations cited earlier, Willis takes it for granted that the only 'real' English is that which is attested as having been produced by native speakers, and similarly McCarthy assumes that there is always only one target to aim at, and that defined by established native-speaker norms. But this notion of what is real English denies the reality of its actual use. For the millions of people around the world trying to learn this language are for the most part doing so to use it as a lingua franca, as a means of international communication, not to identify with, or accommodate to, the socio-cultural values of its native speakers. (e.g. Seidlhofer 2001, 2004). On the contrary, there are many users of English as a lingua franca (ELF) who would want to challenge these values rather than subscribe to them. They would certainly not want to have to recognize the territorial rights of its native speakers as a condition on their learning and using the language. And yet the insistence that the only authentic English is still that which bears the particular idiomatic stamp of native speakers of Kachru's Inner Circle, in Britain or the United States, for example, forces this condition upon them.

Such a condition is not only unwarranted in respect to the purpose of English learning, it also makes the process of learning itself immeasurably more difficult. As we have already pointed out, the particular linguistic realizations of the idiom principle in English, or any other language, are acquired as pragmatic functions through an extended experience of language in use. With idioms, it is this pragmatic functioning that is crucial, and will take precedence over semantic meaning: the segments in an idiomatic phrase will lose their independent semantic value. Indeed there are innumerable idiomatic expressions where the meaning of the separate segments is entirely irrelevant and left unheeded. So, for example, the native speakers' repertoire of idiomatic pre-constructions may include the expressions *he has shot his bolt* or *a bolt from the blue* which they will use without having the least idea what a bolt is, or what is involved in shooting it. Native speaker insiders are not inhibited by such ignorance. Experience has shown them that the phrase works pragmatically very well and that is all that matters: they can dispense with the semantics. But non-native outsiders have not had the benefit of such experience and so the semantics of the segments is all they have to go on. He has shot his bolt. What is a bolt? Beck and call. What is a beck? Par for the course. What, please, is par? Course? What kind of course?

Learners of the language could be advised that they should not trouble themselves with such questions and that so long as they know how the phrase functions, they need not bother about what the words mean because, 'even though they may appear to be analysable into segments', as Sinclair says, actually they are not. But how do the learners know what counts as a 'pre-constructed' phrase and what does not? How do they know how 'semi' the pre-construction is in particular cases? Some idiomatic patterns allow for variation in wording, and so are analysable in some degree. But which patterns? And to what degree? As suggested earlier, you can only learn such things through an extensive experience of the language in use, and this teachers cannot provide. The particular features of the idiomatic usage of native-speaker English are, we would suggest, not only irrelevant for most users of the language – that is to say lingua franca users – but actually unteachable as well.

The idiom principle in ELF

But conformity to these particular idiomatic manifestations is not only a needless requirement for users of ELF, but it actually goes against the cooperative function of the idiom principle itself. As we have already noted, this principle operates dynamically in the on-line pragmatic process of making meaning. It must, therefore, allow for, if not encourage, non-conformity with any preconceived manifestation of this principle where this is necessary, that is to say where shared knowledge of the exact wording cannot be taken for granted.

The point is that these manifestations are effective as cooperative devices within certain native-speaking communities of users because they have common knowledge of their wording and the conditions of their use. But since no such common knowledge can be assumed in the case of countless users of English as an international means of communication, the idiom principle can only realize its cooperative function here if the users are able to develop their own idiomatic realizations as appropriate to the particular interactions they are engaged in. And they will only be able to do this if they have the semantic resource available to them to use to such pragmatic effect. Replication of the idiomatic behaviour of a particular English-speaking community cannot serve the cooperative function of the idiom principle in language use outside these communities.

Sinclair defines the idiom principle by referring to the 'large number of semi-preconstructed phrases' that are available to 'a language user'. But which language user? For users of ELF, availability is usually limited. They may have some of the most commonly occurring fixed phrases available to them (*of course, on time, by the way*) but often not those that native speakers have intuitive access to but which only a concordance can reveal, and the acquisition of which depends on an extensive experience of the language. This being so, ELF users will need to construct what they have to say more atomistically, in a bottom-up fashion, drawing on what is semantically encoded in the grammar and lexis of the language – in other words, by recourse to what Sinclair calls the 'open-choice' principle. Sinclair implies that this is essentially a principle of linguistic analysis that does not apply to what language users actually do. One can accept that this does not apply to native speakers. But it would seem to apply to other users. One needs to recognize that the mode of communication among ELF users may in some respects be very different from that which characterizes the linguistic behaviour of native speakers.

But a primary dependency on the open-choice principle does not preclude adherence to the idiom principle. ELF users will naturally seek to be cooperative by developing pro-tem idiomatic expressions as reference tokens on-line. In other words, they will accommodate to each other in the interests of establishing agreed meaning. At the same time, they will accommodate to each other at an affective level, for the use of these phrases also serve to establish rapport, to identify speakers as members of the group, as insiders in the conversation, and in this respect are also markers of shared territory, expressive of common understanding and attitude. In other words, the co-construction of these pro-tem idiomatic expressions serve not only the cooperative function of communication, but the territorial function of what Aston has referred to as 'comity' (Aston 1988).

ELF idiomaticity: Examples from VOICE

Let us consider some examples, all taken from the corpus of lingua franca speech collected and analysed in the VOICE project – The Vienna Oxford International Corpus of English.[1]

First we look at an example of difficulties that can arise when users aim at a particular idiomatic expression and do not quite get the wording right. Here, S1 is a speaker with a very native-like command of English who produces idiomatic phrases with apparent ease (*across the board, pave the way*). However, when aiming for the expression 'any/every Tom, Dick or Harry' ('any ordinary person rather than the people you know or people who have special skills or qualities' (*Oxford Advanced Learner's Dictionary* 2005)), S1 produces a reduced variant:[2]

S1 [German]:	and i think i would be very much in favor of having COMMON criteria
S8 [Portuguese]:	yes
S1:	applying across the board (.) i'm saying this for another reason also (.) if these courses are to pave the way (.) for [...] (2) you know that quality is very
S5 [Italian]:	very high
S1:	very high so in other words it's not **just any dick and harry** coming (.) from any other country in the world saying i want to study on this program
S5:	o:h no=
S1:	=you have to meet certain quality criteria [...]

The consequence of this choice of phrase is that it is, in effect, not very cooperative: if the interlocutors do not know the idiom, they are in the dark about what meaning is intended; and if they do, this will reflect on the speaker's command of the language and could well result in amusement. In this specific interaction, as so often in ELF talk, the focus seems to be so firmly on the substance rather than the form of what is said that S1's interlocutors only engage with the intended meaning, and the marked phrase passes as if unnoticed (which of course would not be the case in an advanced English-as-a-foreign-language class or exam).

But although ELF speakers may make use of, or attempt to make use of, native-speaker pre-constructions, there are many cases, of course, where, as we have said earlier, ELF users will rely rather on the open-choice principle and produce expressions which deviate from what a native speaker would recognize as the established wording.

In the next few extracts, speakers assemble their own phrases with recourse to the open-choice principle for referring to mental processes of perception:

S5 [Korean]:	a <un> x </un> problem (1) but (.) not a big problem (.) **in my observation** because (.) e:r (1) most american students (1) understand what the (.) the instructor tries to say

S4 [Italian]:	if i can say (.) something **on the base of my experience** (.) i think that we have to (.) to try (.) to build something in doctoral (.) pro<6>gram. </6> S1: <6> hm </6> hm
S1 [Norwegian]:	[...] and of course you have to see to it that (.) the student <@> PASS the courses </@> <!1> (.) a- as well (.) but e:rm (.) e:r that's (.) well (.) internationalization as such. a:nd (.) **well to MY head** <!2> that is not a joint degree but (.) some of the things i've heard today or and <6> yesterday </6> SX-3: <6> <un> xxx </un> </6> SX-m: absolutely
S11 [Slovenian]:	erm i think (1) **i don't see it in my head** (.) how all the groups (er) will are doing different things (.) i'm sorry and one is going to present it (.) <7> because </7> (.)
SX-f:	<7> <soft> hm </soft> </7>

While the phrases highlighted in bold are reminiscent of the idiomatic expressions of users of English as a native language (ENL) such as *in my experience* or *to my mind*, they would be marked as odd in ENL conversations. In the ELF interactions they occur in, however, they are 'made normal' in Firth's terms (1996: 245), and questions of 'nativeness' do not seem to arise – it suffices that they fulfil their communicative purpose. So far, these phrases are individual occurrences, but it cannot be ruled out that one or the other will take hold over time. Thus it might become customary in certain ELF interactions to use *head* and *mind* interchangeably, or to replace *mind* by *head* in variations of ENL constructions. Even if no new fixed phrases emerge, it will be interesting to see whether some free variation between *mind* and *head* establishes itself systematically in ELF.

Next, consider the production of idiomatic coinages on-line that we have been referring to. The following example shows how a non-canonical use of adjective–noun collocations works to this effect. Here, the ELF interactants display some familiarity with what is idiomatically 'normal' but also exploit and at times expand the potential for modification to construct a shared new adjective–noun collocation:

S3 [French]:	we don't have to think ONLY to european master multilingual problems <8> and </8> things like that but we also have to (.)

S1 [Norwegian]: <8> mhm </8>
S3: to think about (.) **endan**<track md1_9>**gered** (.) <9> e:r </9> (.)
S1: <9> mhm </9>
S3: <1> **fields** </1><@> <3> **species** </3> <2> yes </@> @ </2> (.)
SX: <1> **species** </1> SX-f: <3> yeah </3>
S1: <2> yes mhm </2>
S3: erm and also: sciences.

Note too, the territorial imperative at work here, the emerging comity: the interlocutors here explicitly 'collude' in their collocational extension of the attributive use of *endangered* to *field* [of study]. Their mention of *species*, accompanied by laughter, would seem to indicate that they are fully aware that this noun is by far the most frequent collocate of *endangered.*[3] Later on during the same conference, this agreement on an innovative use of the modifier gets further developed by several speakers:

S1 [Swedish]: you you're talking about (.) er: er (.) i saw (.) er two factors the **enDANgered (.) factor** (.) so to say. you have low numbers and you have to have a (.) hh to have critical masses.
[...]
S11 [Danish]: right. i don't <un> xxx </un> i just wanna say that (.) i also think that there should be no (.) exclusion per se. a:nd that small <6> or </6> (.)
S1: <6> mhm </6>
S11: and or er **endangered (.) endangered er programs** (.) could actually benefit tremendously by pooling resources.
[...]
S10 [French]: if there is no (.) confidence between er people from er both <6> inst</6>itution <7> it will </7> be very difficult f- (.) to raise (.)
S1: <6> mhm </6> <7> mhm </7>
S10: er: a **project and program** from the very beginning. (.) <1> er: </1> just choosing the **field** <2> because </2> it's **endangered** o:r er:
S1: <1> mhm </1> <2> mhm </2>
[...]

S9 [Croatian]: the most <track md1_7> natural way to cooperate i think (.) is (.) at the (.) doctoral level plus research. (1) in these (fields). (1) and to combine both somehow. and my second comment regarding the the **endangered fields** is these is not o- these are not only the fields in which you we have a small number of students. (.) i would just like to mention that in in MY case of [place3] **endangered study** is a study of journalism for instance. because (.) we have a lot of ini- initiatives which are of a very low level in the region

[...]

SX: yah

S1: mhm

S10: [...] we didn't (2) talk very much (.) about er a topic (.) er:: (3) we talk er yesterday. er: (.) the: case of er ended- <pvc> **endedgered {endangered}** <ipa> 'endidʃəd </ipa> </pvc> **fields**. er: fields where (.) er in university we have no more strategy (.) for development. [...]

S1: are you talking about the the small areas <5> and the **endangered areas?** </5>

S10: <5> small areas (.) which which are not </5> in generally in (.) development strategy in any institution. (.) except closing. (2)

SX: mhm (3)

S1: mhm. (3)

[...]

S9: so in practice we will need a list of the **endangered disciplines** <4> at at </4> all uni<5> versities </5>

S4: <4> @@ </4>

[...]

S4: <6> industry mathematics (.) yes of course </6>

S9: hh the group theory should be (.) disappeared or not hh <7> this is </7> now the the en- the LIST of **endangered activities** which were (.)

S4: <7> yah </7>

S9: in the history or in the recent history very good (.) and are now **endangered**. (.)

S3: mhm (.)

S9: er <soft> <un> xx </un> </soft>

S1: mhm

S9: mathematics (.) will prevail (.) it's for <1> sure but </1>
S1: <1> mhm </1> mhm
S9: what and er which kind which part of mathematics (.) are **in danger** and which parts are
S1: mhm <2> mhm mhm </2>
S9: <2> e:r in </2> good condition (2)
S1: yeah sh- e: r er w:e had other (.) opinions er?

In the course of this discussion, which lasted about three hours, the collocational range of *endangered* (the 'endangered factor' introduced by S1, still with the rider *so to say*) is collaboratively broadened to include the nouns *activities, areas, disciplines, field(s), program* and *study*, and an in-group consensus is well and truly established. The process that unfolds here before our eyes is variation motivated by the idiom principle, and even the potential seed of a linguistic change, made possible by the acceptance of this particular community of users. How far this might result in actual change will depend on how far this local variation is taken up more widely as representative of the usage of a recognized wider community of users, or 'community of practice' (Wenger 1998).

What we see from these examples is ELF users appropriating the language for their purposes and following the idiom principle in devising wordings to accommodate to each other both in the co-construction both of agreed meaning and rapport. The point is that these wordings do not need to correspond with those of conventional native-speaker idiomatic usage – indeed they will generally only function effectively if they do not. In using English *on* their own terms, ELF users will quite naturally use English *in* their own terms.

Conclusion

What we have discussed in this paper is research in progress: provisional and tentative. The description of ELF is still in its infancy, and much work still needs to be done before its salient features can be specified with any degree of certainty. However, the examples we have discussed give some indication of how ELF speakers co-construct expressions in accordance with the idiom principle so as to cooperate in communication and to engage in a kind of territorial sharing or comity. We will see what further findings reveal. One interesting question is how far stabilization will occur in different groups of ELF speakers in particular domains of use and constellations of first language backgrounds. This remains an open question. And it may turn out that what is distinctive about ELF lies in the communicative strategies that its speakers use rather than in their conformity to any changed set of language norms. We shall see.

Notes

1. The VOICE project supported in its pilot phase by Oxford University Press, is funded by a grant from the Austrian Science Fund. Researchers on the project are Barbara Seidlhofer (director), Angelika Breiteneder, Theresa Klimpfinger, Marie-Luise Pitzl and Stefan Majewski.
2. For the VOICE mark-up and spelling conventions see www.univie.ac.at/voice/voice.php?page=transcription_general_information, the rationale for which is discussed in Breiteneder et al. (in press). The only changes introduced in the ELF examples in this paper are the indication of speakers' first languages in square brackets, as well as deletion of some text '[...]' in order to keep extracts short. The numbering of speakers (S1, etc.) has been left as it appears in the VOICE transcripts.
3. In the British National Corpus, for example, 253 of the 538 occurrences of *endangered* are directly followed by *species*, and the overwhelming majority of all attributive occurrences modify nouns denoting animals or other natural phenomena.

References

Aston, G. 1988. *Learning Comity. An Approach to the Description and Pedagogy of Interactional Speech*. CLUEB.

Breiteneder, A., M. Pitzl, S. Majewski and T. Klimpfinger. (in press). 'VOICE recording – Methodological challenges in the compilation of a corpus of spoken ELF.' *Nordic Journal of English Studies*.

Firth, A. 1996. 'The discursive accomplishment of normality. On "lingua franca" English and conversation analysis'. *Journal of Pragmatics* 26, pp. 237–59.

Hymes, D. 1972. 'On communicative competence.' In J. B. Pride and J. Holmes (eds). *Sociolinguistics*. Harmondsworth: Penguin, pp. 269–93.

Kachru, B. 1985. 'Standards, codification, and sociolinguistic realism: the English language in the Outer Circle.' In R. Quirk and H. G. Widdowson (eds) *English in the World*. Cambridge: Cambridge University Press.

McCarthy, M. 2001. *Issues in Applied Linguistics*. Cambridge: Cambridge University Press.

Pölzl, U. and B. Seidlhofer. 2006. 'In and on their own terms: the "habitat factor" in English as a lingua franca interactions.' *International Journal of the Sociology of Language* 177, pp. 151–76.

Seidlhofer, B. 2001. 'Closing a conceptual gap: the case for a description of English as a lingua franca.' *International Journal of Applied Linguistics* 11, pp. 133–58.

Seidlhofer, B. 2004. 'Research perspectives on teaching English as a lingua franca.' *Annual Review of Applied Linguistics* 24, pp. 209–39.

Seidlhofer, B. and J. Jenkins. 2003. 'English as a lingua franca and the politics of property.' In C. Mair (ed.) *The Politics of English as a World Language. New Horizons in Postcolonial Cultural Studies*. Amsterdam: Rodopi, 139–54.

Sinclair, J. M. 1991. *Corpus, Concordance, Collocation*. Oxford: Oxford University Press.

Wehmeier, S. (ed.) 2005. *Oxford Advanced Learner's Dictionary*. 7th edition. Oxford: Oxford University Press.

Wenger, E. 1998. *Communities of Practice*. Cambridge: Cambridge University Press.

Widdowson, H. 1983. *Learning Purpose and Language Use*. Oxford: Oxford University Press.

Widdowson, H. 1990. *Aspects of Language Teaching*. Oxford: Oxford University Press.

Willis, D. 1990. *The Lexical Syllabus*. London: Collins.

4

Exploring Attitudes towards English as a Lingua Franca in the East Asian Context

Jennifer Jenkins

Introduction

It is a well-established fact that during the past four centuries, the English language has spread around the world, and that as a result, it is used for a wide range of purposes by many millions of people for whom it is not a mother tongue in the traditional sense of the term. This means that there are more English users nowadays in the Outer Circle (i.e. in the countries colonized by the British in the 'second diaspora', see B. Kachru 1992) than there are English users in the Inner Circle (i.e. in Britain and the mother tongue English countries colonized by the British in the 'first diaspora'). English in the individual countries of the Outer Circle, meanwhile, has become English*es*: nativized varieties of English each with its own flavour and characteristics appropriate to its speakers' local social and professional uses and to local institutionalized functions. Thus, we can talk of Indian English, Malaysian English, Singapore English, Nigerian English, and so on.

However, the most extensive spread of English in recent years, in terms of numbers of speakers, has undoubtedly occurred in the countries of the Expanding Circle, such as China, Japan, Thailand, Brazil and Continental Europe. Although English is increasingly being used as a medium of instruction in tertiary and even secondary and primary education in some of these regions, it otherwise serves few, if any, local institutional functions in such places. For this reason, English in the Expanding Circle has traditionally been considered a 'foreign' language, one that is learnt primarily for communication with Inner Circle English speakers, and dependent on Inner Circle norms. This characterization may, at one time, have reflected the primary use of English among Expanding Circle speakers. But English is no longer predominantly a foreign language in these countries: most learners of English in the Expanding Circle no longer learn English in order to be able to communicate with English mother tongue speakers. Instead, they need English to provide them with a lingua franca with which to communicate for both social and professional reasons with speakers of other first languages, particularly those in other Expanding Circle countries. In other words, they are learning, and subsequently using, what has come to be known as 'English as a lingua franca'.

In this article, I begin by defining English as a lingua franca (henceforth ELF) and explaining its ideological differences from English as a foreign language (henceforth EFL). Focusing on the Asian Expanding Circle, I go on to describe some of the features that have been identified as possible features of ELF, along with some of the skills that its proficient speakers demonstrate, in particular, the ability to code-switch and accommodate appropriately in context. I then discuss responses to the notion of ELF, and comment on the implications of ELF research findings for speakers of non-native, nativized and native Englishes.

What is English as a Lingua Franca?

The literature on ELF, it has to be said, is not always clear or unanimous as to the nature of this phenomenon. This is not surprising given that ELF is relatively recent by contrast with EFL. But let us begin with a straightforward definition: we can consider ELF, in essence, a means of communication in English between speakers who have different first languages. Most commentators would agree with this. Where they start to disagree is whether a native speaker of English (henceforth NS) can participate in ELF communication. A minority of scholars (e.g. House 2003) argue that ELF by definition excludes NSs. On the other hand, the majority (e.g. Seidlhofer 2004; Jenkins 2007) believe that NSs can indeed participate in ELF, but that when they do so, the situation is very different from EFL, in that NSs no longer set the linguistic agenda and should not expect the non-native participants in the interaction to defer to NS norms. For this reason, ELF corpora such as the Vienna-Oxford International Corpus of English, or VOICE (see Seidlhofer and Widdowson, this volume) either exclude NSs of English from their data collection or, as in the case of VOICE, restrict the number of NSs that can be present in their data (e.g. VOICE stipulates a maximum of 10 per cent in any interaction). This ensures both that NSs do not distort the data with an untypical number of ENL forms or (wittingly or unwittingly) act as norm-providers, making the NNS participants feel under pressure to 'speak like them'.

This brings me to another area where the literature is not always straightforward: the differences between traditional EFL and ELF. While some scholars and English teaching professionals regard ELF (or EIL, English as an international language, as it is sometimes called) as merely the international spread of *NS* English norms (i.e. in effect, what *EFL* entails), ELF researchers see things very differently. The following table sums up the differences between their ELF perspective and an EFL approach:

EFL	**ELF**
Part of modern foreign languages	Part of World Englishes
Deviations from ENL are seen as deficiencies	Deviations from ENL are seen as legitimate differences
Described by metaphors of transfer, interference and fossilization	Described by metaphors of language contact and evolution
Code-switching is seen negatively as an attempt to compensate for gaps in knowledge of English	Code-switching is seen positively as a bilingual resource to promote speaker identity, solidarity with interlocutors, and the like

As the table demonstrates, the ELF paradigm is almost the complete opposite of an EFL approach to English. To sum up, the overarching difference between the two is that for EFL, native English (or to be more precise, Standard British and American English) are the only acceptable norms to serve as targets for Expanding Circle learners. Any item that 'falls short' of these norms is by definition considered an error. By contrast, for ELF, non-native forms are evidence of the emergence of new kinds of English norms through recently accelerated language contact that is leading, in turn, to accelerated language change (see Jenkins 2006 for a more detailed discussion of EFL vs. ELF).

The current ELF research endeavour is directed at identifying precisely what these new ELF norms consist of. In other words, what sorts of forms do competent ELF speakers produce systematically and frequently that are both communicatively effective and different from the norms of NSs of English? In addition, given the huge potential for contextual diversity in ELF communication, what processes are involved in promoting intelligibility, identity, empathy, solidarity and so on? These are the kinds of questions that are currently being explored through ELF corpora such as VOICE (see Seidlhofer 2001, 2004), the corpus of English as a Lingua Franca in Academic Settings, or ELFA (see Mauranen 2003), and Deterding and Kirkpatrick's corpus of South-East Asian (ASEAN) Englishes, which includes both Expanding and Outer Circle varieties (see Deterding and Kirkpatrick 2006), among several others.

Possible features of ELF

We turn now to consider briefly the kinds of features that are being identified as potential candidates for ELF forms, focusing on the two areas in which most progress has so far been made: lexicogrammar and phonology, and in line with the theme of this volume, on those forms which are found in East Asian Expanding Circle Englishes.

Lexicogrammar

One of the most frequently found features of ELF lexicogrammar in all ELF corpora is zero marking of third person *-s* in the present tense. This feature, which would be described as a 'failure to use *-s*' or 'omission of *-s*' according to an EFL perspective, is one that East Asian ELF speakers share with many others across the Expanding Circle, as well as with some speakers of both Outer and Inner Circle Englishes. In removing the marking of this redundant morpheme, ELF users are continuing a process that has been in progress for almost a thousand years, that is the regularization of the simple present tense endings from the original six inflected endings down to the remaining single one, the third person *-s*. Put like this, zero marking of the *-s* inflection is part of an entirely natural linguistic process, and could be said to represent simply an acceleration (through increased language contact) of a process that is already taking place, albeit more slowly, in the English language, as it is pre-disposed to evolve in this direction (see Breiteneder 2005).

While the 'omission' of this ending is often considered to be caused by a lack of competence on the part of NNSs of English, the empirical evidence suggests that it is nothing of the kind. For although ELF speakers, particularly younger speakers in informal contexts, make extensive use of zero-marked third person *-s*, if an NS of English joins in the conversation, they tend to revert to the *s*-marked form. This demonstrates a sophisticated level of knowledge and skill, in that firstly, they know the NS rule and are able to apply it when they consider it necessary, and that secondly, they are aware that middle-class NSs of English stigmatize its 'omission' (see Cogo and Dewey 2006).

The same kinds of comment can be made about other possible lexicogrammatical features of Expanding Circle ELF. For example, there is a shift in article use particularly, but not exclusively, in East Asian ELF. Speakers systematically employing articles in ways more appropriate to their own than to NSs' use of English, both use articles in grammatical contexts where NSs do not, and vice versa (see Dewey 2007). Again, ELF speakers in East Asia (and elsewhere) tend not to use the cumbersome system of question tag forms employed by NSs of English. Instead, they often use an invariant form, particularly either *isn't it?* or *is it?*, both of which are frequently found in Outer Circle Asian Englishes such as Lankan and Singapore English too (and also as 'innit' among many younger British English speakers of all social groups in informal conversation contexts). Another example is the shift in preposition use with, for example, the regularization of the verb 'discuss' so that it becomes 'discuss about' alongside verbs such as 'talk about', 'speak about' and the like, or 'emphasize on' in preference to the Inner Circle form 'emphasize'. Similarly, prepositions that would be used by mother tongue speakers may be deleted (e.g. 'against' in the multiword verb 'to discriminate against someone').

A final example (though see Dewey 2007 and Seidlhofer 2004 for several other potential lexicogrammatical features of ELF that space constraints prevent me from describing) is the extension of countability to nouns that in ENL are considered uncountable. Thus, for example, ELF speakers from Japan, Korea, China, Thailand and so on are likely to say 'informations, advices, staffs, furnitures', which ENL speakers would regard as errors because they themselves say, for example, 'three pieces of information', 'two members of staff', etc. Again, the ELF way is patently less cumbersome and more elegant. And like many other grammatical ELF innovations, it is again simply the continuation of a natural regularization process that is already in progress (in both Inner and Outer Circles). NSs of English, for example, refer to 'coffees', 'beers', 'accommodations' and so on, while in the Outer Circle, 'staffs', 'furnitures', etc. are already well-established features of nativized Englishes. The issue for the Expanding Circle seems to be, then, that such innovations are acceptable if, and only if, they are first sanctioned by NS use.

Lexis

ELF speakers have also been shown empirically to create new words and collocations. Examples of innovative collocations in VOICE include 'space time' and 'severe criminals', where English NSs would say (I assume) 'spare time' and 'serious criminals'. Again, ELF speakers have been found to convert so-called 'false friends' into what Hülmbauer (2007) prefers to call 'true friends'. For example, whereas 'actually' means 'in fact' in ENL, many European ELF speakers prefer to use it with the meaning 'now', 'currently'. Similarly, they may use the word 'card' to mean 'map' rather than one of its preferred meanings in ENL, e.g. 'greetings card'. ELF speakers are also innovative in their use of morphemes. For instance, among the forms Björkman (2008) finds in her ELF corpus collected at a Swedish university are 'boringdom', 'levelize', 'forsify' and 'discriminization'.

The problem of 'unilateral idiomaticity'

By contrast with features such as those outlined in the previous section, it is in fact certain aspects of NS English that cause intelligibility problems in ELF communication. The first of these is what Seidlhofer (2001) terms 'unilateral idiomaticity', which occurs when one speaker (whether NNS or NS) uses an ENL idiom that the other speaker does not know. Given that idioms are culturally loaded and identity laden, it is perfectly reasonable to assume that the idioms spoken by one linguacultural group (in this case, NS English groups such as British and American) do not travel, and therefore do not have meaning for those from other linguacultures (in this case Expanding Circle groups).

An empirical example of this phenomenon is provided by a French English speaker who had learnt the idiom 'to chill out', and used it in conversation with, first, a Korean English speaker and a few days later, a Japanese English speaker. In both cases, he was met with incomprehension and had to paraphrase using the more transparent non-idiomatic verb 'to relax' (see Dewey 2007). ELF corpora such as VOICE provide copious further examples of this problem, with ENL idioms such as 'Can I give you a hand?' for 'Can I help you?', 'On the house' rather than 'complimentary' and the like, having been found to cause similar responses.

Phonology

Phonology, or accent, is another case in point. My own research into phonology in ELF settings has demonstrated that certain features of ENL pronunciation are detrimental to intelligibility in ELF communication. These are primarily the use of weak forms and other features of connected speech such as elision and assimilation. Those who did not grow up speaking a variety of English that includes such features are unable to recover the full forms for which they are substituted. On the other hand, some features of ENL pronunciation do not actually cause intelligibility problems, but appear not to contribute anything to intelligibility in ELF communication. These include the consonant sounds [θ] and [ð], which are regularly substituted in East Asian ELF varieties by [s] and [z] or [t] and [d] without any loss of intelligibility; word stress, where many Expanding Circle varieties, like Outer Circle Englishes, not to mention American English, before them, are in the process of developing their own stress patterns; and stress-timed rhythm, with most nativized and Expanding Circle varieties exhibiting a preference for syllable timing (see Jenkins 2000).

By contrast, certain features of Expanding Circle pronunciation have been shown empirically to lead to problems in ELF communication. These include changes to many ENL consonant sounds and vowel length distinctions, and consonant deletion. Consonant deletion is, of course, one way in which ELF speakers resolve a problem for most of the world: the fact that NS English, by nature, contains many consonant clusters, whereas the universal preference is for a CVCV (consonant–vowel–consonant–vowel) structure. The alternatives are either to delete consonants within clusters, or to add vowels between consonants. When ELF speakers opt for the former solution and, for example, produce the word 'product' as [pɒdʌk], as did a Taiwanese English speaker in my data, they frequently cause intelligibility problems for interlocutors from first languages that do not employ this consonant deletion strategy. On the other hand, when ELF speakers opt for the second solution and add vowels (as for example, Japanese and Korean speakers of English do), and produce the same word 'product' as [pərɔdʌkʊtɔ] in the case of Japanese English, they rarely meet with the same negative outcome. The same is so when speakers add a vowel to a word-final consonant as in the case of [lʌgɪdʒi] for 'luggage' (Korean English speaker), [tʃeɪndʒi] for 'change' (Japanese English speaker), and suchlike.

Turning to vowel sounds, by contrast with consonants, the majority of vowel qualities favoured by speakers of Expanding Circle English in preference to ENL vowel qualities appear not to cause intelligibility problems in ELF communication unless a change in length is involved (either alone or in combination with a vowel quality modification). However, there is one main exception to this: the sound [ɜː]. There is extensive empirical evidence showing that when this sound is substituted with another long vowel, the result is an intelligibility problem (see Jenkins 2000). The phenomenon occurs most frequently in the case of speakers of Japanese English who tend to substitute [ɜː] with [ɑː], resulting in a word such as 'bird' being pronounced [bɑːd].

In the case of ELF speakers' pronunciation features that *do not* cause intelligibility problems, I have argued elsewhere (e.g. Jenkins 2000) that replacements of ENL forms with ELF speakers' own preferred forms should be regarded as legitimate features of their own local accents and not as errors. Thus, we can speak of a Japanese English accent, a Chinese English accent, a Thai English accent and so on, rather than characterizing any differences from ENL as 'errors' – as they would be described from an EFL perspective. On the other hand, the pronunciation forms that *do* cause problems in ELF communication could be regarded as more appropriate pronunciation targets than General American or Received Pronunciation for learners whose goal is to use English as a lingua franca with speakers from other first languages than their own.

Having said this, it is important to point out the complexity of the ELF situation: with so many diverse Englishes it is not sufficient simply to acquire certain forms and use them indiscriminately. ELF speakers also need a number of skills to enable them to use the forms appropriately *in context*, and it is to these skills that I turn in the next section.

ELF speakers as skilled language users

Recent studies of ELF demonstrate not only that ELF speakers are in the process of developing their own preferred norms, but also that proficient ELF speakers are very skilled users of English. Unlike proficient EFL speakers, they do not merely make use of one particular variety of English (i.e. usually a close approximation of standard British or American English). Instead, they are also able to exploit the English language in more flexible and resourceful ways, responding to the demands of the particular situation rather than rigidly applying one particular code regardless of who they are speaking English with, where, why, and so on. In particular, proficient ELF speakers:

- innovate in English making use of their multilingual resources to create their own preferred forms that are more appropriate in a given context than 'equivalent' ENL forms.
- code-switch for example to signal solidarity with their multilingual interlocutors and to communicate their own bi- or multilingual identities.
- make adept and extensive use of accommodation strategies both for affective reasons (to signal solidarity) and for communicative efficiency, that is to enable them to communicate their meaning more effectively than would be the case if they remained rigidly attached to 'correct' ENL norms.

In the previous sections we considered a number of lexicogrammatical and lexical ELF innovations, and an ELF (vs. EFL) perspective on pronunciation. In this section I will comment on the other two ELF phenomena listed above: accommodation and code-switching.

Accommodation

A point made with increasing frequency is the fact that NSs of English are less intelligible than NNSs in lingua franca communication. Phillipson (2003: 167), for example, argues that '[i]n many international fora, competent speakers of English as a second language are more comprehensible than native speakers, because they can be better at adjusting their language for people from different cultural and linguistic backgrounds'. Many NSs of English, it seems, are so used to the (traditional EFL) notion that it is NNSs of English who should make all the linguistic adjustments in order to understand and be understood by its NSs, that they have not hitherto developed the ability to adjust their English appropriately in intercultural communication in the sophisticated ways that NNSs employ.

Two examples of ELF speakers' use of accommodation strategies will suffice to illustrate this point and demonstrate accommodation being used firstly, to signal solidarity (i.e. the affective motivation), and secondly, to promote intelligibility (i.e. for communicative efficiency). In the following example, two speakers, Japanese and Chinese (L1 Mandarin) are discussing the Chinese revolution:

J: my [specific interest in point
C: [yeah
J: when did language, I mean ... *because [of revolution*
C: [mhm mhm
J: did language change?
C: yeah, [it's changed
J: [specifically, intentionally
C: *because of revolution*, but it also changed from the beginning of the twentieth century

From Cogo 2007: 160–1 (emphasis in original).

The Japanese participant (J) wants to find out when the Mandarin language began to change, and asks whether it changed 'because of the revolution'. In this phrase, she does not use the definite article, as would be the norm in standard native English. A few turns later, the Chinese participant (C) repeats this phrase, and in doing so, also uses zero article, despite the fact that she normally uses the definite article in such grammatical contexts. Cogo concludes that the Chinese participant is accommodating not only by means of her repetition, but also by changing her speech style to resemble that of her Japanese interlocutor, in other words, by converging to signal solidarity.

The second example is phonological accommodation for communicative efficiency, in other words, to promote intelligibility. In this case, convergence is not necessarily on each other's pronunciation. Instead, when conversation partners do not share a particular feature, they tend to accommodate by converging on its standard NS pronunciation (see the previous section for a discussion of phonological items which have been found to be necessary for intelligibility among NNSs of English from different first languages). For example, in a conversation between a Taiwanese and Korean speaker of English, the Taiwanese speaker deleted a large number of consonants during a phase of the conversation when mutual intelligibility was not a priority (e.g. 'quite' as [kwɑɪ], 'different' as [dɪfə]). By contrast, when it was critical for her Korean interlocutor to understand her words, she used very little consonant deletion, whereas she continued to substitute [θ] and [ð] respectively with [s] and [d], substitutions of a kind that the Korean speaker used himself, and which did not cause intelligibility problems for him (see Jenkins 2000 for detailed examples).

On the other hand, where speakers share the same or a similar first language, then there is obviously no need to replace their preferred local variants. Indeed, these are likely to increase as their presence not only increases mutual intelligibility but also serves as a marker of shared identity and thus promotes solidarity. For example, two Japanese speakers, during an exchange of information in which mutual intelligibility was essential to the successful completion of a task, increased their use of word-final [ɑː] in words such as 'whiskers' and 'over', where a standard native English accent would have the schwa sound, [ə] (again, see Jenkins 2000 for further detail).

Code-switching

As mentioned above, another skill of proficient ELF speakers is that of code-switching, which they employ for a number of reasons, including the signalling of solidarity with their multilingual interlocutors and to project their own multilingual identities (and only very rarely to cover for a lexical gap). Both Cogo (2007) and Klimpfinger (2007) provide copious examples of ELF speakers engaged in naturally occurring ELF conversations switching into their own first language, and sometimes of their conversation partner responding in that language (i.e. accommodating to the code-switch). In the example that follows, and a number of others like it, however, the switch is even more sophisticated: the interlocutors switch into a language that is neither of their first languages. For Chako and Anna (pseudonyms) are, respectively, native speakers of Japanese and Italian, but the switch is into Spanish ('galletas' are 'biscuits').

Chako:	Anna ... *galletas*
Anna:	mhm, nice [...]
Chako:	take two
Anna:	no, one is enough (Chako signals with hand to take two, Anna takes two)
Anna	thank you (Chako goes back to her desk) ah, with nuts
Chako:	nuts and chocolate
Anna:	mhm, nice
Chako:	*te gusta*?
Anna:	*mucho*

From Cogo 2007, pp. 174–5 (emphasis in original; transcription simplified).

Cogo interprets the switch in the above case as resulting from contextual elements. Chako uses Spanish as it is the closest language to the L1 of her Italian interlocutor that she knows, thus demonstrating solidarity with Anna. She also uses it because the biscuits are homemade, and she, Chako, speaks Spanish at home, so it seems a more appropriate language to use in what Cogo describes as this 'homely' situation. Obviously, the switch can only be used and responded to appropriately by virtue of the fact that both participants in the conversation are speakers of Spanish as well as English and their own first languages.

Responses, implications and conclusions

The logical conclusion from the ELF research described above is that in English teaching situations in Expanding Circle countries such as Japan, Korea, Thailand and China, learners who plan to use their English in intercultural communication (rather than only with native English speakers) would benefit from awareness raising of the emerging features of ELF, and of the benefits of appropriate use of both code-switching and accommodation strategies. However, at present, the use of ELF features, code-switching and phonological/grammatical accommodations of the kind exemplified above would, of course, be heavily penalized in English language speaking examinations, where conformity to standard native English and intelligibility for a native English listener are still widely seen as the only acceptable goals.

A recent case in point is the new Pearson's Test of English. In an interview with *EL Gazette* in September 2008: 10, a representative of Pearson's said of their new test that in order to create an international exam, they had used test writers from the UK, the US and Australia. In other words, 'international' for this ELT publisher and examination board (as for most others based in the Inner Circle), means the international spread of *native* English. The representative went on to say that because their test is not based on a single model of English, they prioritize intelligibility – for the native listener. In other words, we have the bizarre state of affairs in which tests of the ability to speak English in *international* contexts are, in practice, tests of the ability to speak English in *national* contexts (i.e. in Pearson's case, with native speakers of British, American and Australian English).

While lingua franca use of English among its non-native speakers, despite being the most frequent use of English in the Expanding Circle, seems not even to have been noticed by any of the so-called 'international' examination boards, others involved in ELT, both NSs and NNSs of English, including ELT professionals, applied linguists and even sociolinguists, have responded to the notion of ELF, often very negatively (see Jenkins 2007 for a detailed discussion). Meanwhile, recent research of my own into attitudes towards ELF accents (ibid.) reveals that many English speakers still cling to the notion that only near-native accents, and particularly near-RP and near-GA, are acceptable, even in international settings, and that the quality of an English accent can only be evaluated in relation to its closeness to one of these two NS accents. Thus, in my research, accents such as Swedish and Dutch English were considered far more acceptable than accents such as Japanese and China English. The former kind were described in generally positive terms, with an emphasis on their 'native-like' quality. Meanwhile the latter kind were described in almost unremittingly negative terms, with an emphasis on their differences from RP and/or GA.

While such attitudes might be relevant to EFL (NNS–NS) communication, it is curious that they are also considered relevant to the primarily NNS–NNS interactions of ELF users, as if a conversation between a Japanese and Brazilian English speaker taking place at a conference in Munich should still have to defer to the English spoken among its NSs in London or Los Angeles. Put like this, the idea seems (or should seem!)

absurd. ELF, as we have seen, is an entirely natural development arising from new language contact situations, while attempts to hold back its progress are entirely unnatural examples of linguistic prescriptivism. In this respect, the research into language evolution of scholars such as Mufwene (e.g. 2001) demonstrates clearly how language changes through new contact situations and the extent to which accommodation is involved in the process. Their work has the potential to cast important light on what is currently happening to English in its new lingua franca contact situations, particularly within and across Expanding Circle contexts such as East Asia and Europe. Times have changed drastically over the past few decades, not least in terms of the spread of English, and with these changes comes the need for us to reconceptualize the ways in which we think of notions such as (English) 'speech community' and (English) language 'variety' (see Seidlhofer in press for a discussion of this issue).

Regardless of the many 'ELF-deniers', the signs are, nevertheless, that in the near future, those who occupy the top of the English language hierarchy will no longer be NSs of English, but bilingual speakers of English who have the skills to function comfortably in multilingual communication. The traditional hierarchy of Englishes has, for many decades been as follows:

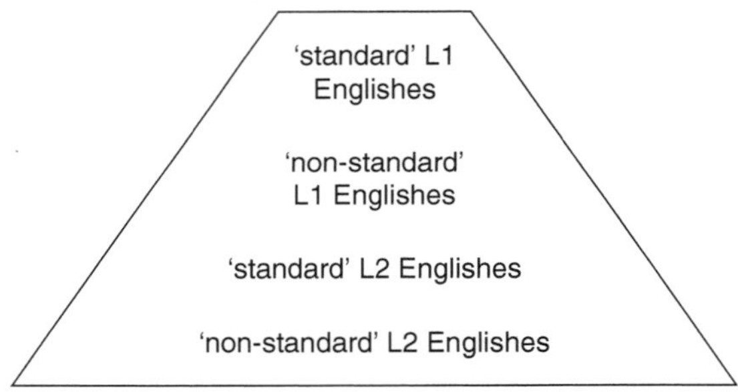

However, by taking into account both the changing demographic and the advantages of being a bilingual speaker of English, we arrive at a very different hierarchy. This time, the varieties of English spoken by its internationally-competent bilingual English speakers are at the top, be their speakers L2 (second language/NNS) speakers of, for example, China-, Korean-, Japanese-English, or bilingual speakers of L1 (first language/NS) English varieties such as North American or British English. In addition, intranational (local) varieties are now at the same level of the hierarchy, regardless of whether they are Inner (native) or Outer Circle (nativized) varieties, as contrasted with the traditional practice of placing Inner Circle standard Englishes above Outer Circle ones:

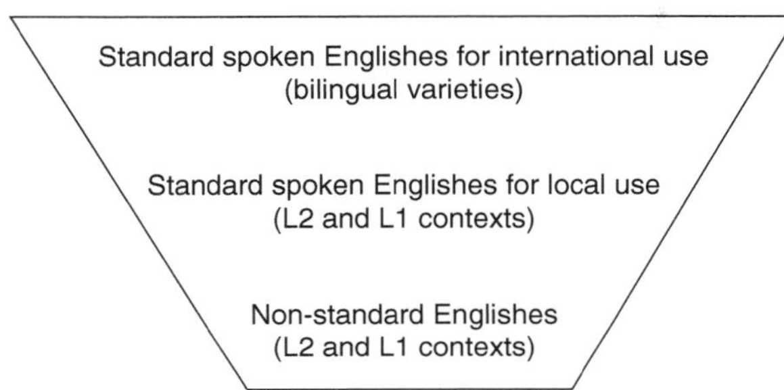

(Both hierarchies from Jenkins, 2009).

Native speakers will soon need to take note of these changes if they wish to participate effectively in international communication. Not only do the majority not speak languages other than their L1 English (and this situation is currently worsening in Britain, where fewer students study an L2 beyond the age of 14), but they also tend to be less competent than many NNSs in their acquisition and use of accommodation strategies, and instead expect NNSs to make all the adjustments. This may in part be the result of their monolingualism. It may also be because, as Hülmbauer points out, NSs are more constrained by the rules of L1 English than NNSs, who have a freer and more flexible use of English because they 'are not influenced by standardising forces to the same extent' (2007: 9).

So where does this leave us? Some years ago, a Japanese speaker of English, Mikie Kiyoi, who was living in Paris, published an article in the *International Herald Tribune* (3 November 1995), an American newspaper produced in Paris (see Jenkins 2000: 228). In the article Kiyoi pointed out that Anglo-Americans need to know 'that the English they speak at home is not always an internationally acceptable English', and asked Anglo-Americans to 'please show us you are also taking pains to make yourselves understood in an international context'. Judging from my previous discussion, it could be argued that not much seems to have changed in the intervening 13 years. And in this respect, it was a pity that Mufwene (2008) missed an important opportunity to apply his knowledge of the role of language contact in language evolution to the notion of ELF. Instead, he told his Japanese audience that in his opinion, English is a 'foreign' not an 'international' language in Japan, and implied that they needed to acquire American English in order to be successful in their lives.

More optimistically, however, scholars such as Honna Nobuyuki have for many years been pointing out from an informed position that native English is not the most relevant for Expanding Circle countries whose speakers learn English for (genuinely) international uses, rather than to communicate with NSs of English (see e.g. Honna and Takeshita 1998; Honna 2008). And there is growing evidence, both scholarly and anecdotal, suggesting that younger English speakers in Expanding Circle countries, particularly in East Asia, are beginning to realize that native-like English is no longer relevant to their international communication needs. Instead, they seem increasingly to wish to make their own decisions about the kind of English they speak, and to project – by means of the influence of their L1 on their English accent – a sense of their own local identity, as well as to develop some kind of hybrid global identity in their English, instead of being told to take on the identity of an NS of English in the US or UK (see Jenkins 2007, Chapter 7 for comments by Chinese, Taiwanese, Korean and Japanese English speakers).

I end with a poem written by a Japanese student studying at a Japanese university after having learnt the facts about the spread of English around the world:

Dear Inner Circle
My English is samurai
My English is sushi
My English is sumo
I'm not gonna follow your English, OK?
My English is Jinglish.

(Poem provided by Nicola Galloway)

In these few short lines, the student not only eloquently expresses the poem's sentiment, but also demonstrates in the penultimate line that s/he is aware of the way NSs speak English informally, and in the first line that the poem is based on knowledge (the concept of the three-circle model). Most importantly s/he takes the term 'Japlish' which, like many similar terms ('Chinglish', 'Hinglish', 'Konglish', etc.) are regularly used to denigrate NNS varieties of English, and subverts it by making it a matter of pride. Perhaps, then, the most sensible conclusion from all that has been said above is that the future of ELF, and of the local Expanding Circle varieties which inform and underpin it, is with the younger generation, and depends critically on their awareness being raised of the sociolinguistic realities of the current spread of English around the world.

References

Björkman, B. 2008. 'So where are we? Spoken lingua franca English at a technical university in Sweden.' *English Today* 24(2), 35–41.

Breiteneder, A. 2005. 'The naturalness of English as a European lingua franca: the case of third person -s.' *Vienna English Working Papers* 14(2), 3–26.

Cogo, A. 2007. 'Intercultural communication in English as a Lingua Franca: a case study.' Unpublished doctoral thesis, King's College London.

Cogo, A. and M. Dewey. 2006. 'Efficiency in ELF communication: from pragmatic motives to lexico-grammatical innovation.' *Nordic Journal of English Studies* 5(2), 59–93.

Deterding, D. and A. Kirkpatrick. 2006. 'Emerging South-East Asian Asian Englishes and intelligibility.' *World Englishes* 25(3), 391–409.

Dewey, M. 2007. 'English as a Lingua Franca: an empirical study of innovation in lexis and grammar.' Unpublished doctoral thesis, King's College London.

Honna N. 2008. 'Challenging issues in English Language teaching in Japan: for self-expressive activities.' Paper given at 'The Respective Roles of English and Local Languages in the School Curriculum', the Inaugural Roundtable of the Research Centre into Language Education in Multilingual Societies, Hong Kong Institute of Education, Hong Kong, 21 June 2008.

Honna N. and Y. Takeshita. 1998. 'On Japan's propensity for native speaker English: a change in sight.' *Asian Englishes* 1(1), 117–37.

House, J. 2003. 'English as a lingua franca: a threat to multilingualism?' *Journal of Sociolinguistics* 7(4), 556–78.

Hülmbauer, C. 2007. 'The relationship between lexicogrammatical correctness and communicative effectiveness in English as a lingua franca.' *Vienna English Working Papers* 16(2), 3–35.

Jenkins, J. 2000. *The Phonology of English as an International Language*. Oxford: Oxford University Press.

——. 2006. 'Points of view and blind spots: ELF and SLA.' *International Journal of Applied Linguistics* 16(2), 137–62.

——. 2007. *English as a Lingua Franca: Attitude and Identity*. Oxford: Oxford University Press.

——. 2009. *World Englishes. A Resource Book for Students* 2nd ed. London: Routledge.

Kachru, B. B. 1992. 'Teaching World Englishes.' In B. B. Kachru (ed.) 1992 *The Other Tongue. English across Cultures*. Urbana and Chicago: University of Illinois Press, 355–65.

Kiyoi, M. 1995. 'Dear English speakers, please drop the dialects.' *International Herald Tribune*, 3 November, and *English Today* 15(2), 55.

Klimpfinger, T. 2007. '"Mind you, sometimes you have to mix" – The role of code-switching in English as a lingua franca.' *Vienna English Working Papers* 16(2), 36–61.

Mauranen, A. 2003. 'The corpus of English as a Lingua Franca in academic settings.' *TESOL Quarterly* 37(3), 513–27.

Mufwene, S. 2001. *The Ecology of Language Evolution*. Cambridge: Cambridge University Press.

——. 2008. '"Global English" vs "English as a Global Language"'. Plenary address at the JACET 47th Annual Convention, Waseda University, Tokyo, 11–13 September 2008.

Phillipson, R. 2003. *English-Only Europe? Challenging Language Policy*. London: Routledge.

Seidlhofer, B. 2001. 'Closing a conceptual gap: the case for a description of English as a Lingua Franca.' *International Journal of Applied Linguistics* 11(2), 133–58.

——. 2004. 'Research perspectives on teaching English as a Lingua Franca.' *Annual Review of Applied Linguistics* Vol. 24: 209–39.

——. In press. 'Common ground and different realities: World Englishes and English as a Lingua Franca.' *World Englishes* 28.

Part II

Cultural Identity, Ideology and Attitudes in Englishes in Asia

5

Pygmalion in Singapore: From Cockney to Singlish

Tony T. N. Hung

Introduction

Bernard Shaw's *Pygmalion* (1912) and its musical offshoot *My Fair Lady* (1956) are among the most enduring (and endearing) dramatic/musical works of the last century, and their popularity continues unabated into the twenty-first century. Apart from their intrinsic dramatic and musical quality, their perennial appeal stems partly from the universal theme of metamorphosis which underlies their plot and characters. More even than in Shaw's time, we live in an age of spectacular 'metamorphoses': Truck drivers can be transformed into film stars and pop idols (like Rock Hudson and Elvis Presley), and film stars into politicians and even presidents and governors (like Ronald Reagan and Arnold Schwarzenegger). There are, seemingly, no limits to how far a person can be 'made over', not only in matters of speech, but in every physical, social and cultural aspect.

For linguists and language teachers especially, *Pygmalion* and *My Fair Lady* (henceforth *P&M*) touch on issues which are even more relevant today than in Shaw's time. The issue of 'standard' vs. 'non-standard' varieties of language has come much more to the fore since the beginning of the twentieth century, with the spread of education and mass media, and the codification and dissemination of what have become widely accepted as national or international pronunciation 'standards', along with the stigmatization of what is perceived (by the privileged classes) as 'non-standard'. In English, RP (or 'BBC English') attained an unprecedented prestige and status in many parts of the world which is only now beginning to show signs of decline, while in Chinese, Mandarin was declared the 'common language' (or *Putonghua*) for all of China, with the Beijing accent assuming the status of a prestige pronunciation, against which other accents of *Putonghua* are measured (to their disadvantage naturally). Issues of language and power, and the survival of 'non-standard' languages or dialects, have thus assumed much greater prominence all over the world since Shaw's time. In a place like Singapore, it has taken the form of the suppression of the other Chinese dialects, such as Cantonese and Hokkien, in favour of Mandarin ('Speak more Mandarin, less dialects' used to be the slogan of the day), the rationale – which was totally fallacious – being that Mandarin was the 'mother tongue' of all ethnic Chinese.[1]

Meanwhile, English has (since Shaw's time) been developing into a *de facto* world language. 'New Englishes' (or 'Outer Circle' varieties) have sprung up all over the world – in India, Singapore, Malaysia, Hong Kong, Philippines, Sri Lanka, West Indies, Africa, etc. – each with (more or less) systematic and homogeneous linguistic features of its own, not to mention sociolinguistic roles and features (cf. Bolton 2002; Brown et al. 2000; Crystal 1997; Hung 1995, 2000; Jenkins 2000; B. Kachru (ed.) 1992; B. Kachru et al. (eds) 2006; McArthur 2002; Schneider 2004, etc.). In the case of Mandarin, there have also emerged a number of 'new varieties' of Mandarin, as people from different parts of China and overseas (in Singapore, Malaysia, Hong Kong, etc.) increasingly acquire the 'common tongue' and use it in their daily lives (cf. Hung 2001).

The rise of international and national pronunciation standards on the one hand, and of regional and 'new' varieties of language on the other, has given added impetus to the spread of linguistic prejudice – a theme as old as the Biblical 'shibboleth' story itself (where people were separated into two groups depending on their pronunciation of the Hebrew word *shibboleth*, with consequences much more lethal than they normally are today). In his day, Shaw was implacably prejudiced against non-standard English of any kind, particularly Cockney (the working class dialect of London). As he put it in his Preface to *Pygmalion*:

> The English have no respect for their language, and will not teach their children to speak it ... It is impossible for an Englishman to open his mouth without making some other Englishman despise him. (*Pygmalion*, p. 1)

This theme was expanded in *My Fair Lady* to embrace other regional varieties of English:

> An Englishman's way of speaking absolutely classifies him,
> The moment he talks he makes some other Englishman despise him.

One common language I'm afraid we'll never get –
Oh, why can't the English learn to
Set a good example to people whose English is painful to your ears?
The Scotch and the Irish leave you close to tears.
There even are places where English completely disappears –
Well, in America they haven't used it for years!

Regrettably, this prejudice against non-standard and regional varieties of English is very much alive and well today. One shudders to think what Shaw himself might have to say about Singapore or Hong Kong English today, or for that matter Australian or New Zealand English. But Shaw – and the 'hero' of *Pygmalion*, Professor Higgins – certainly do not lack latter-day disciples to speak for them. One of these, John Honey (the author of *Does Accent Matter?* and other books in a similar vein), visited Singapore in the late 1980s and made ominous pronouncements (as reported in the *Straits Times*) to the effect that Singaporeans would never 'get away with' their brand of English in the international arena ('charming' though it might be 'at the kampong level'), and that Singapore would lose its competitive edge unless Singaporeans started speaking an 'internationally acceptable' English. (A strange prediction, considering how well Singapore has done internationally over the past few decades, in spite of its alleged linguistic handicap.)

Besides the issues of standard vs. non-standard varieties of English and linguistic prejudice, *P&M* also raises interesting questions about teaching, in particular the teaching of speech. For all his prowess as a phonetician (he is able to tell everybody where they come from by the subtlest clues in their accents), does Higgins really make a good teacher? From the evidence of *P&M*, I would say not. Even setting aside his egoistic 'teacher-centeredness' (boasting that there is not an idea in Eliza's head that he hasn't put there), Higgins completely fails to understand one of the basic tenets in language teaching/learning, i.e. that 'input' does not necessarily equal 'intake'. Thus he forces Eliza to repeat the phrase 'The rain in Spain stays mainly in the plain' endlessly, trying to get her to produce the vowel [ei] (as in RP *pain*), which Eliza, being a Cockney, pronounces as [ai] (as in RP *pine*). Eliza is puzzled as she fails to hear the difference, and asks Higgins 'Didn't I say ([sai]) that?', to which Higgins mockingly replies, 'No you didn't [sai] that, you didn't even [sei] that', and orders her to repeat the phrase 50 times each night before going to bed. Now a modern teacher would (or should) be focusing much more on the learner, and on the differences between the teacher's input and the learner's intake. (In Hung (2000), I gave an example of how Hong Kong learners fail not only to produce the distinction between the long and short vowels in words like *heat* and *hit*, but even to perceive the distinction itself, which may explain their inability to produce the contrast.)

Pygmalion/My Fair Lady transplanted

While *P&M* is a universally popular play/musical, and has been made into two enormously successful movies (*Pygmalion* 1938 and *My Fair Lady* 1964), it is one of those works which are simply untranslatable in any real sense. It is so deeply rooted in a particular language (English with its variety of accents), and a particular culture and society, that any attempt to translate it into another language would result in near-nonsense. Take for instance the following exchange from the opening scene of *Pygmalion*, where Higgins overhears Clara's pronunciation of the word 'pneumonia' with its distinctive 'o' (represented by Shaw as 'ow') and instantly places her in Earls Court (which is not a very fashionable part of London). He blurts it out and elicits an angry response from Clara (who feels humiliated by being thus exposed):

Clara: I shall get pneumownia if I stay in this draught any longer.
Higgins: Earlscourt.
Clara: Will you please keep your impertinent remarks to yourself! (p. 14)

Now this dialogue (and many others in the play) would be utterly incomprehensible if translated into Chinese – or (for that matter) Japanese, Korean, Malay, Tagalog, or any other language:

Clara: 我在這儿再待下去就要得肺炎了。
Higgins: 埃爾斯科特。
Clara: 你這些無禮之言，還是留著說你自己吧!

In fact, it is barely comprehensible even in English in many other parts of the world. *P&M* positively demands to be transplanted and adapted to the linguistic, social and cultural context of other places, rather than merely translated.

There are, to my mind, few places in the world where an adaptation of *P&M* would be more timely and appropriate than Singapore. English has long been established as the dominant official language as well as the *lingua franca* there. Side by side with 'standard English' (however defined), there has emerged a non-standard colloquial form of Singapore English commonly known as 'Singlish'. In some ways, Singlish can be said to be Singapore's answer to Cockney. Though (unlike Cockney) most Singaporeans, from all walks of life and not just the working class, speak Singlish in at least some social situations, it is looked upon with strong disapproval by those in authority, both in the government and the education sector. The following comments by Singapore's leaders (cited in Fong, Lim and Wee 2002) are indicative:

Former Prime Minister Lee Kuan Yew:

- 'Singlish is a handicap we do not wish on Singaporeans.'

Former Prime Minister Goh Chok Tong:

- 'Singlish is poor English that reflects badly on us and makes us seem less intelligent or competent.'
- 'Singlish is not English. It is English corrupted by Singaporeans and has become a Singapore dialect.'

True to their word, the authorities in Singapore have repeatedly curtailed or banned the use of Singlish in the mass media (including TV talk shows, dramas and even commercials), and conducted various campaigns against it – the most recent being the 'Speak Good English' movement launched in 2001 (see its website at: www.goodenglish.org.sg/site/) – fearing that it would irreparably corrupt standard English as spoken in Singapore. The situation is such that, if Shaw had lived in the Singapore of today, he would undoubtedly have written the Preface to *Pygmalion* in much the same vein as the original:

> Singaporeans have no respect for the English language, and will not teach their children to speak it properly... It is impossible for a Singaporean to open his mouth without making some other Singaporean despise him.

In fact, I suspect that Shaw – or at least one side of him – would have felt rather at home with the general ethos of Singaporean society today. He has always been unabashedly didactic in his writings. As he says in the Preface to *Pygmalion*:

> It [*Pygmalion*] is so intensely and deliberately didactic, and its subject is esteemed so dry, that I delight in throwing it at the heads of the wiseacres who repeat the parrot-cry that art should never be didactic. It goes to prove my contention that great art can never be anything else. (p. 5)

In the famously 'paternalistic' society of Singapore, this sentiment would indeed be echoed not only on the stage but throughout society as a whole, and one could easily imagine the Preface to the Singaporean version of *Pygmalion* going something like this:

> It [the Singapore government] is so intensely and deliberately didactic, and its style is esteemed so dry, that I delight in throwing it at the heads of the wiseacres who repeat the parrot-cry that governments should never be didactic. It goes to prove my contention that a great government can never be anything else.

I should imagine that the writing of a play like *P&M* would have attracted the most generous funding from the 'Speak Good English' campaign.

From Cockney to Singlish

What is the object of Shaw's scorn in *Pygmalion*, provoking him into saying that 'it is impossible for an Englishman to open his mouth without making some other Englishman despise him'? It is the sloppy speech habits of Englishmen in general, but most of all Cockney, the working class dialect of London. A 'dialect' is a variety of a language marked by distinctive phonological as well as syntactic and lexical features. The most easily recognizable phonological features of Cockney are these:

- 'shifted' vowels: [iː > əɪ, eɪ > aɪ, aɪ > ɒɪ, ɔɪ > oɪ]
  e.g. *bee* *bay* *buy* *boy*
- intervocalic glottal stop: *little* [lɪʔəl]
- [h]-dropping: *hit him* [ɪʔ ɪm]
- [l]-vocalization: *fill* [fɪʊ]
- [θ] -> [f]: *thin* [fɪn]

(For a detailed description of the Cockney accent, cf. Wells 1982). Cockney is also distinguished by certain lexical and grammatical features, which, though systematic in their own way, differ from standard English and are therefore regarded as 'sub-standard'. For instance, in talking about her aunt's death, and how she was killed by the people who stole her hat, Eliza puts it this way: *'Them what pinched it, done her in'.*

Singlish is not so much a 'working class dialect' of Singapore (though the working class characteristically speak it) as the colloquial form of English spoken by most Singaporeans (other than Lee Kuan Yew, Goh Chok Tong and a few others) in informal situations. On phonological grounds alone, it is not that distinguishable from more standard varieties of Singapore English, other than a greater tendency towards simplification. Some of its most notable phonological features are:

- [θ] → [t]: e.g. *thin* [tin]
- Neutralization of short/long vowel contrasts, as in: *bit/beat, bet/bat, full/fool, cot/caught, cut/cart*
- Glottalization: e.g. *sort of* [sɔʔ ɔf]

(For an analysis of Singapore English phonology, see Brown et al. 2000; Hung 1995, etc.) But it is in its lexical and grammatical features that Singlish is most distinctive. The syntax is much simpler than standard Singapore English, but is nonetheless systematic (for an analysis of Singlish grammar, cf. Deterding et al. 2003; Alsagoff and Ho 1998; the best reference on Singlish vocabulary is the *Coxford Singlish Dictionary,* available online: www.talkingcock.com/html/promo/coxford.htm). For instance, in Singlish there is extensive use of subject omission ('pro-drop'), and of particles like 'lah'. Typical examples of Singlish expressions include *Where got?* and *Cannot lah!* The former is one of the most inimitable expressions in Singlish, and has a variety of uses and meanings, including a retort signifying denial. The latter is simply a case of subject omission and VP ellipsis, and the use of 'lah' for emphatic purposes.

We thus have a near-diglossic situation in Singapore, where the 'standard' form of the language is one imposed from above and essentially exonormative, and where for informal everyday communication the majority of the people use a colloquial, indigenous form of the language which is quite different linguistically. The low regard in which some speakers of standard Singapore English hold speakers of Singlish, and the sense of inferiority sometimes associated with the latter, would make excellent ingredients for a Singaporean version of *Pygmalion* and *My Fair Lady.*

A Singaporean *My Fair Lady*

In the rest of this paper, I shall outline my idea of what a Singaporean adaptation of *P&M* might look like. Of course, someone with more imagination and literary talent than myself would make a much better job of it, and I am not putting forward 'my' version as a 'model' of any sort, but only to show how well *P&M* adapts to Singapore's linguistic, social and cultural context. But whatever shape it might take, I feel that a Singaporean adaptation of *P&M* would need to be written in such a way as to be capable of being interpreted on at least two different levels: at one level, poking fun at the sloppy speech habits of Singaporeans (and hence perceived as a vindication of the 'Speak Good English' movement), and at another level, as a satire on linguistic prejudice. Shaw's *Pygmalion* – in spite of its didactic preface – has always struck me as being somewhat ambivalent between the two. Today, with the benefit of half a century of sociolinguistics behind us, and with English becoming a *bona fide* global language rather than the property of a few traditional English-speaking countries, we can no longer approach this topic from a one-dimensional point of view. (Cf. Jenkins 2000; Hung 2002)

The main characters in our proposed Singaporean version of *Pygmalion/My Fair Lady* (henceforth *SPM*) are as follows:

- *Eliza Doolittle:* Eliza Teo – a Singlish-speaking Tiger Beer salesgirl
- *Professor Higgins:* Prof. John Honeycomb – professor of phonetics, National Institute of Education, Singapore.
- *Colonel Pickering:* Datuk Pek Ker Ling – professor of English (retired), University of Malaya.
- *Nepommuck/Karpathy:* Dr Zee – a phonetics expert from Shanghai.

A word of explanation is called for. Eliza is now a Tiger Beer salesgirl instead of a flower-girl because (unlike London) there are very few flower-girls to be found in Singapore, but hordes of beer girls. As for the Higgins character, in *P&M* he is a private tutor to the rich, earning (as he calls it) a 'fat' living by teaching the *nouveau riches* to get rid of their 'slum' accents. But no one is likely ever to get rich doing the same in Singapore, a much more pragmatic and less class-conscious society than Shaw's London. Therefore, I shall make him a professor of phonetics in the National Institute of Education – which (by general consent) is the last bastion of RP in Singapore. (Any resemblance between the name 'John Honeycomb' and any real person living or dead is, needless to say, entirely coincidental.) Colonel Pickering is now a retired Malaysian academic, while the Hungarian phonetics 'expert' (Nepommuck or Karpathy) is now a Shanghainese – because the story requires him to be a foreigner but of the same ethnicity as Eliza (i.e. Chinese), and because of all the mainland Chinese, the Shanghainese are reputedly the most linguistically and culturally sophisticated. [For the sake of convenience, I shall refer to the characters by their original names in the rest of this paper.]

The opening scene, where Higgins amazes everybody by telling them which part of London they come from ('within two miles, sometimes within two streets') just from their accents alone, obviously poses a problem for *SPM*, as it would be impossible to place anyone geographically within Singapore from their accent. Of course, as an alternative, we could tell a Malay from an Indian or Chinese Singaporean by their respective accents, but in this context it would be all too trivial as their appearances would have given them away in any case. What Higgins the phonetician could do in this scene to impress his Singaporean compatriots would be to identify Chinese Singaporeans from different dialect backgrounds by their English accents, as they do reveal some phonological differences (assuming that they have grown up speaking their native dialects). For example, Teochew speakers typically exhibit the following phonological features:

- [n] → [ŋ], [t] → [k] (in syllable-final position)
  (i.e. [+stop +coronal] → [+back] / ___ #)
  e.g. *sun spot* → *'sung spock'*

The English spoken by Foochow speakers, on the other hand, is typically characterized by:

- [m]/[n] → [ŋ], [p]/[t] → [k] (in syllable-final position)
  (i.e. [+stop] → [+back] / ___ #)
  e.g. *income* → *'ingkang', lipstick* → *'lickstick'*

On account of the immense popularity of *My Fair Lady* (even over *Pygmalion*), I feel that *SPM* would probably work better as a musical than a straight play. One finds that many of the lyrics of *MFL* transfer relatively easily to *SPM*. For instance, here is what Higgins' opening number might sound like (with passing references to other 'New Englishes', and Singapore's pursuit of 'Good English'):

Higgins/Honeycomb:
A Singaporean's way of speaking absolutely classifies him,

The moment he talks he makes some other Singaporean despise him.
One standard language I'm afraid we'll never get –
Oh, why can't Singaporeans learn to
Set a good example to people whose English is painful to your ears?
The Thais and the Indians leave you close to tears.
There even are places where English completely disappears –
Well, in Hong Kong they haven't used it for years!

When Higgins takes on Eliza as a pupil, he tortures her with endless lessons in articulation. In *MFL*, Higgins invented the perfect shibboleth with the phrase *'The rain in Spain stays mainly in the plain'*, which focuses on the familiar [ei] > [ai] shift in Cockney. For *SPM*, the obvious shibboleth would have to involve the voiceless dental fricative [θ], which Singlish speakers invariably pronounce as [t], as in *three* [tri:] (homophonous with *tree*). It is however much harder to think of a counterpart for 'the rain in Spain' using the 'th' sound. Perhaps something like this: The thirty thieves thrived thickly through the throng, which our Eliza would no doubt pronounce as *De tirty tieves trived tickly trough the trong.*

One of the funniest and most revealing scenes in *P&M* is the one where Higgins takes Eliza to his mother's tea party to try her out. By then, she has thoroughly mastered the intricacies of pronunciation – but without the 'proper' vocabulary and grammar to go with it. The effect of speaking in Cockney vocabulary and grammar but with an impeccable RP accent is most amusing. It would be just as easy to achieve a similar effect with Singlish in *SPM*. Imagine a dialogue like the following, spoken in perfect RP but with Singlish grammar and vocabulary:

Eliza: My aunt she die of influenza – so they say lah.
Mrs Hee: Oh no!
Eliza: But I don't believe – I not stupid lah! Where got such thing? She so strong what – how can die of influenza? Cannot lah!

This goes to show how wrong-headed it would be for anyone to believe (as John Honey apparently does) that to be 'internationally intelligible' or to speak 'internationally acceptable English' is basically a matter of pronunciation. It is as much a matter of grammar, vocabulary and discourse as pronunciation – and even where pronunciation is concerned, it is as much a matter of clarity of articulation (which is a universal property not tied to any particular accent) as adopting a so-called 'internationally intelligible' accent (cf. Hung 2002).

The climax of *P&M* is the embassy ball, where Eliza is put to the test by the Hungarian Karpathy ('that blackguard who uses the science of speech/ more to blackmail and swindle than teach'). Unable to 'place' Eliza on account of her impeccable accent, he mistakes her for a Hungarian princess. In *SPM*, we shall make Karpathy a Shanghainese (Dr Zee), and he mistakes Eliza for a fellow Shanghainese – not of royal blood of course (as there is no Chinese royalty), but from an illustrious family. With *P&M* at the back of one's mind, the scene almost writes itself:

<table>
<tr><td>Dr Zee:</td><td>I have found out all about her. She is a fraud.</td></tr>
<tr><td>Hostess:</td><td>A fraud! Oh no.</td></tr>
<tr><td>Dr Zee:</td><td>Yes, yes! She cannot deceive me. Her name cannot be Ms Teo.</td></tr>
<tr><td>Prof. Honeycomb:</td><td>Why?</td></tr>
<tr><td>Dr Zee:</td><td>Because Teo is a Singaporean name, and she is not Singaporean.</td></tr>
<tr><td>Hostess:</td><td>But she speaks English so well.</td></tr>
<tr><td>Dr Zee:</td><td>Too well. Can you show me any Singaporean who speaks English as it should be spoken? There's no such thing.</td></tr>
<tr><td>Hostess:</td><td>But if she is not Singaporean, what is she?</td></tr>
<tr><td>Dr Zee:</td><td>Shanghainese.</td></tr>
<tr><td>All:</td><td>Shanghainese!</td></tr>
<tr><td>Dr Zee:</td><td>Shanghainese. And related to the Soong family.</td></tr>
<tr><td>Prof. Honeycomb:</td><td>Did you speak to her in Shanghainese?</td></tr>
<tr><td>Dr Zee:</td><td>I did. She was very clever. She said 'Please speak to me in English: I do not understand Cantonese.' Cantonese! She pretends not to know the difference between Cantonese and Shanghainese…</td></tr>
</table>

This scene makes the same point as the original, i.e. that native speakers of a language (whether the English in Shaw's time, or Singaporeans in our time) tend to be sloppy in their speech habits, and that it is only foreigners who are well schooled in the language who speak it as it should be spoken. Though obviously exaggerated, it does have a certain logic, which is partially reflected by previous studies which have shown that, to an international audience, educated 'non-native' varieties of English may in fact be more intelligible than 'native' varieties (cf. Smith and Rafiqzad 1979).

A (semi-serious) postscript

The ending has always been regarded as the weakest part of *P&M*. In the original play, Shaw insisted on an anti-romantic ending, where Eliza leaves Higgins and marries that weakling Freddie, a most unsatisfactory ending as she is by then so far above him in every way. The 1938 *Pygmalion* movie and the musical *My Fair Lady* changed that by having Eliza return to Higgins at the end, with Higgins uttering that famous closing line, 'Where the devil are my slippers, Eliza?' Though obviously better than the original, there is still something slightly contrived about it. In the Cantonese version of *P&M* produced in the 1990s, Higgins actually runs after Eliza and proposes to her, which is the worst possible ending of all, as the 'real' Higgins would rather be damned than do any such thing.

The problem is neatly solved in *SPM*, by one of the most inspired bits of social engineering ever invented by humankind: the SDU (Social Development Unit).[2] The SDU comes to the rescue and arranges everything. Eliza marries Higgins, as naturally as day follows night, and has three children (or more – depending on the latest official target in Singapore). And to top it all – *none of them speak Singlish*, naturally!

Acknowledgements

An earlier version of this paper was given in Waseda University in 2004. I am grateful to members of the audience for their stimulating comments, particularly to Professor Yasukata Yano – whose urbane wit and erudition may one day (I hope) inspire a Japanese adaptation of *My Fair Lady* worthy of a true linguist.

Notes

1. While Mandarin is the *official* and *national* language of China (and Taiwan), this is of course not the same as saying that it is the 'mother tongue' of all Chinese. It is the mother tongue only of the Chinese from the northern parts of China, while Cantonese, Teochew, Hokkien, Hakka, etc. are the mother tongues of the others. It is surely ironic that the Chinese dialects should have continued to thrive in mainland China and Taiwan (where Mandarin is the national and sole official language), while they are driven almost to extinction in Singapore (where Mandarin is not the national or even the first official language).
2. The Social Development Unit is the government's dating and 'match-making' service for single professionals in Singapore – probably the only one of its

kind in the world. The government also offers incentives for educated couples to have up to three or four children.

References

Alsagoff, L. and C. L. Ho. 1998. 'The Grammar of Singapore English.' In Foley J. A. et al. (eds) *English in New Cultural Contexts: Reflections from Singapore,* 127–51. Oxford: Oxford University Press.

Bolton, K. (ed.) 2002. *Hong Kong English: Autonomy and Creativity.* Hong Kong: Hong Kong University Press.

Brown, A., D. Deterding, and E. L. Low (eds) 2000. 'The English Language in Singapore: Research on Pronunciation.' Singapore Association for Applied Linguistics. *Coxford Singlish Dictionary.* Available online at the 'Talkingcock' website, www.talkingcock.com/html/promo/coxford.htm

Crystal, D. 1997. *English as a Global Language.* Cambridge: Cambridge University Press.

Deterding, D., E. L. Low, and A. Brown (eds) 2003. *English in Singapore: Research on Grammar.* Singapore: McGraw Hill.

Foley J. A. et al. (eds) 1998. *English in New Cultural Contexts.* Singapore Institute of Management/Oxford University Press.

Fong, V., L. Lim and L. Wee. 2002. 'Singlish: Used and abused.' *Asian Englishes* 5(1),18–39.

Honey, J. 1989. *Does Accent Matter?* London: Faber & Faber.

Hung, T. T. N. 1995. 'Some aspects of the segmental phonology of Singapore English.' In S. C. Teng (ed.), *The English Language in Singapore: Implications for Teaching.* Singapore Association for Applied Linguistics.

——. 2000. 'Towards a phonology of Hong Kong English.' *World Englishes,* 19(3), 337–56.

——. 2001. Phonological features of Hong Kong Mandarin. *Proceedings of the 7th International Conference on Chinese Phonology,* pp. 396–403. National Chengchi University, Taipei.

——. 2002. 'English as a global language and the issue of international intelligibility.' *Asian Englishes,* 5 (1), 4–17.

Jenkins, J. 2000. *The Phonology of English as an International Language.* Oxford: Oxford University Press.

Kachru, B. (ed.) 1992. *The Other Tongue: English across Cultures* (2nd ed.). Urbana, IL: University of Illinois.

Kachru, B., Y. Kachru and C. L. Nelson. (eds) 2006. *Handbook of World Englishes.* Oxford: Blackwell.

McArthur, T. 2002. *Oxford Guide to World English.* Oxford: Oxford University Press.

My Fair Lady [Movie, 1964]. Directed by G. Cukor. Warner Studios DVD, ASIN #630522577X.

Pygmalion [Movie, 1938]. Directed by A. Asquith. Home Vision DVD, ASIN #0780023536.

Schneider, E. W. et al. (eds) 2004. *Handbook of Varieties of English.* (2 vols.) Berlin: Mouton de Gruyter.

Shaw, G. B. 1912. *Pygmalion.* Reprinted London: Longman (1957).
Smith, L. and K. Rafiqzad. 1979. 'English for cross-cultural communication: the question of intelligibility.' *TESOL Quarterly,* 13(3), 371–80.
'Speak good English' Movement: www.goodenglish.org.sg/site/
Wells, J. C. (ed.) 1982. *Accents of English.* Cambridge: Cambridge University Press.

6
Japanese English for EIAL: What it should be like and how much has been introduced

Morizumi Mamoru

The issues of English as an international auxiliary language (hereafter EIAL) have been taken up in this half century interwoven with various aspects, such as language, culture, politics, economics and society, and have cast a great influence on foreign language teaching at school. This complex theme has been studied both theoretically and practically by numerous earlier scholars and educationalists (see, for example, Crystal 1997; Hino 2003; Honna 1990; Jenkins 2003, 2007; Kachru 1991; Kirkpatrick 2007; Quirk and Widdowson 1985; Yano 2001). In this article,[1] I take up three issues: the basic standpoints for considering Japanese English for EIAL; its perspectives in terms of linguistic materials such as sounds, vocabulary and expressions; and its introduction to the English textbooks for middle schools in Japan, and explore what perspectives and problems we have in the matters.

Before I go into the main discussion, let me refer to my basic idea toward the term, EIAL, English as one of the international auxiliary languages (see Smith 1976), which I dare to use in this article. EIAL is a rather old term and it may even sound archaic. More popular terms for English used in the world today may be EIL (English as an international language) advocated by Smith (1983) and others, EGL (English as a global language) by Crystal (1997) and others, and ELF (English as a lingua franca) by Jenkins (2000) and others.[2] There are also IE (international English) and WE (world Englishes). It seems to me, however, that the terms 'international language', 'global language' as well as 'international English' and 'world Englishes' sound too strong and assertive; they even make me feel the 'power' of English. In order to avoid or lessen this power and assertiveness, I dare to use the term 'auxiliary' to emphasize the auxiliary role of the English language as an international language. Besides, the term IAL (international auxiliary language) has often been used for artificial languages, including Esperanto, and it appears to mean that we should make this new language our own (Sapir 1949: 45–64). Jenkins' and others' ELF does not sound so strong and assertive to me compared with the other terms, but I would rather hesitate to use the term 'lingua franca', as it implies the locality of the Mediterranean area from its Latin origin and its imperial past.

What I want to claim through this denomination, which may sound too minute and insignificant, is that the very natural idea that English should not be the sole language for international communication should be reflected in the terminology. This is the case not only with English but also any other languages. If one particular language is always used for international communication, the values and viewpoints are inclined to be unified (McKay 2002: 20; Phillipson 1992: 67–74). It is often said that a language is a mere tool and has nothing to do with mind and spirit. A tool, however, has something to do with values and ways of thinking, and this will be discussed extensively later in this article. No one denies that English has its present powerful status and that it has been used as one of the strongest international auxiliary languages. We cannot disregard this. However, we do not need to accelerate the tendency. We should give this mission to other languages too. This claim leads to the variety of Englishes. Thus, the argument about the perspective of EIAL is inevitably related to views and beliefs about the relation of language and internationalization. 'To discuss EIAL is to examine our views of English or linguistic sensitivity as a whole' (Morizumi 2007: 45).

Standpoints of EIAL

As for the standpoints that accept and promote the circulation of EIAL such as Japanese English which is used by NNSs (non-native speakers of English), we have to consider the following two points. The first point is whether the model we have is mono- or polymodel. The second point is what the norm of EIAL is, that is to say, whether we should have the exonormative model (NS – native speakers of English – model) or the endonormative model (NNS model). At the base of this discussion is whether we should consider globalization as unity or diversity. Since globalization should have both aspects of unity and diversity, this choice of two alternatives is a matter of degree: the one side does not preclude the other completely. The discussion of dichotomy should be roughly

Table 6.1 Three different standpoints of EIAL

	Quirk	**Kachru**	**Jenkins**
Number	Monomodel (Unity-oriented)	Polymodel (Diversity-oriented)	Polymodel (Diversity-oriented)
Norm	Exonormative (NS Model)	Endonormative within the Outer Circle?	Endonormative (NNS Model)

divided into three: the positions of Randolph Quirk, Braj Kachru and Jennifer Jenkins, which could be put into the form of Table 6.1.
Quirk insists that EIAL should be English which can serve as the standard of English used all over the world and that it should be one particular variety of the native speakers' English, while Kachru and Jenkins claim that non-native speakers of English outnumber the native English speakers and that English used by non-native speakers can be a model of EIAL. Here is a dichotomy of a mono- vs. polymodel argument.

This argument of mono- vs. polymodels goes back to the question of which of the two, unity or diversity, we should take for globalization. Quirk is in the position to claim unity, saying that we need a single standard model for EIAL, that is to say, EIAL should be taken up as a singular form. The reason Quirk prefers a single model is expressed in his article written as early as the late 1980s.[3] He writes as follows:

> It seems likely, indeed, that the existence of standards (in moral and sexual behaviour, in dress, in taste generally) is an endemic feature of our mortal condition and that people feel alienated and disoriented if a standard seems to be missing in any of these areas. (Quirk 1985: 5–6)

On the other hand, some people claim that there should be more than one standard or model for EIAL. One of the representatives of this position is B. Kachru. He calls Quirk's claim 'the nativist monomodel position' and his own 'the functional poly-model position' and explains the latter as follows:

> The functional poly-model position entails the use of theoretical and methodological frameworks which relate the formal and functional characteristics of English in the Outer Circle to appropriate sociolinguistic and interactional context. (Kachru 1991: 183)

Another basic stance is a dichotomy of the exonormative or endonormative attitude toward English used as an EIAL. Quirk claims the exonormative attitude, while Jenkins allows the endonormative position for EIAL which is realized in her concept of ELF. She defines ELF as English used among NNSs and implies it should naturally have some characteristics reflecting the languages and cultures of the speakers who use it.

> ELF (English as a Lingua Franca) emphasizes the role of English in communication between speakers from different L1s, i.e. the primary reason for learning English today; it suggests the idea of community as opposed to alienness; it emphasizes that people have something in common rather than their differences; it implies that 'mixing' languages is acceptable (which was, in fact, what the original *lingua francas* did) and thus that there is nothing inherently wrong in retaining certain characteristic of the L1, such as accent, ... (Jenkins 2000: 11)

This follows the notion that the model of EIAL should be polymodel and the norm is endonormative. Kachru is the same as Jenkins in the polymodel position, but he is rather ambiguous in the respect that the norm is completely endonormative, because it seems that Kachru's main concern is concerning the Englishes used in the Outer Circle, and not extended to those in the Expanding Circle. Jenkins points out this attitude of Kachru's as follows:

> Kachru does not extend his criticisms of Quirk's attitude to expanding circle Englishes...In other words, because the expanding circle Englishes (unlike the outer circle Englishes) do not have a substantial number of country-internal functions (if any), Kachru does not recognize the legitimacy of ELF varieties. (Jenkins 2007: 11)

EIAL should have polymodels and varieties according to languages and cultures of the NNS. We should, however, have something in common among Englishes we use for the sake of intelligibility. Jenkins calls the common features of ELF pronunciation the Lingua Franca Core. Based on this standpoint of Jenkins's, I will discuss the substance of Japanese English for EIAL, and introduce how it appears in the subject matters of school textbooks.

Some features of Japanese English for EIAL

Having discussed my standpoints of Japanese English for EIAL, I will now turn to the issue of what the substance of Japanese English for

EIAL is. If we consider the past one generation and name a few examples of advocates who suggested that Japanese people should use English different from that of NSs, we have Suzuki Takao's 'Englic', Watanabe Taketatu's 'Japalish', and Oda Makoto's 'Englanto'. All of them recommend Japanese people to use Japanese English, but none of them elaborate on what it really looks like. Suzuki (1975) says that Englic should be free from NS English, but does not say anything about what it should be really like. Watanabe (1983) mentions the received norm of his Japalish, but the argument is rather rough and too expanded, for example, saying that /si/ should be replaced by /ʃi/, or advocating the use of gestures and so on. Oda (1989), from his various experiences in foreign countries, recommends us to use our own English, but his argument is biased regarding the content of our speech or writings, namely, messages we send to the counterparts. Thus, although all of them explain why we should have Japanese English, none of them say what it should actually be like, which we will discuss in the following section.

Three linguistic materials taken up for discussion

Generally speaking, linguistic materials to be discussed should be writing systems, sounds, vocabulary, grammar, expressions[4] and discourse. In this article, however, I explore sounds, vocabulary and expressions, because these three reflect more characteristics of 'Japaneseness' compared with the other three: the degree of the variety is expected to be larger in sounds, vocabulary and expressions than in writing systems, grammar and discourse. The former three are more changeable according to the variety and needs of EIAL and it would be extremely difficult to limit the change, while the latter three would not give us serious problems even if we apply the NS English systems to the EIAL systems. Or rather, if we added some characters such as the Japanese Kana, the Korean Hankul, or Russian Alphabet to the present writing system of the English Alphabet, the writing system of EIAL would be too confusing for communication, so we would be better off leaving the present system as it is.[5] The same discussion would be true with the basic grammar such as the word order. If the word orders were different from EIAL to EIAL, it would lead to confusion. For example, if we adopted the Japanese syntax of S+O+V for EIAL in addition to the English S+V+O, it would give us a lot of turmoil. Thus, they are resistant to changes. Some rules such as the third person singular for verbs and the concord of number (singular or plural) for nouns, however, may not raise serious problems for EIAL.

As for the style of discourse or the organization of utterances or sentences, any language or culture has both inductive and deductive patterns and uses them according to TPO (time, place and occasion). Although it is often said that English-speaking people are likely to say the conclusion first, while Japanese people have a tendency to say it at the end (Toyama 1992: 10–17), this inclination is a matter of degree or style. Japanese people may often say or write the conclusion first according to the needs of the situation, while more often than not English-speaking people occasionally adopt the logical or literary process of introduction, development, turn and conclusion which was originated from the organization of Chinese poetry. Therefore, for the current purpose of considering Japanese English for EIAL, we will put aside writing systems, grammar and discourse, and focus on sounds, vocabulary and expressions, to which we shall now turn.

Sounds

Sounds are the most changeable aspect of EIAL. This is because they are quite possibly subject to the influence of the vernacular: we cannot get rid of some particular sound habits which have been acquired through our mother tongue. What should we keep in mind when we consider sounds for EIAL? What are the cores among a variety of sounds of EIAL? Concerning these questions, I will make four points, three of which accord with Yano's claim that Englishes in the Expanding Circle such as Japanese English should be a 'plainer, simpler, and more regular English' (Yano 2001: 128–9).

First, I take up the point that comes before the problems of pronunciation of each sound – the articulation of our voice. Some peoples such as the Japanese do not use much energy when they speak; they are inclined just to mutter. It is necessary for them to articulate clearly so that the counterparts can listen to what they say. This applies not only to EIAL but also to their mother tongue.

Second, the pronunciation of EIAL should be in accord with the spelling. The English language is notorious for its irregularity between sound and spelling. If English words were pronounced as they are spelled, it would lighten the burden imposed on NNSs. For example, for such words as 'often' and 'suggestion' which have two pronunciations /ɔ́fən/ /sədʒéstʃən / and / ɔ́ftən/ /səgdʒéstʃən/ respectively, the latter should be adopted for EIAL. For such words as 'privacy'/práivəsi/· /prívisi/ and 'globalization' /gloubəlaizéitʃən/· /gloubəlizéitʃən/, the choice of the pronunciation should accord with the rule of phonics: the former will be adopted respectively. As is well known, some vocabularies such as 'you', 'live', 'get', 'water', 'girl', all of which are often used for daily life, are irregular in the rule of phonics.[6] If we pursue the goal of ownership for all people who use them in EIAL, we should regularize the link between spelling and pronunciation.

Third, some pronunciations which NNSs do not have in their L1 can be substituted by similar sounds of their L1. Some examples of the latter point are [t] and [d] sounds for [θ] and [ð] sounds, as seen in 'thank', 'thick', 'this' and 'that'. What we call the dark [ɫ] is substituted by [ʊ] sound in the case of 'little', 'apple', 'castle', etc. Another example is [p] substituted for [f]. It is said that the first Japanese Americans, who went to the United States of America in the Meiji Era, were not able to pronounce the [f] sound: they said /hláuə/ for 'flower' and /hráidei/ for 'Friday' and could not make themselves understood. Then they began to use [p] instead of [f], saying /pláuə/ and /práidei/, which settled the problem. The sounds [f] and [p] are similar in that they are labial. When Japanese people pronounce [p] sound with their little aspiration, the sound is almost the same as [f] sound. As for the substitute sound for 'th', an article in *Newsweek* introduced J. Jenkins's remark, saying that [θ] used by international airplane pilots is shifted into [t]:

> Linguist Jennifer Jenkins, an expert in world Englishes at King's College London[7] asks why some Asians, who have trouble pronouncing the "th" sound, should spend hours trying to say "thing" instead of "sing" or "ting." International pilots, she points out, already pronounce the word "three" as "tree" in radio dispatches, since "tree" is more widely comprehensible. (*Newsweek*, 7 March 2005 'Who Owns English?')

Fourth, although GA (General American) is generally adopted for the audio material for textbooks in Japan (Hardy 2006: 29), in a case where there are two kinds of pronunciation for some words, NNSs can choose easier varieties for them to pronounce. For instance, the sound of -ar- in 'car' and 'park' are pronounced as [ɑː] in RP (Received Pronunciation) and [ɑː*r*] in GA. In such a case, the former should be adopted by some Asian NNSs such as Japanese speakers of EIAL, because r-colouring is very difficult for them to pronounce. The diphthong in 'home', 'coat' and 'so' is pronounced as [əʊ] in RP and [oʊ] in GA. In this case, the latter is easier for Japanese people: they have the [oʊ] sound in the Japanese language. So Japanese English for EIAL adopts the [oʊ] sound. Thus we adopt either RP or GA from NNS convenience. EIAL is a mixed language in this respect. This discussion comes from some examples of Japanese speakers, but it does not refer to, say, Indians who are likely to pronounce almost every r-sound in the spelling. Thus EIAL is different according to the NNS. We have to acknowledge this kind of variety when we speak and listen to EIAL.

Among the prosodic features, such as stress, rhythm and intonation, stress (and consequently, rhythm) should be regarded with more attention than intonation. If we speak Japanese English for EIAL with Japanese syllable-timed accent which is based on pitch rather than stress, the communicability range will fall. For example, if we say /bi-ju:-ti-f-l/ ('beautiful') with the correct pronunciation of each phoneme but with the Japanese flat accent, both NSs and NNSs from Asian countries will have great difficulties in identifying the word. On the other hand, if we say /bju:-chi-hu-ru/ with the imperfect pronunciation of each phoneme but with the stress on the right place, the extent of the understanding of both native and non-native speakers will go up. Compared with pronouncing phonemes correctly, putting stresses on the right places is much easier for Japanese people, so it will not produce a serious problem for them to adopt this practice for Japanese English for EIAL. Intonation would not be a big problem for all Englishes including Japanese English, because it is near universal that we have only two main kinds of intonation, rising intonation and falling intonation. The former is generally used for interrogative utterances, while the latter is more often used for declarative or assertive utterances. Consequently, we should not need to pay attention so much to intonation.

Vocabulary

Issues concerning the vocabulary of Japanese English for EIAL would be roughly divided into three. First, we have some words and phrases which are specific to the Japanese tradition and culture. These words and phrases have been used as 'loan words' in English without translation, because there are no equivalent terms to them in English. Some examples are 'sushi', 'kimono', 'judo', 'noh', 'zen' and so on, which were once written in italics but nowadays they are more likely to be written in the ordinary type. As is seen in the examples such as 'dango' (conferring secretly among the parties concerned for negotiation or bid), 'nemawashi' (manoeuvring behind the scenes for obtaining one's objective) and 'tsunami' (a tidal wave caused by an earthquake), some words reflect the present day social and political customs in Japan and the specific meteorological features found in Japan. About 200 words of this kind are included in a dictionary such as *Webster's Third New International Dictionary*. When we use this kind of vocabulary for those who are not accustomed to Japanese culture, we need to add some annotation such as 'sushi or a rice ball with a slice of raw fish on it' or 'kimono or Japanese traditional costume with wide sleeve, worn with a broad sash'.

Second, in Japanese there are words and phrases called 'wasei eigo' or 'English made in Japan'. They are 'English-like Japanese words', which have been written in Japanese katakana syllables. They are sometimes written in the Roman alphabet, and thus mistaken for English. Some of the typical examples are 'cooler', 'consent', 'gasoline stand', 'morning call', 'sharp pencil', etc., meaning 'air conditioner', 'electrical outlet', 'gas station', 'wake-up call' and 'mechanical pencil' respectively. They look like or sound like English words and phrases in both spelling and pronunciation. *CIDE* (*The Cambridge International Dictionary of English*) has included about 150 of these words and phrases together with similar vocabulary from other non-English native countries and regions. In principle, we should not use this kind of English-like Japanese when we speak with those people who do not know this situation. These words and phrases do not make any sense in English or they have special meanings which are different from the original English. The reason I write 'in principle' is that there is some possibility that some of these words and phrases will be used in Japanese English for EIAL in the future, because they possibly add some new meanings to the native speakers' English words.

Here is an episode illustrating this possibility. In the late 1980s, when we used the term 'comic movies' for Japanese 'manga eiga' in *the New Crown English Series*, a series of junior high school English textbooks authorized by the Ministry of Education, Culture, Science, Sports and Technology in Japan (Hereafter MEXT), of which I was in charge as one of the writers, an ALT (Assistant Language Teacher), who is a native speaker of English, insisted that there was no such expression as 'comic movies' in English, and that it should be corrected as 'comedies' or 'funny movies'. But, Japanese 'comic movies' are not only comedies and funny movies, but also romances, adventures and serious human dramas. Thus we used the term as it was. This was what happened more than twenty years ago, when the idea of 'Englishes' was not so popular in Japan. Now we would express the term as 'manga movies' using the Japanese term 'manga', which is now used as a loan word in English and a lot of languages in Asia. Thus, in the vocabulary of Japanese English for EIAL we may have a lot of examples whose meanings are quite new to other people including the native speakers of English.

Third, in using the rest of the vocabulary except for the above-mentioned two groups of special words and phrases, we may as well be careful with the differences of meaning between an English word and a Japanese word which is regarded equivalent. For example, there are some differences between 'teacher' and its Japanese translation 'sensei' in terms of their object, function and association. The objects of these two words are different: the English 'teacher' means 'school teaching staff', while the Japanese 'sensei' implies not only 'school teaching staff' but also 'medical doctor, parliamentary member, master of some arts or sports'. There are differences in function: the Japanese school teachers are expected to take more care of children's daily life than teachers in English speaking countries.[8] As for association, a primary school teacher in English-speaking countries is often referred to using the pronoun 'she', while this is not so in Japan. This means that the visual association of the English 'primary school teacher' is a woman, which reflects the situation that the majority of primary school teachers in English speaking countries are women. Thus, the Japanese 'sensei' is not equivalent to the English 'teacher'. All NNSs have the same problems in translation of their L1 into English (for details, see Morizumi 2004). So, when they use their variety of EIAL, they should keep in mind an Italian old saying 'The translator is the traitor'.

Expressions

Even if a sentence or an utterance has no problem in terms of grammar and usage, it can be regarded as 'not English-like' or even 'incorrect' from the viewpoints of English traditional and cultural values. Our greatest concern in admitting and promoting the diversity of EIAL is the 'right or wrong' discussion of this kind of expression. The issues of pronunciation in which Japanese people have difficulties, or such grammatical issues as the rule of the third person singular or concord of number (singular or plural) are only the matters of 'formal rules'. Although we have some difficulties or troubles in observing those rules or codes, it does not give us suffering or conflict in heart and mind. When it comes to a matter of expressions of our values and ways of thinking, however, the discussion is not so simple, because it has something to do with our identity.

Our values and ways of thinking are reflected in our language. In other words, language expressions, whether spoken (utterances) or written (sentences), reflect our moral-codes or logic. Let's take an example of expressions in which the Japanese sense of modesty, or virtue of reserve, is reflected. Japanese people are likely to say when they serve something to eat to their guest: 'There is nothing, but please help yourself' and/or 'This isn't very delicious, but please help yourself' (Morizumi and Petersen 1989: 9–18; Morizumi 2006: 12). Many native English speakers might say that these expressions are not English-like when considered from the standpoint of English values or logic. They would say, 'If there is nothing, how can I help myself?' or, 'If something is not delicious, why serve it?' As for the latter expression, Naotsuka (1980) surveyed how the expression was accepted by some Asians and Europeans. She asked what they thought about the utterance. Most Asians including Koreans and Chinese replied affirmatively, saying they would often say this, while most Europeans answered with responses varying from 'This doesn't make any sense' to 'The person who speaks this way is insincere'. With this result, Naotsuka suggests that we should not use this kind of expression. It is certain that, generally speaking, many native speakers of English may not condescend to their guest like this when they serve something to eat to him or her. Instead, they may say, 'This is very delicious. I hope you'll like it.' Maybe there are some Japanese people who would like to speak as most English native speakers speak, and it is all right for them to speak that way. It lacks balance, however, if this kind of expression which reflects cultural values and ways of thinking is totally banned in the Japanese use of EIAL.

In addition to the expressions resulting from the above-mentioned reserved attitude of Japanese people, there are other kinds of expressions which Japanese people are inclined to use in their daily life.[9] For example, Japanese people sometimes ask someone they meet for the first time, 'How old are you?' and 'Do you have any children?' It is very important for many Japanese people to know whether their partner in dialogue is senior or junior, or having a child or not, for they decide on a way of talking or the contents of the topic according to the human relations in terms of age and family condition. Morioka (1981) insists that these questions are unsuitable for conversation among NSs of English, and should be avoided. She calls them 'conversation stoppers', and states that Europeans, including NSs of English, cannot continue a conversation when they are asked these questions. These questions may interfere with privacy for Europeans, including NSs of English, but to make these expressions 'conversation stoppers' when we are using EIAL with various peoples in the world is to force us to observe one kind of values and logic. In every culture there are some expressions and questions which require us to consider TPO (time, place and occasion) when we use them. If Japanese people cannot express their traditional Japanese way of thinking or feeling in EIAL, they would lose their sense of self-identity. More radically speaking, it leads to the rejection of their way of life. If EIAL is a 'container' to carry various messages, it should be 'stateless'. It should be 'neutral' in accepting any kind of values and logic. Japanese English for EIAL is one of the Englishes used as an international auxiliary language, and it should include Japanese ways of thinking (Morizumi 1995: 13–15; see also Park, this volume).

Identity of EIAL

I have so far discussed what Japanese English for EIAL should be like in terms of sounds, vocabulary and expressions. As one of the conclusions of this discussion, we can say, naturally, that NNS Englishes should be different from NS Englishes. Reportedly,[10] Ling Yu-tang, a Chinese (Taiwanese) man of letters who stayed in Japan for some time before the Second World War, once said 'In order for the majority of Japanese people to speak English fluently, either they should become un-Japanese-like, or English should become un-English-like.' This is an extreme argument, but the reality it addresses is admirably expressed. It is already illustrated with NNS Englishes in Singapore, India and the Philippines. For example, the mesolect and the basilect of Singaporean English are quite different from NS Englishes, mainly because they are used by the general public in the country. On the other hand, becoming good speakers of English could mean losing their identity to NNSs as implied in *the Course of Study* issued in 1947 and 1951 by MEXT, referring to the objectives of English learning or teaching in Japan. It said as follows:

> To learn English is not to memorize many English words but to make our mind and heart work in the same way as English speaking people do. (*The Course of Study* 1947)
>
> The objectives of English teaching are ... to develop an understanding of, appreciation for, and a desirable attitude toward the English speaking peoples, especially as regards their modes of life, manners, and customs. (*The Course of Study* 1951)

What is said in the above quotations is 'a relic from Japan's past', but it implies that learning a foreign language has something to do with forming our mental behaviour. It is often seen that those NNSs who live in English-speaking countries for a long time are sometimes English-people-like in their attitude and behaviour. This phenomenon is seen in a larger scale in the Outer Circle where English is used as a second or an official language. For example, it is reported that many elites in Singapore who speak 'good English' or the acrolect are Western-oriented and lacking in Singaporean identity. The issues of EIAL are relevant not only to the users' identity but also to their social status or social differential (Okumura et al. 2006: 131). Tanaka (1978: 341) says,'I sincerely wish that our study of linguistics will help break the prejudices of language and liberate persecuted people ...' To extend this, we hope that our study and practice of EIAL will help protect the general public in using their own English. The following section will investigate how the issue is being dealt with in Japanese English textbooks.

EIAL as seen in textbooks for middle school

The last point I take up in this article is how much of the idea or discussion of EIAL has been introduced to, or recognized by, the learners of English in Japan. I am afraid that such sociolinguistic aspects of language learning as the issues of EIAL have not been fully taken up in English education. So, when our students go out of school into the real world and encounter Englishes used in various parts of the world, they are surprised, embarrassed, or have superiority or inferiority complexes.[11] They have an inferiority complex about their pronunciation and grammar toward NSs, and meanwhile a superiority complex toward NNSs in the world. It is said that some Japanese speak English like NSs do in pronunciation and grammar although the content of their speech is poor in both quality and quantity. To avoid these unnecessary anxieties and complexes, and to enhance the adequate sense or views of languages and cultures, it is indispensable for them to be informed about the reality and principles of EIAL while they are in school. That is why I have conducted a survey about the topics of EIAL introduced in high school English textbooks in Japan.

How should the issues of EIAL be introduced and taught in English classroom instruction? One of the best ways in the Japanese context is to take up the issues in the subject matter of the textbooks authorized by the MEXT.[12] If the topic of the text is about what Englishes used in the world are like and about how we should cope with the situation, students can be ready to meet the issues while studying English in school. An overview of the English textbooks for junior and senior high schools in Japan shows that the concept of the EIAL has been treated to some extent as their topics or subject matters, although very few concrete examples of EIAL are introduced. We shall now examine some of the examples, starting with the junior high textbooks.

Junior high school textbooks

Among the six kinds of present textbook series authorized by the MEXT, I will take up the *New Crown English Series,* which have shown more interest in EIAL than the other five.

It is in a lesson titled 'The Last Lesson' of *New Crown English Series 3* that the topic of an international language was taken up for the first time in the course of the history of junior high school English textbooks in Japan. This version was published in 1980, when the topic of EIAL was not so popular in Japan, so this topic itself was quite controversial at that time. The lesson is based on A. Daudet's 'The Last Lesson', the theme of which is the 'importance of a mother tongue'. The last part of the text is as follows:

> At one time English was the language of one particular nation. It was the language of England, but it is no longer so. Many peoples in the world have used English as a common language for a long time, and you can call it an international language. (Nakamura and Wakabayashi et al. 1980: 89)

Another example is 'The Story of English' in *Let's Read 3* of the 1992 version of *New Crown English Series 3,* which takes the history of the English language for its subject matter. This is the first example in which the term 'Englishes' appeared in either junior or senior high English textbooks in Japan.

> Now English is not merely the language of Britain. It is not only that of the United States either. It is the language of a variety of people throughout the world. Australians speak Australian English, Indians speak Indian English, and so on. This is the age of 'different Englishes'. (Morizumi et al. 1992: 69)

A picture of a drugstore in Australia is attached to the text. The drugstore is run by a Chinese-Australian owner and it has a shop sign 'Mixed Business' which means 'drugstore'. The caption of the picture says 'The shop owner uses the expression "Mixed Business" which has not been used in NS English.'

The last example is in a lesson with the title of 'Life in Australia' of the latest version *New Crown English Series 2* (2006). The lesson takes up Australian English with a dialogue between an Australian girl and a Japanese boy whose uncle has been to Sydney on business. The last utterance, suggesting the variety of Englishes in the world, is the main message of this text on this page. The dialogue goes as follows:

Ken:	My uncle went to Sydney last week. He stayed for five days.
Emma:	A short trip. Did he understand Australian English?
Ken:	No. He didn't understand it at first. But he learned 'Ta.' It means 'Thank you.'
Emma:	Right. Did he learn 'G'day mate'?
Ken:	Yes. It means 'Hello.'
Emma:	Right. English is different in different countries.

(Takahashi et al. 2006: 6)

This is not an example of NNS varieties of English, but, as the last utterance of the text implies, the main theme of this lesson is that English spoken even in the Inner Circle is partly different from country to country, or from region to region, the fact of which is often not introduced in English education in the countries in the Expanding Circle like Japan. Another significance of the introduction of Australian English is to show that Australian accent including the pronunciation of /mait/ instead of /meit/ for 'mate' is not inferior to RP or GA. Unfortunately there are a lot of people in Japan who have the prejudice that British and American Englishes are better to teach than the other varieties of English in the Inner Circle. A junior high school textbook published in the early 1980s wrote as follows:

> The language of Australia is English, but most Australians speak it with an Australian accent. For example, they say, 'I'll go to the hospital to die!' Their 'today' sounds like 'to die'. (Ito et al. 1981: 45)

The text requires arguments in two ways; first, the existence of Aboriginal languages is ignored in the first sentence, and second, the episode of pronunciation of 'to die' and 'today' suggests a slur or mockery toward Australian English unless we are very careful in explaining it. Thus, we must treat this text as a negative example of EIAL. We will now examine some examples from the senior high school textbooks.

Senior high school textbooks

Senior high school textbooks are divided into six types or subjects according to the variety of the language activities or skills taken up: *Oral Communication I, II, English I, II, Reading and Writing.* In this article, the textbooks of *English I* and *II* (which are general textbooks with four skills taken up and have 37 kinds published respectively) and *Reading* (which has 26 kinds) are taken up for this survey, and the following four examples are analysed.

'Singlish Bad, English Good' of *Crown English II* (lesson 9) refers to Singapore's the 'Speak Good English Movement'. The text begins like this:

> The Singaporean Government says that Singlish is no good, and that their people must learn how to speak good English. Is it possible for the government to make their people speak good English? (Shimozaki et al. 2006: 85)

The title of this lesson implies that Singlish is bad and English is good, which is rather biased from the principles of EIAL and the viewpoint of linguistic sensitivity. The message of this text, however, is not imbalanced as is suggested in the above interrogative sentence of the first paragraph. In the latter part of the text, Larry Smith's remark on EIAL is quoted:

> 'Now it's not native speakers that are moving English forward,' said Larry Smith, a professor of international English. 'It's the non-native speakers, the people in Singapore, the people in Malaysia.' (Shimozaki et al. 2006: 87)

The next example comes from *Unicorn English II.* In the first three sections of lesson 10 'English as a World Language', the development of English is introduced, and in the latter two sections, the issues of the standard English and 'a style of English which has been influenced by their native languages' is taken up as the main topic. The tone of the whole text emphasized the latter point, that is, the good points of the standard English are mentioned, but the discussion is followed by an opposing argument with the conjunction 'however', supporting or justifying the varieties of English. The text concludes as follows:

> For now, certainly standard English is the most practical to learn for international communication. However, when you have a chance to speak English with someone, don't worry if your English is not always "correct" or "perfect." (Yasuyoshi et al. 2006: 144)

The message of the last sentence may be encouragement to the students, but there seems to be an assumption that English used by NNS is 'incorrect' or 'imperfect' (Jenkins 2007: vii; Kirkpatrick 2007: 6–7).

'English: A Small Beginning' of *Prominence English II* (lesson 1) explains the process by which a small language of England has come to be one of the biggest international auxiliary languages. In the latter part of the lesson, the role of English is mentioned in the following way:

> However, English has become a second language in countries like India and Singapore, where it is used in government, in education, and on radio and television. In these countries, English is a very important language, often, unifying many different groups of people. (Nakada et al. 2004: 9)

'English as an International Language' of *Encounter Reading* (lesson 3) discusses the reasons English has become an important international language, and in the last section it is implied that English has achieved its global status not because of its linguistic features but because of other factors.

> Languages rise and fall in world status for many kinds of reasons – political, economic, social, religious, literary – but linguistic reasons do not rank highly among them. (Watanabe et al. 2004: 44)

In 'Englishes' of *Exceed English Reading* (lesson 5), the issue of EIAL is taken up from the viewpoints mentioned in this article. It is based on an article of *Newsweek* (7 March 2005) and, in the last section the issue of identity is discussed as seen in the following:

> Values are different from nation to nation. When we put into our values into English, we may need to change some English logic. For example, consider the following utterances which some Japanese are likely to say:
>
> *There is nothing, but please help yourself.*
> *This isn't very delicious, but please help yourself.*
>
> These expressions are based on the Japanese sense of modesty. If we could not express our traditional Japanese way of thinking or feeling in English, we would lose our sense of self-identity. In order to have English really internationalized, we may have to put our local identities in the English we use. (Morizumi et al. 2008: 82)

As for the textbooks for EIAL at the tertiary level in Japan, very few have been found except for reading materials whose main topic is 'language and culture' or 'sociolinguistic aspects of language' as are seen in some of the textbooks including McConnell (2000). In these textbooks for reading comprehension, one or two chapters are allotted for the topic of EIAL or Englishes, just as seen in junior or senior high school textbooks. There are some cases, however, where some varieties of Englishes are introduced through TV news or newspapers on the Internet. But those Englishes used in the major TV stations and newspapers such as Channel News Asia, *The China Daily, The Korean Times* and *The Times of India* do not always reflect the real local variety of EIAL especially in terms of pronunciation.

Teaching materials to be desired

What is clear through an overview of the textbooks published in Japan is that there are some textbooks in which the principles of EIAL have been mentioned, but almost none of them have taken up concrete examples. One of the most complete and exhaustive textbooks for EIAL is Jenkins (2003), in which both principles and practices of EIAL are treated in a full-scale way with questions to the students, who can check and confirm the philosophy of EIAL and acquire practical competence to meet the situation of Englishes in the world. It is desired that a textbook or reference book like Jenkins's should be written in each country in the Expanding Circle. What needs to be kept in mind in editing such a book is to accompany varieties of audio materials of EIAL. An example for this goes back to as early as Trudgill and Hannah (1982), which has the audio material of the Inner Circle Englishes including RP and Canadian English. It has no audio examples of the Expanding Circle Englishes, but we cannot expect too much if we consider the year 1982 when the book was published. One of the latest books, with audio CD attached, is Kirkpatrick (2007), which has several NNS audio materials such as Filipina, Singaporean, Cambodian, Bruneian, Indonesian, Malaysian and Vietnamese Englishes, all of which are introduced under the name of 'English for a lingua franca'. There are some published in Japan, one of which is Nakatani (2004) in which more than half the examples among the 14 are of NNS varieties. If we have both written and listening materials for EIAL available in school education – primary, secondary, and tertiary levels respectively – students can recognize that we are in the era of Englishes, through which our solidarity and identity are enhanced as well as our linguistic and cultural sensitivity.

Notes

1. This article is an English version of Morizumi (2008) with some revision. I owe it to Professor YANO Yasutaka: He kindly asked me to contribute to this

volume, and his works on 'Englishes', including Yano (2001), were very helpful for me to organize the article. I also thank Professor MURATA Kumiko and Professor Jennifer Jenkins for their useful comments and advice to complete the article.

2. Different naming is sometimes used by the same scholar. L. Smith once used the term of EIAL and Jenkins adopted the term of EIL in some of their earlier works respectively.
3. It was in the early 1980s when the concept of 'Englishes' became popular in the world. Pride (1981) *New Englishes*, Platt et. al (1982) *The New Englishes*, Trudgill and Hannah (1982) *International English*, and Todd (1984) *Modern Englishes* were published in this period.
4. I use the term 'expressions' for 'ways of speaking' which are specific to each language and culture. For example, Japanese people are likely to say 'Work hard', while English-speaking people might say 'Take it easy', when they see off someone who is going to take some competitive examination.
5. However, code-mixing is observed for creative purposes such as in advertising. See Bhatia, this volume, for example.
6. This kind of irregularity can be seen in irregular conjugation of content words of English. Almost all irregular nouns, verbs and adjectives are of the basic daily life vocabulary.
7. Currently, 'at the University of Southampton'.
8. Cf. 'A Comparative Survey of Friendship Relation and Daily Life Consciousness of High School Students in Japan, USA, China and South Korea' published by Japan Youth Peaceful Institute, March 2005.
9. Varieties of expressions which are specific to Japanese culture have been translated into English in Yamagishi (1998). Many of them should be examined for the right or wrong discussion for Japanese English for EIAL in the point whether the Japaneseness should be reserved in the translation or not.
10. Cf. Professor Ohashi Katsuhiro's remark at a symposium 'Nihon no eigo-kyoiku ni okeru riso to genjitsu' or 'The Ideal and the Reality of English Education in Japan' (Kinoshita M., Ohashi, K. and Morizumi M. et al.) for JACET Kyushu•Okinawa Chapter Annual Conference, 11 October 2003.
11. Cf. 'World Englishes no kangae wo jugyo ni' or 'To Introduce the Concept of World Englishes in Our Classroom Instruction', the resume of Professor Shiozawa Tadashi's keynote speech for the symposium in JACET 46th Annual Conference, 9 September 2007.
12. MEXT authorizes textbooks for junior and senior high school every four years. As of April 2008, there are six kinds of junior high school textbooks authorized by the Ministry. In senior high school, there are six subjects for English: *Oral Communication I, II, English I, II, Reading and Writing*, among which *English I* and *II* are most widely used. There are now nearly forty kinds of *English I* and *II* textbooks.

References

Crystal, D. 1997. *English as a Global Language*. Cambridge: Cambridge University Press.

Hardy, T. 2006. 'Constructing Identities in a Language Textbook in Japan: Stake Holders and Issues' in *Obirin Synergy No. 6*, Tokyo: J. F. Oberlin University Graduate School.

Honna, N. 1990. *Asia no eigo* or *Englishes in Asia*. Tokyo: Kuroshio Shuppan.

Hino, N 2003. 'Kokusaieigo kenkyu no taikeika ni mukete – Nihon no eigo-kyoiku no shiten kara' or 'For Study of Systemization of EIL – With Special Reference to English Education in Japan' *Asian English Studies No.5*. Tokyo: Japan Association for Asian Englishes.

Jenkins, J. 2000. *The Phonology of English as an International Language*. Oxford: Oxford University Press.

——. 2003. *World Englishes: A Resource Book for Students*. London: Routledge.

——. 2007. *English as a Lingua Franca: Attitude and Identity*. Oxford: Oxford University Press.

Kachru, B. 1991. 'World Englishes and Applied Linguistics' in Tickoo (ed.). *Languages and Standards: Issues, Attitudes, Case Studies*. Singapore: RELC.

Kirkpatrick, A. 2007. *World Englishes*. Cambridge: Cambridge University Press.

McConnell, J. 2000. *Language and Culture in the 21st Century*. Tokyo: Seibido.

McKay, L. 2002. *Teaching English as an International Language*. Oxford: Oxford University Press.

Morioka, K. 1981. *Hikakubunnka no eikaiwa* or *English Conversation for Comparative Culture*. Tokyo: Kenkyusha.

Morizumi, M. 1995. 'Sekaikyotsugo toshiteno eigo wo donoyoni toraeruka' or 'How Should We Consider English as a World Common Language?' in *The English Teachers' Magazine*. 44(4). Tokyo: Taishukanshoten.

——. 2004. *Tango no Bunkatekiimi –'Furendo' wa 'tomodachi' ka* or *Cultural Meaning of English Words – Is 'Friend' equal to 'Tomodachi'?* Tokyo: Sanseido.

——. 2006. 'What Are the Ultimate Purposes of English Education? – Three Kinds of Education Imposed on TEFL in Japan' in L. Yiu-nam et al. *New Aspects of English Language Teaching and Learning*. Taipei: Crane.

——. 2007. 'Chu•ko no kyokasho niokeru <kokusaieigo>' or 'International English as Seen in the Middle School English Textbooks in Japan' in *The English Teachers' Magazine* 56(5). Tokyo: Taishukanshoten.

——. 2008. 'Nihonjin no tame no EIAL' or 'Japanese English for EIAL' in *Asian English Studies No. 10*. Tokyo: Japan Association for Asian Englishes.

Morizumim, M. and M. Petersen. 1989. 'Komyunikeshon to bumpo•hyogen' or 'Grammar and Expression for Communication' in *ELEC Bulletin, No.92*. Tokyo: English Language Education Council.

Nakatani, M. 2004. *Namatta eigo no risuningu* or *English around the World*. Tokyo: The Japan Times.

Naotsuka, R. 1980. *Obeijin ga chinmokusurutoki* or *Mutual Understanding of Different Cultures*. Tokyo: Taishukanshoten.

Oda, M. 1989. *Oda Makoto no eigo gojuppo hyappo – Jimae no eigo wo dotsukuruka* or *Oda Makoto's Fifty Steps and a Hundred Steps – How Should We Make English of Our Own?* Tokyo: Kawaibunkakenkyujo.

Okumura, M. et al. 2006. *Taminzokushakai no gengoseijigaku – Eigo wo mon-onishita shingaporujin no yuragu aidentiti* or *Linguistic Politics in Multi-ethnic Society – Wavering Identity of Singaporeans who Master English*. Tokyo: Hitsuji Shobo.

Phillipson, R. 1992. *Linguistic Imperialism*. Oxford: Oxford University Press.

Platt, J., H. Weber and M. L. Ho. 1984. *The New Englishes*. London: Routledge.
Pride, J. (ed.) 1982. *New Englishes*. Rowley: Newbury House.
Quirk, R. 1985. 'The English language in a global context.' In R. Quirk and H. G. Widdowsons (eds) *English in the World. Teaching and Learning the Language and Literature*. Cambridge: Cambridge University Press, pp. 1–6.
Quirk, R. and H. G. Widdowson. (eds) 1985. *English in the World: Teaching and Learning the Language and Literature*. Cambridge: Cambridge University Press.
Sapir, E. 1949. *Culture, Language and Personality*. Berkeley: UCP.
Smith, L. E. 1976. 'English as an international auxiliary language', *RELC Journal*, 7(2), 38–42.
——. 1983. *Readings in English as an International Language*. Oxford: Pergamon Press.
Suzuki, T. 1975. *Tozasareta gengo・nihongo no sekai* or *A Closed Language・A World of Japanese*. Tokyo: Shinchosha.
Tanaka, K. 1978. *Gengo kara mita minzoku to kokka* or *Peoples and States as Seen from Language*. Tokyo: Iwanami Shoten.
Todd, L. 1984. *Modern Englishes, Pidgins and Creoles*. Oxford: Blackwell.
Trudgill, P. and J. Hannah. 1982. *International English*. London: Edward Arnold.
Toyama, S. 1992. *Nihonngo no hasso・Eigo no hasso* or *Japanese Ways of Thinking・English Ways of Thinking*. Tokyo: NHK Books.
Watanabe, T. 1983. *Japalish no susume: Nihonjin no kokusaieigo* or *Let's Go with Japalish – An International Language for Japanese People*. Osaka: Asahishinbunsha.
Yamagishi, K. 1998. *Eigo ni narinikui nihongo wo kou yakusu* or *How to Translate Japanese Culture into English*. Tokyo: Kenkyusha.
Yano, Y. 2001. 'World Englishes in 2000 and beyond' in *World Englishes* 20–2.

High school textbooks authorized by the MEXT

Ito, K. et al. 1981. *New Horizon English Series 2*. Tokyo: Tokyoshoseki.
Morizumi, M. et al. 1992. *New Crown English Series 3*. Tokyo: Sanseido.
——. 2008. *Exceed English Reading*. Tokyo: Sanseido.
Nakada, S. et al. 2004. *Prominence English II*. Tokyo: Tokyoshoseki.
Nakamura, K. and S. Wakabayashi, et al. 1980. *New Crown English Series 3*, Tokyo: Sanseido.
Shimozaki, M. et al. 2006. *Crown English II*. Tokyo: Sanseido.
Takahashi, S. et al. 2006. *New Crown English Series 2*. Tokyo: Sanseido.
Watanabe, S. et al. 2004. *Encounter Reading*. Tokyo: Shubunkan.
Yasuyoshi, I. et al. 2006. *Unicorn English II*. Tokyo: Bun-eido.

7
Characteristics of Korea English as a Glocalized Variety*

Kyung-Ja Park

Introduction

Today English is spoken globally across cultural and geographical boundaries. People from different cultural backgrounds speak different varieties of English. As the number of people who use English as a first language (FstL), a second language (SL), or a foreign language (FL) increases, inevitably the number of varieties of English, especially spoken English, increases. The purpose of learning English as an international language is not to blindly imitate native speakers of English (NSE) but to understand and to be understood clearly.

The goal of this paper is to highlight distinctive features of Korea English (KE) and to demonstrate the importance of acknowledging KE as a legitimate variety of English (glocalized English: GlcE) in order for both native speakers' English (NSE)[1] and non-native speakers' English (NNSE) to be mutually 'intelligible, comprehensible and interpretable' (Smith and Forman 1997).

We would like to propose to use the term Korea English (KE) rather than either Korean English or Konglish. KE refers to the spoken English used by most educated Korean speakers when communicating internationally as well as intra-nationally. It has common cores of normative English with Korean traits and nuances in pronunciation, lexicon, syntax and discourse, distinct from other types of English. The term focuses on the unique characteristics of the spoken English used by Koreans. In Park (2006) and Park and Nakano (2007), I called this variety of English 'glocalized English' (GlcE).

In Korea, English is regarded as the most indispensable foreign language because it is a prerequisite for professional success as well as a tool for global interaction. Today English in Korea plays an important role in education, business and government. According to Sohn (1999: 12), almost 90 per cent of loan words in Korean have come from English since the end of the Second World War. This indicates that English loan words are deeply rooted in everyday communication in Korea.

Moreover, since 1997, English has been taught from the third grade of elementary school under the premise that, to become a successful global citizen, English should be mastered. In addition, there are numerous TV programmes that offer instruction in English to elementary and secondary school students as well as to adults. English employed in Korean English textbooks for secondary school students has very distinctive linguistic and paralinguistic features not found in other varieties of English. At the university level, an increasing number of universities in Korea are offering content courses in English. In addition, several universities in Korea have opened dual degree programmes with overseas universities. The government has also taken a step forward to pave the way for English to be a second language. According to *The Korea Herald* (23 October and 11 November 2003), developing communicative competence in English is the main reason for the establishment of English-only villages in Korea.[2] Thus, English seems to be one of the prerequisites to become a successful global citizen.

In the business world, English plays a key role in various aspects. For example, companies conduct interviews in English when hiring new employees. These companies also have their own English language programmes to enhance the English communicative competence of their employees. For business in Korea, English is regarded as a communication tool for inter-cultural interactions and international business transactions (IBT).

English in Korea, with more than one hundred years of educational history,[3] is more than just another foreign language; it is a language with a common set of English rules and expressions with uniquely Korean nuances. English in Korea is different from other foreign languages in Korea such as French, German, Spanish, Russian, Japanese, Chinese, and so forth. English has penetrated and has been assimilated into Korean life itself. English, as it is used in Korea, has been tremendously impacted by Korean culture and language. Speakers routinely use a mixture of English and Korean words, insert English words into a Korean sentence, code-switch from Korean to English, and use English with distinct glocalized flavours of Korean culture and language. English ubiquitously abounds in formal educational settings and international interactions.

If we consider other Englishes, such as those of Singapore, India and Hong Kong, we see that they have undergone different developmental stages as they became employed as a means of intra-/international interactions and communications, and as a medium of instruction and an official language. The same holds true for KE. Therefore, although it seems a bit premature to claim that English is used as a second language in Korea, the English used by Korean speakers is now well under way to becoming employed as a second language.

There have been two views on the nature of KE: (1) KE is neither institutionalized nor codified (Song 1998), and (2) KE is codified 'serving as the endonormative standard for English education in Korea' (Shim 1994, 1999; Baik 1994, 1995). Those who advocate codified KE provide the high school English textbooks of Korea between 1987 and 1995 as evidence that in lexico-semantic, morpho-syntactic and pragmatic aspects, there are major differences between American English and KE (Shim 1994, 1999 among others). Even though these differences produce grammatically correct English, NSEs find them unacceptable due to their unusual and awkward 'foreignness', according to Shim (1999). However, for KE speakers, they are features of codified Korea English observable in Korean high school English textbooks (Shim 1999: 250–6).

On the other hand, Song (1998) asserts that it is premature to describe KE as undergoing a language shift requiring that Korean be completely forfeited in favour of English. Language shift from Korean to English has not happened yet, according to Song. The reason is that in Korea (1) English is neither employed as an official language nor a medium of instruction at school, and (2) English is not used for intra-national communicative purposes.

However, two questions arise. The first question concerns the qualification for a language to be an SL. For example, are the above-mentioned two factors necessary and sufficient criteria for a language to be considered as an SL? The second question is how to deal with SL and FL. Should SL be considered as a continuum of FL or vice versa (Davies 2005; Richard et al. 1993)? Is it possible for speakers of English as an FL to become speakers of English as an SL?

Considering the current Korean situation in which English proficiency is considered to be an index of a successful life and career, it is more plausible for Koreans to use English as a communication tool at work since there is an increasing number of domestic and foreign companies in Korea which promote the use of English or adopt English as a primary language at work. The high demand for English proficiency brings about the infamous 'English Divide' (Baker et al.

2001; Tan 2007: English Chosun. Com, 18 July 2007). This new term can be interpreted as 'the gap between those who are proficient in English and those who are not' and is known to create tension in a community. Just as the 'Digital Divide' marginalized those without access to digital information, the English Divide is likely to make social and professional advancement more difficult for those with weak or non-existent English language skills.

As Korean society becomes a knowledge-oriented society and English becomes the communication tool as well as the medium of written information, it is inevitable that English will become a criterion distinguishing the power class from the other class. It is not uncommon to see young Korean children talking in English. Private English kindergartens are flourishing into a profitable business in Korea. An increasing number of students from elementary school to university are going abroad to study in an English-speaking country. It is inevitable that this trend will continue for some years. If that is the case, then in about ten years, speaking English is likely to be a necessary condition not only for university admission but also for employment in Korea. Moreover, starting in 1997, English has been taught from the third grade.

Many universities encourage or even require that content-based courses be conducted in English. For example, at one university in Seoul, more than 30 per cent of all classes are conducted in English. The percentage is expected to rise in the future. According to the *Korea Times* (6 February 2006), in 2006 Seoul National University started offering 10 per cent of liberal arts classes in English to raise students' basic academic knowledge as well as their English proficiency. Quite recently (MBC TV News, 4 November 2006) Korea's Minister of Education and Human Resources announced that by 2015 secondary school teachers will be required to teach English in English. To establish their proficiency, the national qualifying examination for English teachers will include a written essay and an oral interview in English, as well as English listening comprehension tests. Another note is that English proficiency is needed more than ever for government jobs. Considering all these facts, it is reasonable to think that Korea is now in the process of moving from English as a foreign language (EFL) to English as a second language (ESL).

Something else we should consider is that, if most educated KE speakers consistently employ certain forms, phrases, grammar, sentences and so forth, those forms should be regarded as norms as long as they are understandable and not grammatically incorrect. It is true that due to Westernization, Korean culture is changing and becoming multicultural.

However, Korea is still preserving and cherishing many of its unique cultural features and customs which greatly impact how people speak.

According to Crystal (1997), the global status of a language can be achieved if the language is used either as a primary language of the majority or as the priority foreign language. If we accept his definition of global language, it seems evident that KE should be regarded as a GlcE because KE is spoken by the majority of educated Koreans as a priority foreign language. KE, as a glocalized variety, also has its own characteristics due to its unique nature of culturally loaded linguistic and paralinguistic phenomena, to which we shall now turn.

Characteristics of KE

Distinctive features of the expressions used by Korean speakers of English (KSEs) include not only specific expressions but also unique culture-laden linguistic and paralinguistic phenomena. Some of the problems foreigners might encounter when communicating with KSEs (when managing IBT, for example[4]) illustrate some characteristics of KE. These problems show that KE used by the majority of educated Koreans as a priority foreign language is now well into the process of becoming a glocalized variety.

Although there are many signs that Korean culture including business culture is becoming more multicultural due to globalization (for example, more firms are run by managers who are not citizens of the country of origin of the firm), there are still some lingering differences. As we are living in this globalized world, 'mutual intelligibility, comprehensibility, and interpretability' (Smith and Forman 1997) are more important than ever. Opportunities for cross-cultural communicative interactions are presented more than ever for both NSEs and non-native speakers of English (NNSEs). In such circumstances, the overriding goal is to minimize misunderstanding and to achieve successful communication, for which understanding and awareness of the culture-specific orientations of Koreans and the Korean value system are essential.

The Korean value system reflected in KE

Korea has a unique history steeped in Confucianism (Kim 2006: 3–4), thereby producing a distinctive culture and value system. Thus, foreigners are advised to understand Korea's history and culture if they want to successfully engage in communicational interactions with Koreans.

Confucianism is the basis of the social code for proper behaviour in Korea (Kum 2006). That is, obedience and respect for superiors and elders, regard for humility, sincerity and courtesy, and belief that community comes before the individual are very important in everyday life (Sohn 1986). Thus, Korea's Confucian beliefs and the Korean value system are the keys to Korean culture. The Korean value system is deeply based on 'indirectness, hierarchism, formalism, collectivism, and emotionalism' (Sohn 1986: 445) which are all interrelated as reflected in English employed by Koreans. Korean culture is reflected in KE which in turn is also influenced by the Korean language. In the following, I will elaborate on five notions which are deeply embedded in the Korean value system, drawing on two different kinds of data I collected from 2004 to 2006 (hereafter, EFF and EFS, respectively).[5]

Indirectness and modesty

First, Koreans usually prefer to speak indirectly out of politeness. Old Korean proverbs state that it is a virtue not to openly express one's opinions or feelings but to show humility by remaining silent (Sohn 1986). Even in conversations, long silences are not only tolerated but often appreciated and recommended. This is why Americans often think Koreans are unfriendly and cold whereas Koreans often think Americans are direct, talkative or rude (Sohn 1986). Thus, one should try to save the other's face whenever possible and not to criticize others in public.

For example, foreigners are likely to be faced with situations where Koreans avoid such expressions as 'I disagree', 'I don't like you', 'I have a different view on that', 'I cannot agree with you', 'I don't agree with you', and so forth. This is because disagreement is expressed indirectly to save and not threaten face (Park and Nakano 1999: 22–3).

Generally speaking, Koreans also deny the positive evaluation to show modesty and politeness in expressive acts. In Korea, speech acts such as thanking, apologizing and offering condolences are not as expressive as in English in either the number of forms or the frequency of use as well as their expressive intensity (Sohn 1986). Americans most frequently acknowledge a compliment with 'Thanks (a lot)', or 'Thank you very much' while Koreans are likely to deny it. So when somebody says that 'Oh, this is very good', 'You did a good job', 'Your dress is very pretty', you are not supposed to accept it (Sohn 1986).

Seniority and hierarchism

Second, an important characteristic of the Korean value system stems from the fact that seniority is very important in Korea. Age is one of the most important elements in the choice of honorifics and speech styles as well as nonverbal behaviours. Seniority counts in all aspects of life. This affects everything from the organization of Korean business to communication and negotiation systems. For example, knowing a person's age allows one to select the appropriate expressions and styles in Korean. Koreans ask about age because they consider this information basic to normative and effective communication. The expressions used by Koreans such as 'What is her age?' (EFS) and 'Her age is thirty-two.' (EFS) are not grammatically incorrect or ill-formed but they sound 'foreign' to NSEs because English speakers would not ask about a person's age in business or other social settings (see Morizumi, this volume, for similar Japanese tendencies).

There are several ways of expressing respect to one's seniors (Sohn 1986). First of all, by using honorific lexical items one can show respect. For example, 'meal' in Korean has two different lexical items: one is a plain form, 'bab',[6] and the other honorific form, 'jinji' (in the olden days 'sura' is used only to a king). Secondly, there is also an honorific suffix which can be attached to verbs. For instance, 'gada' is a plain verb form meaning 'to go'. However, if you use an affix, '-si' to the verb stem 'ga', then you have an honorific form, 'gasida'. Finally, you can use both an honorific lexical item and an honorific affix by putting an honorific affix to an honorific lexical verb of 'to sleep' as in 'jumu-si-da'. The plain verb form is 'jada'. Moreover, one can always show respect to one's elders not only linguistically but also para-linguistically. Especially when sitting for meals, it is always advised to wait for one's seniors to pick up the spoon and chopsticks or to say 'meonjeo deuseyo (please start first)' (Lim et al. 2003).

An interesting example showing hierarchical relationships as an important Korean value system can be taken from address terms. Americans prefer informal and comfortable relationships because they are practical. Koreans show respect to their seniors and elders by adding an honorific suffix '-nim' to a lexical item or by using honorific lexical items or both honorific lexical items and suffix. For example, address terms are hierarchical and formal in Korean whereas English titles do not appear to have strong hierarchical connotation. A director of a university library is called 'gwanjang' when the addressor is older or higher-ranking person. However, he or she is called 'gwanjang-nim' by a younger or lower-ranking person. The difference between these two titles is that the suffix '-nim' is added to show respect. Thus, their use of deferential and plain forms of address and reference are determined mostly by 'the hierarchical dimension' not by 'the dimension of solidarity' (Sohn 1986: 452). That is, what name or title you are going to use is not determined by how close you feel to the person you are talking to, but by if that person is higher or lower in status, or older or younger in age. Moreover, in Korea 'once "gwanjangnim", forever "gwanjangnim" ', no matter what you do subsequently.[7]

Formality

Third, formality rather than informality and practicality is emphasized in the Korean value system. This is also related to hierarchism as is shown in the previous example of 'gwanjang(nim)'. An interesting example to show Koreans' preference of formality can be illustrated by the address term, 'gyosu-nim' (EFS) meaning 'professor'. In Korea, university students never address their professors by their first names regardless of situations. They are addressed either by the title alone as in 'Prof.' or by the title followed by the last name as in 'Prof. Park'. In Korea one can easily encounter a situation where someone is addressed as 'Prof.' by his or her family members. This is why some Korean students in America are reluctant to address their professors by their first names even though they are asked to do so.

Collectivism

Fourth, collectivism is also emphasized in the Korean value system. Koreans are more group-oriented and they value the group they belong to (Lee 2007). Koreans are more conscious of others' opinion than their own. Korean people are generally believed to be good negotiators. Therefore, it is good to be prepared to be patient and gentle but firm at the negotiating table. It is not good to push your position too hard. Sensitive issues and details may be saved for future discussions, preferably by a third person, if available. However, sufficient time is necessary because major decisions are usually made collectively. Group consensus is more valued than independent action. As an example, to questions like 'Who did it?' and 'Who would like to do this?', Koreans automatically respond 'We did it' (EFS) and 'We would like to do it' (EFS) instead of 'I did it' and 'I would like to do it'. 'Koreans also say "our company," "our son," "our school," and "our hometown" instead of saying "my company," "my son," "my school," and "my hometown" ' (Sohn 1986).

Emotionalism

Fifth, the Korean value system also emphasizes emotionalism. The ways Koreans express emotions are also different from Americans (Kim 1978), and it is reflected in the Korean language which, in turn, is also reflected in KE. In Korea, one of the most important values is the sense of 'jeong (정, 情)' which does not have any equivalent in English (Sohn 1986). It means 'love, affection, caring, sentiment, sympathy, feeling, concern, or all of them'. This distinctive concept of 'jeong' affects Koreans' behaviour in many ways. 'Hanbeon jumyeon jeong eobsda' (Sohn 1986) means 'You don't have *jeong* when you give someone only one helping of food.' Many times, Korean people put more food on their guests' plates even without asking, saying 'Please eat more', or 'You should eat more'. This might be considered unfamiliar and strange or even rude in America, but it is actually an expression of intimacy, affection and caring in Korea (Sohn 1986). Similarly, Koreans express personal concern when they ask questions such as 'Are you unmarried?' (EFS) 'What age is she?' (EFS) 'What is your job?' 'Where do you live?' (EFS) 'How much is your monthly salary?' (EFF) 'Can you lend me some money?' (EFF) etc. without being considered rude (see Morizumi, this volume, for similar Japanese characteristics).

Personal emotional factors are also considered to be important in Korea. Thus, one can frequently encounter such English expressions employed by KSEs as 'Please give me special consideration (jalbutagdeurimnida or teugbyeolhi butagdeurimnida)', (EFS) 'I need your special consideration. (teugbyeolhi bwajuseyo)' (EFS). Koreans tend to rely on one's emotion. Therefore, meeting face-to-face rather than simply on paper or by phone is very important. Koreans tend to rely on oral agreements whereas Europeans and Americans emphasize written contracts (Coyner 2007). Foreigners often face such expressions as 'I will see you and talk with you later (najunge manabebgo malsseum deurigesseumnida)' (EFS) and 'I will come by and see you for a talk (mannaseo iyagi hajiyo)' (EFS) employed by KSEs. This does not necessarily mean that Koreans regard written contracts as unimportant. However, Koreans tend not to hesitate to renegotiate agreements if conditions change whereas Europeans tend to think that the deal is final when the contract is signed (Coyner 2007). In such East meets West encounters, Western logic may not be as effective as an emotional common denominator. Koreans are very sensitive about their state of good feeling, *gibun*. In the end, everyone will benefit when a good mood is created. I will list some other characteristics of KE which reflect both the Korean language and culture.

Other features of KE: Reflection of language and culture

The Korean value system is clearly reflected in KE. Responses to negative questions in KE also illustrate this point. These responses can be considered as one of the most puzzling problems foreigners face when communicating with KSEs. In Korean a yes/no response depends on agreement or disagreement with the content of the question whereas a yes/no response is based on one's own action in British and American English (Hahn 1981). That is, as a response to the question of 'Didn't you go there?' *Yes* in Korean means that 'I didn't go there' but *Yes* in American English means that 'I did go there'.[8] Many other expressions used by KSEs clearly illustrate how cultural and social perspectives are different depending on Englishes used cross-culturally. Two more examples from KE will be briefly discussed in the following:

First, the word order of Korean language is reflected in the expressions where Koreans focus on the characteristic rather than the person.[9] The following expressions are widely used by KSEs while NSEs would not use them:

(1) The price is very expensive. (EFS)
(2) His height is very tall. (EFS)
(3) His eyes are round shaped. (EFS)

Second, borrowings from English and other languages as well as coinages are fondly employed by KSEs although their meanings and sometimes their parts of speech are far different from the original ones. The word 'arbeit' (EFS) is an example. This is a German word (verb) meaning 'to work'. However, for Korean speakers, this word is commonly used as a noun meaning 'part-time job'. Another example of borrowing frequently employed by KSEs in universities in Korea is the word 'cunning' (EFS). This word is commonly used as a noun meaning 'dishonesty'. An ingenious example of coinage by KSEs is the compound word, 'eye + shopping' (EFS) meaning 'window shopping'. This is a frequently used expression employed by KSEs. It is so pervasively used in both oral and written forms in Korea that it seems to be naturally accepted even by NSEs in Korea. 'Eye shopping' means that they do not buy things but just look or see things with their eyes in order to please their eyes. Another ingenious example of the English coinages by KSEs is the compound word, 'behind + story' (EFS), meaning 'background information'. This compound word appears to be created by KSEs by analogy of the phrase, 'behind the scene'. This is also very frequently used in Korea in such a natural way that even NSEs in Korea seem to be fond of it.

Thus, KE spoken by KSEs reflects Korea's distinctive value system and cultural and social perspectives.

Concluding remarks

In conclusion, due to Korean culture, language and the unique features of English spoken by Koreans, communication breakdown is possible when foreigners are engaged in communicational interactions (IBT, for example) with KSEs in Korea. In order to have successful and smooth interactions in Korea, it would be helpful to be aware of KE and to understand Korea's culture and value system. Not only is it important to respect other people and other cultures but also it is the spice of life enriching it and making it more colourful, fruitful and worthwhile.

Successful global communication can be achieved by overcoming national and cultural barriers and by recognizing both NSEs and NNSEs on equal status. The concept of NSEs which seems to instil an inferiority complex in most learners should be abandoned because in this globalized world both NSEs and NNSEs have equal rights to membership in English used globally. The diversity of glocalized Englishes (GlcEes) is enriching the language in many aspects and is reflected in the way the language is changing.

If we accept the view that it is the local variety of English that leads to difficulties when communicating with interlocutors from different cultural backgrounds, then integrating cross-cultural elements into the language learning environment is very important. That is, language has to be learned in conjunction with culture. As Humboldt (cited from Corder 1967) stated, we cannot really teach language but merely provide learners with favourable 'conditions in which it will develop spontaneously in the mind in its own way' in order to communicate clearly in appropriate cultural contexts.

Some might argue that it is premature to state that KE is a GlcE because English is not used intra-nationally. However, it is only a matter of time before KE will serve the purpose of GlcE considering that (1) the rapidly increasing number of Koreans are learning English, (2) Koreans are learning English from grade three, (3) many universities in Korea are encouraging or even requiring classes be conducted in English, (4) proficiency in English is required to obtain a good job, (5) more parents send their children either to overseas schools or to private English institutions in Korea to make them learn English, and, most importantly, (6) the government strongly urges secondary school teachers to conduct English classes in English.

For successful communicational interactions in Korea, it is important for foreigners to be aware of cross-cultural differences as well as linguistic differences. Korean culture reflected in the language is a source of misunderstanding due to the different value systems. Differences are reflected and observed in KE. It would be strongly recommended that those who want to have successful interactions in Korea learn characteristics of KE in order not to offend, be offended by, or be misunderstood by their Korean interlocutors.

List of abbreviations

EFL: English as a foreign language
ESL: English as a second language
EFF: an example taken from the data collected from the conversation with my friends in Fall 2006.
EFS: an example taken from the data collected from the university students that I and other Korean instructors taught in Seoul, Korea, from 2004 to 2006.
Fst L: first language
FL: foreign language
GlcE: glocalized English
GlcEes: glocalized Englishes
IBT: international business transactions
KE: Korea English
KSE: Korean speakers of English
NNSE: non-native speakers of English
NSE: native speakers of English
SL: second language

Notes

*This chapter is a shortened and revised version of an earlier chapter entitled 'Directionality issues in teaching English with reference to expressions by non-native speakers of English' published in the Journal of PAAL 10(1). I would like to thank Prof. Kumiko Murata and Dr Susan Iwamura for their valuable comments on this version.

1. Currently there seems to be different concepts of NSEs.
2. English-only villages in Korea are villages specifically created for purposes of teaching English to Korean speakers while building students' cultural awareness to promote their English skills. Students can get short-term English immersion in a live-in environment where only English is spoken. The first English-only village in Korea was opened in August 2004 in Ansan, Gyeongido Province.
3. The official English education in Korea started in 1883 at DongMunHag (동문학, 동문學), the first foreign language institute in Korea (Park et al. 2001).
4. According to the report of Korea International Trade Association (IITA, 29 January 2008), Korea has achieved an important landmark in trading as of

18 December 2007, exceeding Hong Kong in terms of exports. This means that Koreans who have engaged in international business transactions (IBT) have more opportunities to communicate in English, the lingua franca, with their overseas partners and vice versa.

5. EFF – collected from the conversation with my friends in Fall 2006
EFS – collected from the university students that I and other Korean instructors taught in Seoul, Korea, from 2004 to 2006.
6. For the transcriptions of Korean examples, 'New Romanization' proposed by the government in 1999 is adopted in this paper.
7. I think I have to give an example from my personal experience. I had an opportunity to serve as the director of the university library from 2000 to 2002. During those periods I was addressed as 'gwanjangnim' both in formal and informal situations. Even now I am no longer in the position of 'gwanjang', I am still addressed as 'gwanjangnim' both in formal and informal situations.
8. Examples of paralinguistic and linguistic features (or problems) are mainly adopted from (1) the talk I delivered at Plenary Session #7, 'English as an International Language in Asia Pacific Region' on Wednesday 4 August 2004, at EWC/EWCA 2004 Tokyo International Conference, (2) my presentation on Korean English at the CCDL Symposium held 20–23 December 2004, at Waseda University, (3) the conversations among my friends in Fall 2006, (4) the data collected from the university students that I and other Korean instructors taught in Seoul, Korea, from 2004 to 2006 and (5) The Lecture Series on Korean English, Women's Place in Korea and Culture [DVD] (2003), planned and coordinated by Multimedia Education Room, College of Liberal Arts, Korea University Television Network, Seoul, Korea. The Lecture Series on Korean English is also available at Waseda University's homepage (http://oic.wls.jp/index-e-02.html).
9. The Korean language belongs to the Ural-Altaic family. It has Subject–Object–Verb (SOV) order which is characterized by having postpositions, not prepositions.

References

Baik, M. J. 1994. 'Syntactic features of Englishization in Korea.' *World Englishes.* 13(2), 155–66.

——. 1995. *Language, Ideology, and Power: English Textbooks of Two Koreas*. Seoul: Thaekaksa.

Baker, S. and I. Resch, in Paris, with Karlisle, K. in Rome and Schmidt, K.A. in Stuttgart. 2001. 'The Great English Divide: In Europe, speaking the lingua franca separates the haves from the have-nots.' *Businessweek,* 13 August 2001.

Corder, S. P. 1967. The significance of learners' errors. *International Review of Applied Linguistics (IRAL),* 5, 161–9.

Coyner, T. 2007. 'Korean Concepts of Negotiating', *Korea Times*. 4 October 2007.

Crystal, D. 1997. *English as a Global Language*. Cambridge: Cambridge University Press.

Davies, A. 2005. *A Glossary of Applied Linguistics*. Edinburgh: Edinburgh University Press.

Hahn, K-J P. 1981. 'The Development of Negation in One Korean Child.' Ph.D. Dissertation, University of Hawaii.

Kim, J-Y. 2006. *The Korean Civil Service System*. Seoul, Korea: Bubwoo Publishing Co.

Kim, K-H. 1978. 'The Language of Emotion of Americans and Koreans.' Ph.D. Dissertation. Keimyung University.

Kum, J-T. 2006. *Hangug Yugyoyi Hyeonsil Insiggoa Byeonhyeog Ron (Understanding of Confucianism in Korea and its Reformation)*. Seoul, Korea: Jibmundang.

Lee, K-Y. 2007. 'Korea English.' In Park and Nakano (eds), *Asia Englishes & Miscommunication*. Seoul, Korea: Korea University Press, pp. 241–315.

Lim, J., K-J. Park, H. K. Lee and S-H. Chung. 2003. 'Korean culture.' In *The Lecture Series on Korean English, Women's Place in Korea, and Culture* [DVD]. Planned and Coordinated by Multimedia Education Room, College of Liberal Arts, Korea University, Produced by Korea University Television Network. Seoul, Korea.

Park, K-J. 2006. 'Directionality issues in teaching English with reference to expressions by non-native speakers of English.' *Journal of Pan-Pacific Association of Applied Linguistics,* 10(1), 1–20.

Park, K-J. and M. Nakano. 1999. 'A study of pragmatic functions of refusal expressions among Japanese and Korean learners of English', *Bulletin of the Institute of Language Teaching, Waseda University,* 54, 1–9, The Institute of Language Teaching, Waseda University.

——. (eds) 2007. *Asia Englishes and Miscommunication*. Seoul, Korea: Korea University Press.

Park, K-J., H. K. Lee, and C-E. Kim 2006. 'Korean English.' ms. submitted to be published in *WE and Mis-communication*: DCC, Waseda University.

Park, K-J., Lee, H. K., Noh, K. H., Kim, S. C., Kang, B. N., Kang, H. S., Ju, Y. K., Shin, B. S., Park, H. S., Chung, D. S., Noh, K. S., Kwak, H. Y., Seong, G. B., Choi, T. H., Lee, E. J., Lim J. Y., Han, H., Cho, I. J., Kim, H. B., You, S. H., Lee, M. S., Choi, S. Y., Chang, B. M., Lee, J. K., Kim, C. H., Kim, S. H., Kim H. J., Maeng, E. K., Shin, K. C., Kim J. W. and Chung, E. H. (2001). *Yeongeo gyoyug ibmun (An Introduction to English Education: What are the problems about English Education of Korea)*. Seoul, Korea: Bagyeongsa.

Park, M-S. 1979. *Communication Styles in Two Different Cultures: Korean and American*. Seoul: Hanshing Publishing Co.

Richard, J. C., J. Platt, and H. Platt. 1993. *Dictionary of Language Teaching & Applied Linguistics*. London: Longman.

Shim, R. J. Y. 1994. Englishized Korean: structure, status, and attitudes. *World Englishes,* 13(2), 225–44.

——. 1999. Codified Korean English: Process, characteristics and consequence. *World Englishes,* 18(2), 247–58.

Smith. L., and M. Forman (eds). 1997. *World Englishes 2000*. Honolulu, HI: University of Hawaii Press.

Sohn, H-M. 1986. *Linguistic Expeditions*. Seoul: Hanshin Publishing Company.

——. 1999. *The Korean Language*. Cambridge: Cambridge University Press.

Song, J. J. 1998. Forum. English in South Korea revisited via Martin Jonghak Baik (1994, 1995), and Rosa Jinyoung Shim (1994). *World Englishes,* 17(2), 263–71.

Tan, M. 2007. The English Divide, *Asian Journal. Com*. 29 August 2007.

Part III

Englishes in Asian Academic and Business Contexts

8
Academic Writing in World Englishes: The Asian Context

Yamuna Kachru

Introduction

It is evident that children acquire language in the course of their overall development through infancy to pre-teen years unless there are physiological (e.g. total loss of hearing) or environmental causes (e.g. forced isolation of the child) that prevent such acquisition. However, the linguistic competence acquired in natural socio-cultural settings does not necessarily include literacy skills. These skills depend on socio-cultural traditions that include writing in addition to oral performances of various sorts, e.g. in the community (i.e. community meetings), religious events (reading and writing of scriptures, delivering sermons, etc.) and ritualistic acts (performing specific rites according to manuals of the tradition). Competence in writing is acquired with deliberate effort in institutional settings such as the family, the school, the monastery, or wherever. It involves instruction and, usually, practice over a long period of time, and the rate of success in achieving writing competence varies considerably within any given population. Each literate culture has its own conventions of writing, and it is instructive to look at these closely if one is interested in understanding the process of writing, the cultural context of the product, and the cultural value assigned to writing.

This paper has a limited goal of exploring the interaction of culture and conventions of writing in order to understand the current concern with writing in English all across the world, especially in academic settings.[1] Within academic writing the study of manifestation(s) of the genre, or set of genres, of academic writing across languages and cultures absorbs a great many professionals in English studies. The focus of this paper is on writing across disciplines, including those of scientific–technical fields. I first discuss the concept of culture in the context of writing followed by a brief discussion of the theoretical underpinnings of the analysis. Subsequently, a sketch of the mutual relevance of culture and academic writing in the light of available research on writing in world Englishes is presented.

Culture

Culture is said to be intimately involved in norms of human behaviour. Behaviour in culturally appropriate ways includes verbal interaction in socially defined contexts in a socio-culturally suitable code or codes. Such interactions have also to conform to notions of appropriacy held in the community. For instance, in a bi-/multilingual situation, it is legitimate to mix and switch shared languages/dialects in verbal interactions, as is common in Asia, whereas in a monolingual situation, mixing and switching would be unacceptable since it would hamper intelligibility and cause consternation. How various speech acts such as apology, compliment, invitation, persuasion, etc. are performed, and which code/codes are selected for such speech acts depend on the socio-cultural norms of the group participating in interaction. Some examples may make this clear. In the Hindi speech community of India the following code choices are more likely: a poetry reading session would involve Hindi, worshipping in a Hindu temple setting would usually be done in Sanskrit, and legal proceedings in a higher court of law would be conducted in English. In a speech act of expressing one's gratitude, the speech acts of blessing, complimenting, or thanking may all be appropriate depending upon the context of situation (Firth 1957). That is, the following are all possible as expression of gratitude:

1. Expressing gratitude (Y. Kachru 1995b)[2]
   a. Informal situations:

      Blessing (if expressing gratitude to a younger person), appreciation of inherent qualities or effort or help rendered (if equal), expression of one's helplessness and grateful acceptance of favour (if superior in status)

   b. Formal situations:

      Thanks.

The notion of communicative competence (Hymes 1970) refers primarily to the ability to use language(s) in socially appropriate ways.

As children acquire communicative competence in a language or languages shared in their speech community, they also acquire a social identity, and within the framework of the social identity, a personal or individual identity. In the normal course of events, it is difficult for one to assume new subtractive identities that replace the original one(s). That is why we have, e.g., Asian Americans, Bangladeshi British and Turkish Germans, all labels acknowledging additive, dual, identities.[3]

As is well known, literacy is not universal, and was not widespread until very recently in human history. Even now, there are societies and cultures where literacy plays no role in the life of the community, e.g. rural societies in South Asia, sub-Saharan Africa and other regions of the world. Literacy practices vary a great deal across cultures and require careful study, as has been shown by Heath (1983), Scribner and Cole (1981), among others. This paper is concerned with one set of genres, that of argumentative or persuasive writing, within what is known as the overarching genre of academic writing. The next section discusses the underlying theoretical approach briefly.

Culture and meaning potential

In the theoretical formulation of systemic grammar, the concept of *meaning potential* is central. It is defined in terms of culture: what people can mean and can do, to paraphrase Halliday. The context of culture defines the potential, or the range of possibilities, and the context of situation determines the actual, or the choice that takes place (Halliday 1973). This is true of linguistic structure as well as rhetorical patterns and structure of texts. Language is essentially an interrelated set of texts in which meaning potential is actualized: people express meanings to realize some social goal relevant to their socio-cultural context.

Looking at academic writing in this framework then suggests the following: rhetoric or how thoughts are organized in words, sentences and paragraphs is a matter of socio-cultural convention. Recent research in technical translation studies has shown that even when using another language, readers and speakers prefer the rhetorical patterns they have been socialized in and judge the other language documents employing criteria familiar to them (Uljin 1996). St Amant (1999), writing about technical manuals instructing consumers in the use of their target products, observes that rhetorical organization of texts across cultures differs at every level: sentence, paragraph and text. Whereas American writers are instructed to write short sentences and make sure that the specific content of the sentence is expressed directly in a main clause with no clutter of preceding subordinate clauses, Southern Europeans prefer longer sentences giving more detailed information. Similarly, Americans are taught to organize their paragraphs such that first a general premise is introduced, subsequent paragraphs present arguments in support of the general premise logically, and the conclusion establishes the final outcome of the arguments that constitutes proof of the general premise. Many Asian traditions, including those of China, Japan and India, prefer a different organization such that observations of phenomena and arguments based upon these observations are presented first and subsequently a conclusion is drawn based upon the evidence presented. Whereas in the context of American business communication, writers are expected to come to the point to be made first, Japanese and Latin American business texts may begin with a polite, solicitous comment directed at the target audience before coming to the point of the text.

Similarly, textual or generic structure is a socio-cultural construct in addition to being a linguistic construct. It is true that genres reflect disciplinary conventions, as claimed in the literature on genre analysis (see Bhatia 1993; Swales 1981, 1985, 1990). But, there is nothing sacrosanct about the current practices in any tradition, including the Anglo-American tradition of writing. The ancient Indian mathematical tradition utilized *sūtra* (aphorisms) and *šloka* (verse) forms very effectively in explaining mathematical concepts and setting mathematical problems (See Datta and Singh 1962 for a history of Indian mathematics). The pluralistic grammatical tradition in India has both *aṣṭadhyāyi* of Pāṇini (Katre 1987), which codified Vedic Sanskrit in order to ensure its preservation for religious and ritualistic purposes, and *tolkāppiyam* in Tamil, which codified the language of orally composed and transmitted Sangam literature, obviously with an aesthetic purpose (Murugan 2000). Thus, defining the generic structure with reference to just the discipline, with no regard to the socio-cultural purposes for which the disciplinary genre is developed, does not seem to illuminate the nature of either a genre or a text as an exemplar of a genre.

The meaning potential of rhetorical conventions and generic structures across cultures is an area which has attracted little attention of researchers in genre studies and writing in a second language, or ELT professionals. Researchers in world Englishes have just started to explore the area within a restricted range of text generation (e.g. works cited in Y. Kachru 1997b).

Argumentation in academic writing

Having established the approach to writing that is assumed here, I will now turn to the notion of argumentation. It is not easy to define what is meant by argumentation in the context of writing in English. There is a great deal of disagreement among researchers with regard to viewing the nature and purpose of argumentation. In the teaching of composition, those who follow the traditions of Greek rhetoric and formal logic tend to use the term 'persuasion' rather than 'argumentation', or use the two terms interchangeably. Others make a clear distinction between argumentation and persuasion (see Y. Kachru 1997b for further details). In spite of differences, there is widespread acceptance in the academia that there is something called argumentative-persuasive writing and there have been attempts to describe this text type in several sub-disciplines including those of rhetoric, writing in a second language, business and technical communication, and writing in English across languages and cultures.

Argumentative/Persuasive writing

I will briefly examine the realization of the abstract notion of argumentative text type in published literature. Argumentative pieces have been characterized either in terms of linguistic structure of sentences in the text, or speech acts of utterances. For instance, according to the grammatical structural approach (Werlich 1976), the dominant sentence type in an argumentative piece is the quality-attributing sentences (e.g. *The problem is complex*); clause expansion types are causal, concessive and nominal; sequence type is contrastive; text structuring is deductive, inductive and dialectical; and the tense form is present. According to Biber (1986), argumentative texts contain infinitives, suasive verbs (e.g. *command, demand*), conditional clauses, split auxiliaries, and prediction, necessity and possibility modals. In terms of speech acts, Aston (1977) assigns two types of values to speech acts in an argumentative text: an illocutionary value and an interactional value. He further maintains that argumentative texts are characterized by representatives in terms of illocutionary acts, and the interactional relationships between acts are of four types: explanation, evaluation, instances and metastatements. Tirkkonen-Condit (1985) draws upon van Dijk (1980), Kummer (1972) and Aston (1977) and suggests the following view of argumentative text: it has a superstructure – the schematic form that organizes the global meaning of a text; it is a problem-solving process; and its goal is to convince the audience of the points made in the text (see Teo 1995: 17–39 for a detailed discussion of this model).

It is clear that text types are not exclusive. For instance, Parret (1987: 165) observes that there is overlap between argumentation and narration: 'nobody can deny that argumentation and narrativity overlap in many sequences of discourse as well as of everyday language…' Hatim (1991: 190) notes: 'texts are multifunctional, normally displaying features of more than one type, and constantly shifting from one type to another'. According to Beaugrande and Dressler (1981: 183), the major difficulty in text typology is that 'many actualized instances do not manifest complete or exact characteristics of an ideal type'. Biber (1986: 390) supports this conclusion: 'the identity of the salient text-type distinctions in English is an unresolved issue'. It has been suggested that in view of the difficulty of identifying text types, the notion of text type be seen as an abstraction. Although the abstract notion of text type is useful in research, it is worth keeping in mind that text types usually overlap in real life (see Teo 1995: 8–10). This is true not only of English, but also of other languages.

Cultural values and argumentation

Coming back to cross-cultural concerns, it is not clear that all languages and cultures share the text types described or posited in English. For instance, according to a standard textbook on grammar and composition published by the National Council of Educational Research and Training, India (Vyas, Tiwari and Srivastava 1972: 209), the argumentative essay is not a distinct text type in Hindi. The section on composition mentions the following categories of essays: descriptive (*varṇ anātmak*), narrative (*vivərə ṇātmək*), deliberative (*vicārātmək*), explanatory (*vyāk^{h}yātmək*) and imaginative (*kəlpənātmək*), and further reduces it to three groups: descriptive (including narrative), deliberative (including explanatory) and imaginative. Argumentation is one sub-type of deliberation or explanation; it is not a distinct category. The 'deliberative' is not necessarily equivalent to the Anglo-American 'argumentative' essay. In an argumentative text the goal is to convince the audience that the view put forward in the text is right and that all competing opinions lead to undesirable consequences. In the deliberative text, on the other hand, the points in favour as well as those opposed to a particular position are put forward so that the audience is informed on all facets of an issue, and the decision as to which one of the positions presented is right or wrong is left to them. The advice given to students in Vyas, Tiwari and Srivastava (1972) is as follows: '[F]or elaboration [i.e. the body of the essay: YK], material should be categorized carefully to facilitate the sequential presentation of points. Everything that is said must be proved by arguments, facts, events, or quotation [citing authority: YK] and they should be arranged in such a form that *readers can easily arrive at the conclusion desired by the writer'* (emphasis added). The purpose is not to *provide solutions* and *convince* the audience of their rightness; rather, it is to *lead* the readers to find the right solutions. Thus, deliberative essays are indirect by design. The instruction to students conforms to the Indian tradition. According to Heimann (1964: 170–1):

> The method applied in Indian epistemology is that of gaining higher knowledge through discussion. One standpoint is first pronounced, and then confronted and denounced by a second, a third and further *pakṣas* 'wings' or 'viewpoints'. Finally the highest, or at any rate the at present no-more-refutable notion is reached. The Indian textbook of philosophical systems, the *sarva-darśanasaṃgraha,* 'the compilation of all viewpoints', is so arranged that the first mentioned is the worst, and the last the best, from the vedāntic standpoint which is here proclaimed. It is divergency which helps to elucidate the comparatively higher, i.e. wider grasp of the problem in hand. *Saṃvāda,* 'discussion', instead of *vivāda,* 'dispute', is the methodical means of gathering all the different facets of the truth, which is only indirectly and gradually approachable.

It is not the case, in spite of the myths perpetrated about other cultures in the academic-writing-in-English circles, that Eastern – including Indian – writers do not have a concept of argumentation (see Sen 2005 for the healthy tradition of argumentation in India). In Indian philosophy, the notion of argumentation is well developed (Datta 1967). In the Sanskrit tradition, the word for cognition in general is *jñāna,* the word for valid cognition is *pramā,* and that for the source of valid knowledge is *pramāṇa*. Perception (*pratyakṣa*), inference (*anumāna*), authority (*śabda*) and postulation (*arthāpatti*) are all recognized as valid sources of knowledge. An important distinction is made between the psychological process of inference that takes place in one's own mind and the demonstrative form of inference used for convincing others. The demonstrative form has five steps:

2. (i) Clear enunciation of the proposition to be proved (*This hill has fire*)
   (ii) Statement of reason (*This hill has smoke*)

(iii) Statement of universal relation, supported by concrete instances (*Whatever has smoke has fire, e.g. the fireplace. Whatever has no fire has no smoke, e.g. the lake*)
(iv) Application of the universal relation to the present case (*The hill has such smoke (which is invariably accompanied by fire)*)
(v) Conclusion (*Therefore, the hill has fire*).

The validity of a theory is also indirectly established by indirect hypothetical argument (*tarka*), which consists in showing that the supposition of its contradiction leads to undesirable consequences.

In other Asian traditions, there are yet other methods of conducting arguments. The Chinese tradition is different from the Indian; it is characterized by the historical method, and attention to language (Hughes 1967). It was believed that one indispensable method of achieving knowledge was the historical method. It was also realized that thought is conditioned by language and that language as communication fails unless it is disciplined and controlled. Thus, philosophy became (a) a critique of language, of communicated meaning and (b) a checking of this critique by a critique of history. The purpose of the 'double-harness' writing was not as much to convince as to point to the fact that the only sound approach to inward experience or objects of outward attention was from a double angle of vision. Similarly, the goal of 'linked pearl' writing, where two general propositions were followed by a third, introduced by the logical connective *therefore* which did not correspond to facts, was to drive the audience to reconsider the nexus of the two initial propositions and the conclusion from them. Linked pearl was a methodological device for stirring criticism of accepted knowledge. That this tradition still lives on in the current generation of Chinese Americans is illustrated by the following story about Peter, a Chinese American (Fox 1994: 117–18):

> ... his thesis is upfront and pretty clear, the gist of it being that eastern medicine should be taken seriously by the west because "it works." Evidence follows [for some pages] ... after these few pages the story is abandoned and the rest of the paper is taken up with the history of eastern medicine and its many categories and types without any more reasons to believe it works and without any particular conclusions ... "I know it is digressive," he says. "And I want to do something about that. But I don't want to cut any of this – it's too important ... There is something intuitive about eastern medicine," he continues, "an understanding of subtlety, of balance. Such things cannot and are

> not tested scientifically. Careful observations of patients' reactions to herbs and other remedies, accumulated over thousands of years, have created this practice – not in a systematic sense, but through an accumulation of wisdom." ... Instead of saying that eastern medicine is based on unsystematic observation that nevertheless became increasingly complex, organized, and remarkably effective over centuries, he has laid out the complicated typology and let the audience observe it and draw their own conclusions.

The way Peter, a modern Chinese American, writes is reminiscent of the way Chinese philosophers thought about the sources of knowledge and imparting knowledge.

A tradition that has virtually no similarity with any other tradition is the Japanese tradition. In the Japanese tradition, according to Nakamura (1967: 189), 'Kakinomotono-Hitomaro composed a famous poem in which he said, "In our land covered with reed and rice-ears, they have not argued since the time of the gods."' There are no attempts at disciplining the language, either. Nakamura goes on to say that 'the value of ways of Japanese expression lies more in aesthetic and intuitive aspects than in exactly logical ones' (p. 191). According to Moore (1967c: 295), 'Japan has been worldly and realistic from the very beginning.... This probably [is] the most significant clue to the wide range of attitudes that constitute the Japanese perspective.' Japan has adapted many different points of view (e.g. Buddhist thought from India, Confucianism from China), but '[T]he basis of such adaptation has not been intellectual. It has been strictly in terms of practical suitability for Japanese life.... Like the Indians and the Chinese, the Japanese stress harmony and tolerance – and try more than the others to minimize both practical and intellectual cleavages and confrontation.... In most of the adjustments to life, whether they are in philosophy, religion, or practical affairs, there are clear intellectual incompatibilities, but to the Japanese mind they are not – in the name of intellectual and practical harmony (and tolerance)' (Moore 1967c: 294). Harmony and aesthetics are two principal characteristics of Japan. Moore (1967c: 296) sums up the discussion thus: 'In comparison with other cultures, the aesthetic has been considered to be the essentially unique expression of spirituality in Japan, as is ethics in China, religion in India, and possibly reason in the West.'

The above, of course, are sweeping generalizations, and have to be looked at as such. One has to remember that the cultural values and traditions outlined above have also contributed to the modernization of societies in China, India and Japan; these regions are definitely in the modern scientific and technological age. But, the fascinating story of modernization of these societies and cultures and their adaptation of the processes of modernization belong to another context.

Argumentation for persuasion requires critical thinking. It is misleading to claim that certain cultures lack abilities involved in such thinking since they concentrate more on social harmony and conformity to socio-cultural norms. Generally, this is the perception in the Anglo-American institutions of tertiary education and considerable academic writing research is oriented to such views as it is claimed that critical thinking requires individualistic and adversarial practices (Ramanathan and Atkinson 1999). However, an empirical study by Stapleton (2001) shows that the quality of critical thought is dependent on the topic content, with the familiar topic generating better critical thinking as evidenced by the depth and range of argumentation and a variety of types of evidence. Furthermore, the judgment that L2 writers (in this case, the Japanese) lack critical thinking abilities may partly be the result of non-shared cultural assumptions between L2 writers and L1 evaluators of their writing. Part of the non-shared assumptions may also involve the conventions of generic structure of academic writing, which is discussed briefly next.

Generic structure of academic writing

Following the discussions in Bhatia (1993) and Swales (1990), it is reasonable to propose that a piece of argumentative writing may consist of the following six components: a specific theoretical proposal that ensures resolution of an issue under debate, which constitutes a problem for existing theory or theories; the methodology demonstrating the relevance of the proposed hypothesis to the solution of the problem; counterarguments to the proposal and the methodology; refutation of counterarguments; a conclusion claiming better fit between the proposed theory and the solution of the problem as compared to the earlier theory or theories. Essentially, this means the argumentative text has the following structure: (1) a hypothesis; (2) data and arguments that support the proposal; (3) counterarguments; (4) a demonstration of non-applicability of counterarguments; (5) a conclusion claiming the validity of the proposed solution. Using the terminology of the genre analysis, we may refer to these structural components as moves. Note that the first move, proposed solution, may have not only a discussion of the theoretical framework adopted for the study, but also the historical background explaining why the particular framework is the most appropriate one for resolving the problem at hand. It may also have a review of some of the earlier attempts to resolve the problem which either did not succeed or succeeded only partially. Actually, most scientific writing in the Anglo-American tradition has both these submoves. Thus, a review of literature and a critique of earlier research is an integral part of any academic paper, whether for publication or to satisfy a course requirement in an institution of higher education.

A brief illustration of conducting genre analysis in terms of the text elements is presented below. In view of consideration of space, the example is that of an abstract rather than a full argumentative text. An abstract answers four questions for the readers of the article: the purpose of the research, what was carried out, what the findings were and what is to be concluded from the findings. Bhatia (1993: 78–9) proposes four *moves* to correspond with the four elements identified above: 1. Introducing Purpose, 2. Describing Methodology, 3. Summarizing Results and 4. Presenting Conclusions.

The relevant text is as follows:

> We explore the predictors of early mastery versus error in children's acquisition of American Sign Language. We hypothesize that the most frequent values for a particular parameter in prelinguistic gestures will be the most in early signs and the most likely sources of substitution when signing children make errors. Analyses of data from a longitudinal study of the prelinguistic gestures of five deaf and five hearing children and a longitudinal study of four deaf children's early signs have revealed evidence of significant commonalities between prelinguistic gestures and early signs. This apparent continuity between prelinguistic gesture and early sign reflects constraints operating on the infant – in all likelihood, motoric constraints – that seem to persist into the first-word period in both major language modalities. In sign, as in speech, the products of first sign use building blocks that are available to the prelinguistic child. (From Cheek, A., K. Cormier, A. Repp and R. P. Meier (2001) 'Prelinguistic gesture predicts mastery and error in production of early signs.' *Language* 77(2), 292)

Analysis into moves:

Move 1: We explore the predictors of early mastery versus error in children's acquisition of American Sign Language. We hypothesize that the most frequent values for a particular parameter in prelinguistic gestures will be the most in early signs and the most likely sources of substitution when signing children make errors.

Moves 2 and 3: Analyses of data from a longitudinal study of the prelinguistic gestures of five deaf and five hearing children and a longitudinal study of four deaf children's early signs have revealed evidence of significant commonalities between prelinguistic gestures and early signs.

Move 4: This apparent continuity between prelinguistic gesture and early sign reflects constraints operating on the infant – in all likelihood, motoric constraints – that seem to persist into the first-word period in both major language modalities. In sign, as in speech, the products of first sign use building blocks that are available to the prelinguistic child.

The features of this abstract that are noteworthy are the following: The theoretical framework is not mentioned explicitly. It is left implicit as part of the shared knowledge between the writers and the readers: the framework is based on theories of language acquisition, including sign language acquisition. No critique of earlier research follows, as the paper suggests exploring a new area. The inclusion of moves 2 and 3 in the same sentence in the abstract is also noteworthy. The phrase, '[a]nalyses of data from a longitudinal study of the prelinguistic gestures of five deaf and five hearing children and a longitudinal study of four deaf children's early signs' is a description of the methodology followed in the study; the rest of the sentence, 'have revealed evidence of significant commonalities between prelinguistic gestures and early signs', sums up the results of the study. The last sentence presents some conclusions from the study.

An argumentative text contains all the four moves of the abstract discussed above; in addition, it also has the structural elements mentioned in the first paragraph of this section. Normally, the method of presenting an argument in writing is a learned behaviour; the skill does not manifest itself spontaneously, no matter how talented or proficient a user of a language one is. This is clear if we look at some writing samples of high school students from India.

Scientific writing in high school in India

I did some preliminary analysis of a very small sample of scientific writing of higher secondary students enrolled in a well-known school in a metropolitan city. My aim was not to look for errors in the student writing, as I believe, following Bertrand Russell (1926: 113) that '[w]herever avoidance of error is the chief thing aimed at, education tends to produce an intellectually bloodless type'. The report presented below is about what I found in terms of rhetorical organization of the essays and I hope to raise awareness of educators so that their attention is drawn to the issues involved.

What is observable from samples of writing is that most scientific reports that the students of class XII turn in have a weak generic structure. For example, one of the reports submitted to fulfil the requirement of a project report on mutual induction has the following structure: 1. Objective, 2. Introduction, 3. Faraday's discovery, 4. Electromagnetic induction, 5. Components used, 6. Transformer, 7. Coils, 8. Diodes, 9. Observations, 10. Precautions, 11. Conclusion.

The objective states,

> The objective of the project is to find the effect of mutual induction by the use of two long solenoids and a transformer and hence detecting the flow of current in one of the coil (*sic*) by developing an induced e.m.f.

It gives no indication of what the researcher expects to find or if he or she has any hypothesis about the phenomenon.

The Introduction and other parts, as expected, are descriptive and then the conclusion states:

> From above observations, it is found out that E.M. F. induced in the secondary coil is inversely proportional to the distance between the two coils i.e. (*sic*) when the distance between the primary and secondary coil is more and vice versa. This implies that the mutual induction of the two coils depends upon the distance upon the distance (*sic*) between the primary and secondary coil (*sic*).

A reader cannot be sure if this is an unexpected result or a predicted result of the experiment. The statement of the objective did not indicate what was expected; the conclusion does not specify the nature of the result. This is what I have referred to as a weak generic structure, as a well-developed generic structure would be more explicit and lead the readers to the conclusion the writer wishes them to draw.

A report submitted for a biology project on dental diseases is purely descriptive; it lays out the information about dental diseases, and dental procedures to treat them. All the biology and chemistry reports basically presented simple application of existing theoretical formulations and described the experiments and their results. As such they had the following structural elements: Introduction, describing the theoretical formulations they were applying; list of apparatus and/or objects used for the study; procedures carried out; and finally, results obtained.

The weak generic structure of scientific writing at the high school level clearly indicates that it takes time for learners to become part of a scientific community by learning to control the discourse conventions of that community. This is not surprising, as analyses of Michael Faraday's texts by Anderson (2006) shows that a great deal of struggle is involved in making words do what scientists want them to do in order to formulate scientific theories and establish their identities.

The Indian scientific-technical writing in its generic structure is close to the Anglo-American tradition as illustrated by the example of the demonstrated form of inference in argumentation to convince others of one's position (see 2 above). There is one exception based on cultural difference: previous scholarship is discussed with respect and without explicit challenge to one's illustrious predecessors. No claim is made about one's personal achievement; rather, the findings are presented as an addition to knowledge generated by previous scholarship.

Teaching academic writing in English across cultures

I am not familiar with research on conventions of scientific writing in other Asian countries. I have not seen much interest in research on the generic structure of scientific writing in India; there is little information available on how much of the Indian way of thinking is reflected in scientific and technical literature. There has been some research on academic and creative writing in Indian English and some of the major Indian languages (see e.g. B. Kachru 1986, 1987, 1992, 2005; Y. Kachru 1983, 1987, 1988, 1996, 1997a, 2001; Pandharipande 1983) and other Asian contexts (e.g. Kamimura and Oi 1998 and the relevant references in Y. Kachru and Nelson 2006), but I have not come across any studies on scientific-technical writing. Science and technology are flourishing in India, China, Japan and elsewhere and there are often reports of original and innovative inventions in the newspapers and journals. It is important to explore how the thinking behind them is articulated.

The earlier tradition in academic fields, such as grammar, philosophy, scientific disciplines, was that described in the preceding section on cultural values and argumentation where the Indian tradition of argumentation is discussed. In technical areas, the tradition was that of apprenticeship and oral instruction. This was true of even the most complex technical tasks such as carpet weaving in the North and manufacturing of mats in the South, and executing the intricate designs in cotton and silk *sarees* and gold and silver jewellery in all parts of India. The weaving and manufacturing involved intricate motifs and numerous colours and yet the execution was precise in each case. That tradition still lives, but in modern institutions of higher education, the medium of written language and how conventions have been developing in various languages and areas of research is worth studying.

I would like to briefly consider the implications of the traditional values discussed in the paper for the teaching of academic writing in English in the Asian context in general. Most studies that deal with educational implications of research in writing suggest that it is desirable for all users of English to learn the preferred conventions of academic writing in Inner Circle (Anglo-American) Englishes (e.g. Swales and Feak 1994).[4] This is because, as Rubin (1995: 5) observes, the 'tendency to treat demographic markers in writing as sources of interference is predicated on the notion that communicative success and positive evaluation requires "unmarkedness" in discourse styles... [v]oiceless, genderless, identity-less prose is the most desirable'. Academic writing is more and more dictated by the need for developing evaluation criteria for writing from the point of view of teachers of English, who are guided by the methods and practices of the ELT establishment from the Inner Circle. Very little awareness of the wider perspective of the use of English as relevant to non-Anglo-American and non-European contexts has so far arisen in professionals of any Circle of English.

If we take the wider perspective, an alternative view of what the needs of the field of English education relevant to the Outer and Expanding Circles are becomes obvious. While it is perfectly legitimate to make all writers aware of the rhetorical patterns preferred in Inner Circle English, i.e. the Anglo-American and European traditions, it is equally legitimate and desirable to make English educators aware of the different rhetorical conventions of world majority learners and users of English. Just as no language is more or less logical than another, no rhetorical pattern is more or less logical as compared to others (Y. Kachru 1995a).

Conclusion

The concerns of Inner Circle publishers, who are the gatekeepers of most publications in academic fields, are understandable. But that should not determine the fate of academic writing and homogenize it to an extent where a creative process is reduced to automatic slot filling. To quote Fox (1994: 21):

> [The] world-wide strategies of indirection – linguistic, rhetorical, poetic, psychological – create a richness that to world majority students makes the spare, relentless logic of the western tradition seem meager in comparison.

Diversity and richness is surely more desirable than rigidity and a drab sameness in general. The English language, as a language of wider communication, has become pluricentric, and carries the weight of various socio-cultural identities. Some researchers and educators engaged in ELT have shown awareness of this fact (e.g. Hinkel 1999, 2005; Savignon and Berns 1984). As someone involved in teacher education, I see a great challenge and a great opportunity in this situation. It is time educators from all parts of the world, i.e. all Circles of English, begin contributing to the diverse and rich pluricentric tradition of research on academic writing in world Englishes.

Notes

1. Almost all major publishers of English books, including prominent university presses in the UK and USA, have published multiple titles on academic writing within the past two decades and the trend shows no sign of slowing down (see e.g. Bailey 2001; Craswell 2004; Hamp-Lyons and Heasley 2006; Jordan 1999; Oshima and Hogue 2005; Silva and Matsuda 2001).
2. Some appropriate expressions in Hindi are as follows:

A. To a younger addressee
  a. jīte/jītī raho!
     live (m)/ live (f) remain
     May you live long!
  b. xuš raho!
     happy remain
     May you be happy!
  c. īšvar tumhẽ lambī umr de!
     god you (dat) long life give (opt)
     May God grant you long life!

B. To an equal
  a. tumhāre/āpke d^{h}airy kī dād denī hī
     your (fam)/your (h) patience of acclamation (f) give (f) emph
     paṛegī.
     fall (fut f)
     One has to commend your patience.

b. tumne/āpne baṛī taklīf kī.
you erg/you (h erg) much (f) trouble did (f)
You went to a lot of trouble.

c. tumhārī/āpkī madad kab^{h}ī nahī̃ b^{h}ūlū̃gā / b^{h}ūlū̃gī.
your (f) /Your (h f) help ever not forget (fut m)/ forget (fut f)
I will never forget your help.

C. Formal
d^{h}anyavād/šukriyā!
Thank you!

3. Identity is a complex notion; numerous other identities beside ethnic identities, e.g. religious, regional, national, linguistic and gender, are equally involved in verbal behaviour across cultures, as discussed in a number of recent publication. One such study is Joseph (2004) that discusses language and ethnic, national and religious identities in various regions of the world.
4. B. Kachru (1985: 12–13) proposes the concept of Three Concentric Circles of English to capture the origin, historical diffusion and current profile of the English language in the world. In this conceptualization, the Inner Circle comprises the 'mother country' – England and the British Isles – and the areas where the speakers from Britain took the language with them as they migrated – Australia, New Zealand and North America. The Outer Circle comprises the countries where the language was transplanted by successive waves of businessmen, colonial administrators, educators and missionaries, and is now nurtured by the vast majority of indigenous multilingual users, e.g. India, Nigeria, Pakistan, The Philippines, Singapore. They use English as an additional language for their own purposes, which include many national and international domains. The Expanding Circle represents the countries where the language is still spreading, mainly for serving the need for an international medium in business and commerce, diplomacy, finance, higher education in science and technology, and other such spheres, e.g. People's Republic of China, Japan, Korea, Thailand, and the countries of Europe, the Middle East and Latin America. English in this Circle, however, is also finding increased use in intranational domains of academia, media and professions such as medicine, engineering, etc.

References

Anderson, R. 2006. 'The Crafting of Scientific Meaning and Identity: Exploring the Performative Dimensions of Michael Faraday's Texts.' *Perspectives on Science* 14(1), 7–39.

Aston, G. 1977. 'Comprehending value: aspects of the structure of argumentative discourse'. *Studi Italiani di Linguistica Teorica ed Applicata* 6, 465–509.

Bailey. S. 2001. *Academic Writing: A Handbook for International Students*. London and New York: Routledge.

Bhatia, V. K. 1993. *Analyzing Genre: Language Use in Professional Settings*. London: Longman.

Biber, D. 1986. 'Spoken and written textual dimensions in English: Resolving the contradictory findings.' *Language* 62, pp. 384–414.

Craswell, G. 2004. *Writing for Academic Success*. London: Sage Publications.
Datta, D. M. 1967. 'Epistemological methods in Indian philosophy.' In Moore (1967b), pp. 118–35.
Datta, B. and A. N. Singh. 1962. *History of Hindu Mathematics*. Bombay: Asia Publishing House.
Firth, J. R. 1957. 'A synopsis of linguistic theory.' In F. R. Palmer (ed.) 1968. *Selected papers of J. R. Firth, 1952–59*. London: Longman.
Fox, H. 1994. *Listening to the World: Cultural Issues in Academic Writing*. Urbana, IL: National Council of Teachers of English.
Halliday, M. A. K. 1973. *Explorations in the Function of Language*. London: Edward Arnold.
Hamp-Lyons, L. and B. Heasley. 2006. *Study Writing*. Cambridge: Cambridge University Press.
Hatim, M. 1991. 'The pragmatics of argumentation in Arabic: The rise and fall of a text type.' *Text* 11, 189–99.
Heath, S. B. 1983. *Ways with Words: Language, Life, and Work in Communities and Classrooms*. Cambridge: Cambridge University Press.
Heimann, B. 1964. *Facets of Indian thought*. London: George Allen and Unwin.
Hinkel, E. (ed.) 1999. *Culture in Second Language Teaching and Learning*. Cambridge University Press.
——. 2005. *Research in Second Language Learning and Teaching*. Ed. Eli Hinkel. Mahwa, NJ: Lawrence Erlbaum.
Hughes, E. R. 1967. 'Epistemological methods in Chinese philosophy.' In Moore (1967a), pp. 77–103.
Hymes, D. 1970. 'On communicative competence.' In Gumperz, J. J. and Hymes, D. (eds), *Directions in Sociolinguistics*. New York: Holt, Rinehart and Winston, pp. 38–71.
Jordan, R. R. 1999. *Academic Writing Course*. London: Nelson/Longman.
Joseph, J. E. 2004. *Language and Identity: National, Ethnic, Religious*. Basingstoke, UK: Palgrave Macmillan.
Kachru, B. B. 1985. 'Standards, codification and sociolinguistic realism: The English language in the Outer Circle.' In Randolph Quirk and Henry Widdowson (eds) *English in the World: Teaching and Learning the Language and Literatures*, Cambridge: Cambridge University Press, pp. 11–30.
——. 1986. *The Alchemy of English: The Spread, Functions and Models of Non-Native Englishes*. London: Pergamon Press. [South Asian Edn by Oxford University Press, 1989]
——. 1987. 'The Bilingual's Creativity: Discoursal and Stylistic Strategies in Contact Literature.' In Smith (1987). New York and London: Prentice-Hall. pp. 125–40.
——. (ed.) 1992. *The Other Tongue: English across Cultures*. Urbana, IL: University of Illinois Press. (2nd edition)
——. 2005. *Asian Englishes: Beyond the Canon*. Hong Kong: Hong Kong University Press.
Kachru, Y. 1983. 'Linguistics and written discourse in particular languages: contrastive studies: English and Hindi.' *Annual Review of Applied Linguistics* 1982, 3, 50–77.
——. 1987. 'Cross-cultural texts, discourse strategies and discourse interpretation.' In Larry E. Smith (1987), pp. 87–100.

——. 1988. 'Writers in Hindi and English.' In Purves, A. C. (ed.) *Contrastive Rhetoric: Theory and Case Studies. Written Communication Annual,* vol. 3. London: Sage Publications, 109–37.

——. 1995a. 'Contrastive rhetoric in world Englishes.' *English Today,* 11, 21–31

——. 1995b. 'Lexical exponents of cultural contact: Speech act verbs in Hindi-English dictionaries.' In B. Kachru and H. Kahane (eds) *Cultures, Ideologies, and the Dictionary: Studies in Honor of Ladislav Zgusta.* Tübingen: Max Niemeyer Verlag. pp. 261–74.

——. 1996. 'Kachru revisits contrasts.' *English Today,* 12, 41–4.

——. 1997a. 'Cultural meaning and contrastive rhetoric in English Education.' *World Englishes,* 16(3), 337–50.

——. 1997b. 'Culture and argumentative writing in world Englishes.' In Smith and Forman (1997), pp. 48–67.

——. 2001. 'World Englishes and rhetoric across cultures.' *Asian Englishes: an International Journal of the Sociolinguistics of English in Asia/Pacific,* Winter 2001, 54–71.

Kachru, Y. and C. L. Nelson. 2006. *World Englishes in Asian Contexts.* Hong Kong, Hong Kong University Press.

Kamimura, T. and K. Oi. 1998. 'Argumentative strategies in American and Japanese English.' *World Englishes,* 17(3), 307–23.

Katre, S. M. 1987. *Astadhyayi of Panini: In Roman Transliteration.* Austin, TX: University of Texas Press.

Kummer, W. 1972. Aspects of a theory of argumentation. In E. Gulich and W. Raible (eds), *Textsorten.* Frankfurt, Germany: Anthenäum, pp. 25–49.

Moore, C. (ed.). 1967a. *The Chinese Mind: Essentials of Chinese Philosophy and Culture.* Honolulu, HI: The University Press of Hawaii.

——. 1967b. *The Indian Mind: Essentials of Indian Philosophy and Culture.* Honolulu, HI: The University Press of Hawaii.

——. 1967c. *The Japanese Mind: Essentials of Japanese Philosophy and Culture.* Honolulu, HI: The University Press of Hawaii.

Murugan, V. 2000. *Tolkappiyam in English-Translation, with the Tamil Text, Transliteration in the Roman Script, Introduction, Glossary, and Illustrations.* Chennai; Institute of Asian Studies.

Nakamura, H. 1967. 'Consciousness of the individual and the universal among the Japanese.' In Moore (1967c). pp. 179–200.

Oshima, A. and A. Hogue. 2005. *Writing Academic English.* New York: Addison-Wesley.

Pandharipande, R. V. 1983. 'Linguistics and written discourse in particular languages: contrastive studies: English and Marathi.' *Annual Review of Applied Linguistics* (1982), 3, 118–36.

Parret, H. 1987. Argumentation and narrativity. In F. H. van Eemeren, R. Grootendorst, J. A. Blair and C. A. Willard (eds), *Argumentation: Across the Lines of Discipline.* Providence, RI: Foris Publications, pp. 165–75.

Ramanthan, V. and D. Atkinson. 1999. 'Some problematic "channels" in the teaching of critical thinking in current L1 composition textbooks: Implications for L2 student writers.' *Issues in Applied Linguistics* 7, 225–49.

Rubin, D. L. (ed.) 1995. *Composing Social Identity in Written Language.* Hillsdale, NJ: Lawrence Erlbaum Associates.

Russell, B. 1926. *On Education, Especially in Early Childhood.* London: George Allen and Unwin.

Savignon, S. and M. Berns. 1984. *Initiatives in Communicative Language Teaching.* Reading, MA: Addison-Wesley.

Scribner, S. and M. Cole. 1981. *The Psychology of Literacy.* Cambridge, MA: Harvard University Press.

Sen, A. 2005. *The Argumentative Indian: Writing on Indian History, Culture and Identity.* London: Allen Lane.

Silva, T. and P. K. Matsuda (eds) 2001. *On Second Language Writing.* Mahwah, NJ: Lawrence Erlbaum.

Smith, L. E. (ed.) 1987. *Discourse across Cultures: Strategies in World Englishes.* London, Prentice-Hall.

Smith, L. E. and M. Forman. (eds) 1997. *World Englishes 2000.* Honolulu, HI: University of Hawaii Press.

St Amant, K. 1999. 'When culture and rhetoric contrast: Examining English as an international language of technical communication.' *IEEE Transactions of Professional Communication* 42(4), 297–300.

Stapleton, P. 2001. 'Assessing critical thinking in the writing of Japanese university students: Insights about assumptions and content familiarity.' *Written Communication* 18(4), 506–48.

Swales, J. M. 1981. 'Aspects of article introductions.' In *Aston ESP Research Report No. 1, Language studies Unit.* Birmingham, UK: University of Aston in Birmingham.

——.1985. 'A genre-based approach to language across the curriculum.' In Makhan L. Tickoo (ed.) *Language across the Curriculum,* Singapore: SEAMEO Regional Language Centre, pp. 10–22.

——. 1990. *Genre analysis – English in Academic and Research Settings.* Cambridge: Cambridge University Press.

Swales, J. M. and C. B. Feak. 1994. *Academic Writing for Graduate Students: A Course for Non-native Speakers of English.* Ann Arbor: University of Michigan Press.

Teo, A. 1995. 'Analysis of newspaper editorials: A study of argumentative text structure.' Ph.D. dissertation, University of Illinois at Urbana-Champaign.

Tirkkonen-Condit, S. 1985. 'Argumentative text structure and translation.' Ph.D. dissertation, University of Jyvaskyla, Finland.

Uljin, J. M. 1996. 'Translating the culture of technical documents: Some experimental evidence.' In D. C. Andrews (ed.) *International Dimensions of Technical Communication.* Arlington: VA: STC, pp. 69–86.

van Dijk, T. 1980. *Macrostructure: An Interdisciplinary Study of Global Structures in Discourse, Interaction and Cognition.* Hillsdale, NJ: Lawrence-Erlbaum Associates.

Vyas, B. S., B. N. Tiwari and R. N. Srivastava. 1972. *hindii vyaakaraN aur racnaa.* (Hindi grammar and composition). Delhi: National Council of Educational Research and Training.

Werlich, E. 1976. *A Text Grammar of English.* Heidelberg, Germany: Quelle and Meyer.

9

Standards and Linguistic Realities of English in the Malaysian Workplace*

Saran Gill

Introduction

When researching into the word 'standards', I typed in the search term 'standards' in the computer at the university library and when the 'enter' key was pressed, I obtained the following impressive list:

Accounting – standards
Air-pollution – standards
Health personnel – standards
Auditing – standards
Blood banks – standards
Library bindings – standards
Building materials – standards
Data processing – standards
Material publications – standards
Computer industry – standards.

It is obvious from the above listing that standards are an essential component and permeate every aspect of our lives. They provide a point of reference so that one journeys through life with a clear and purposeful sense of direction. Without standards in all these fields, there would be no benchmark to measure against – no yardstick to compare levels of achievement or required sets of criteria. Unfortunately in the long list of items, there was no listing for the category 'standards and language'.

Why are standards a problematic topic to approach in the field of English language use? First, this stems from the nature of the language itself. This is because language is not a fixed commodity; it is a means of communication that reflects cultures, expressions and emotions of various speech communities. What one speech community may define as appropriate may not be so to another group of people. Second, in the field of language education, especially English language education, 'standards' has been a sensitive and controversial word. If we trace the changes over time of the way in which varieties of English and the issue of standards have been discussed in Malaysia, we will be able to understand the reasons for this. We can divide this development into three main phases:

Dependent/exonormative phase
Independent/liberation and expansion phase
Knowledge-driven international/endonormative phase.

English in Malaysia with the development of its varieties and the issue of standards has progressed and altered through a long historical journey. This started with a period of colonialism with its inherent dependence on the colonial masters, leading on to a period of independence and the exuberance of liberation and expansion, and presently we find ourselves in a post-independence phase of consolidation and pragmatic progress, driven by the knowledge-economy to meet the global challenge of international communication in increasingly competitive markets.

Dependent/Exonormative phase

In the context of the Outer Circle countries, many of whom were closely linked to the British because of exigencies of history, the standard that they referred to for English was the native-speaker standard – the speaker of Received Pronunciation. There was a dependence on the home country from which the language originated. Therefore, in terms of standards, it was the exonormative model that was referred to as the focal point for pedagogical and communicative standards.

In the syllabus of the 1970s, for Malaysian schools, it was stated that, 'for all practical purposes the minimum level is simply where the communicational intent is successfully conveyed, irrespective of the linguistic finesse. The maximum level is of course native-speaker ability' (English Syllabus in Malaysian schools, Forms 4–5, 1975: 4).

Since we are discussing the issue of standards, it is the maximum level that we shall concern ourselves with. As we are looking at the dependent stage, it would be enlightening to trace the opinions of those we were dependent on for maximum levels of successful communication to analyse their viewpoints and to assess whether those viewpoints have changed over time.

Quirk, for example, recommended a 'single monochrome standard' for all users. He said,

> The relatively narrow range of purposes for which the non-native needs to use English (even in ESL countries) is arguably well catered for by a single monochrome standard form that looks as good on paper as it sounds in speech. (Quirk 1985: 6)

This stance, articulated in 1985, reflects how viewpoints have not changed over the years. As far back as 1927 a similar strong stand was articulated:

> On the question of what words and idioms are to be used or to be forbidden, we cannot afford any kind of compromise or even discussion with the semi-demi-English-speaking population overseas. Their choice is to accept our authority or else make their own language. (From the *New Statesman* 25 June 1927, cited in Fernando 1986: 198)

We are now in the New Millennium and English is used all over the world; it belongs to everybody and yet opinions have not changed. If we look at recent expressions on the above topic, we observe a similar stance, though articulated in a more refined manner. Nonetheless, no matter what the style, the basic message is the same, as reflected in the following quotation:

> One way of managing the complex attitudes and responses to English by the world public to the benefit of Britain is through more careful 'brand management.' A debate would be timely on how Britain's ELT providers can cooperatively prepare for the need **to build and maintain the British brand and how the promotion of English language goods and services relate to the wider image of Britain as a leading-edge provider of cultural and knowledge-based products** (my emphasis). The way English is promoted and marketed may play a key role in positioning Britain as one of the 21st century's forward-thinking nations. (Graddol 1997: 63)

The common agenda in all these stands is very clearly that of promoting British English to the world. There is a clear message of ownership, control and promotion of the English language by the British, for the British, to the rest of the world. In the above discussion, the messages are expressed by a British politician and linguists through different forms that have similar underlying premises in the semantic content.

These are:

1. Adopt our language totally; otherwise develop your own.
2. As a linguist, acknowledge the existence of other varieties but advise non-native learners that it is not beneficial to use them.
3. Ignore all other language developments and solely market our brand for their consumption and for our survival.

This is further supported and expanded on by Quirk when he says,

> There are only the most dubious advantages in exposing the learner to a great variety of usage, no part of which he will have time to master properly, little of which he will be called upon to exercise, all of which is embedded in a controversial sociolinguistic matrix he cannot be expected to understand. (Quirk 1985: 6)

Learners in the Outer Circles (Kachru 1985) are not intentionally or formally exposed to the great variety of usage. It is a linguistic phenomenon that develops naturally within the society. In the Malaysian scenario, this is manifest through the natural cross-fertilization between Bahasa Malaysia, English and various other ethnic languages, such as Tamil and Cantonese. In this context, English cannot help but be influenced by the various other languages and sociolinguistically develop into a number of different varieties. Malaysians use the Malaysian varieties at hand naturally and effortlessly. Therefore, it is clear that the 'sociolinguistic matrix' is either viewed controversially or accepted as a perfectly normal phenomenon depending on where one comes from and what one's agenda is.

This 'sociolinguistic matrix' in which Malaysians and many other peoples in the Outer Circle contexts are submerged leads us to the second phase of the development of the sub-varieties of Malaysian English called the independent/liberation and expansion phase.

Independent/Liberation and expansion phase

In the liberation and expansion phase, English has been watered and fertilized and has branched out into colourful foliage in terms of varieties.

Kachru, in discussing the diffusion of English, described it as 'The Second Diaspora of English' in that the 'seeds' of resultant varieties of the language showed this diversity (Kachru 1992a: 230).

Kachru talks about linguistic pluralism and says of the acculturation and nativization of English in the various Outer Circle countries that they 'bring to English a unique cultural pluralism and a linguistic heterogeneity and diversity which are unrecorded to this extent in human history' (Kachru 1992a: 230).

In the Malaysian context, this diversity has been reflected by works mainly in the area of the lexico-semantic and phonological varieties of Malaysian English, such as Platt and Weber (1980), Wong (1983, 1991), Baskaran (1987) and Anthonysamy (1997).

In the researchers above, the investigations were largely conducted in the socio-cultural framework of the use of English in the local Malaysian context, very often in informal social contexts. Over time, this liberated linguistic phase provided recognition and a strong sense of confidence for the use of the varieties of Malaysian English as a means of communication within the country for intra-national communication.

At the same time, Malaysians have been constantly reminded that even though we have adopted and used the English language for various functions and purposes and it has 'acquired unparalleled functional and societal depth' (Kachru 1994: 3), the main value of the English language for Malaysians is for international communication.

The seemingly big divide between the liberation and expansion phase – the pluralistic development of varieties of language and the post-independence phase of adopting a pragmatic approach of seeing to the needs of the country – also led to a period of confusion among members of society. This is expressed by a number of the letters written to a prominent English daily newspaper about standards of English used in Malaysia.

The letter that sparked off the great debate was the following:

> In my five years of English teaching in various institutions in Malaysia, one of the greatest forces working against my efforts has been the influence of sub-standard models on my standards.
>
> However hard I try to raise my students' performance in the language, I am constantly disheartened by the awareness that they will walk out of my class and into a morass of slipshod, incorrect English usage as they meet with other speakers of what is increasingly becoming a pejorative term – 'Malaysian English.' (King in *The Star*, 1990: 16)

A typical contrasting response to the above is reflected through the following letter:

> We must appreciate that a Chinese has his own 'twang', just as a Malay has his and an Indian too. And it just cannot do to profess an 'English twang' in your spoken English. And when a Chinese meets another Chinese or a Malay meets another Malay, or an Indian meets another Indian, their English will not be the English which a person who knows no language other than English will speak; their English will be interspersed with words in their own language, and in their own particular 'twang'. So to be 'in tune' and 'in' with his colleagues, he will speak English the way they do. (Pro Bono Publico in *The Star*, 1990: 17)

Through an analysis of the various letters, it can be clearly seen that two differing opinions emerged from these letters. The first expressed anxiety over the standard of English and the manner in which it has developed into different sub-varieties, and the fear that it might reduce Malaysia's ability to communicate internationally; the second, in direct contrast, felt that the development of varieties of Malaysian English is a sociolinguistically acceptable feature of language development and therefore all criticisms regarding Malaysian English were unjustified.

What the above displays is language use for different domains – one in all its liberating, colourful form of the use of the language between Malaysians and the other the varieties that are used for the domain of international communication.

Knowledge-driven international/endonormative phase

This then takes us to the most important phase of linguistic development for a nation that needs the English language as an international language and a language to be able to access knowledge and information in the field of science and technology – the knowledge-driven international phase.

Malaysia recently implemented a major change in language policy from Bahasa Malaysia to English for the disciplines of science, maths and technology. This is to help it develop a generation of Malaysians who are able to acquire information and knowledge directly in English, as it is through English that there is a proliferation of international publications. (See Gill 2005 for a detailed discussion of the reasons that the major change was instituted.) It has now been five years since the implementation and presently Malaysia is at language policy crossroads, uncertain whether to continue with the policy or revert to Bahasa Malaysia as the language of instruction for these disciplines. The Ministry of Education which is responsible for these decisions on language policy in the education system is organizing round table dialogues. The aim of these dialogues is to provide voice and space to various members of society to articulate their experiences of the impact on the ground of the implementation of English as language of instruction for science and maths. The participants of the round-table dialogues include key members of community, academics and researchers, teachers, representatives from parent-teacher associations and non-governmental organizations, the Ministry of Education aims to bring on board all the experiences and opinions of these various parties and to balance this with the needs of the nation to be able to come up with a decision that would have considered both short and long-term needs of the peoples and the nation (*New Straits Times*, 2008).

No matter what decision is made with regard to language policy in Malaysia, it is essential for Malaysians to be able to express their ideas and arguments clearly and confidently in various business, trade and diplomatic interactions. This is because the dominant language that is used in the field of business, trade and industry is English. The language use in these domains has not been legislated in recognition of the fact that English is an international language and is the language used by most multinationals and Malaysia needs to develop economically through foreign direct investments brought in by multinationals and others who largely communicate in English.

Given that we need Malaysians to be able to communicate intelligibly on the international scene, we need to investigate as a starting point the speech quality of executives in the Malaysian workforce. The focus here has moved from research on the use of the language in social contexts and in informal workplace contexts to the use of English in formal situations in the workplace. What is used in the social contexts is also what is used in informal situations in the workplace. But the important question that should be posed is whether these sub-varieties of English are regarded as acceptable and appropriate for use in formal situations in the workplace.

We will have to consolidate – to make more secure and firm the emerging realities of the flourishing sub-varieties of English and the issue of standards in the workplace. This will require investigating the issue of the acceptability and appropriacy of the various sub-varieties of Malaysian

English in the workplace. Our process of consolidation should be guided by principles of linguistic pragmatism and attitudinal change (Kachru 1985: 25). Linguistic pragmatism is essential because we need to adopt a pragmatic attitude with regard to the appropriacy and acceptability of the sub-varieties of English for different situations in the formal workplace; attitudinal change because the standards that we used to aspire to are no longer standards that are appropriate or acceptable for our socio-cultural contexts.

What we have to do now is to explore our speech-fellowship-specific realism, (Kachru 1985) which in this paper is the formal workplace, to consolidate issues related to standards and emerging realities in the knowledge-driven international/endonormative phase.

Issue of standards

During the liberation/expansion phase, when there was new-found freedom, there were some linguists who felt that the issue of standards should not be discussed. Standard Malaysian English as referred to in the article 'Standards and Pedagogical Norms for Teaching English in Malaysia' (Gill 1993: 222) was strongly criticized in the following manner:

> Although frequently cited, Standard ME does not operate as a formalised model. As a researcher who has explored this area, I have yet to meet any species of linguistic animal called standard ME, nor have I met others who have seen it, although many claim to know how it looks. (Venugopal 1994: 329)

Granted, more research needs to be carried out to formalize this entity called Standard ME but it would be more pragmatic to recognize it and take steps to formalize it rather than criticize it. A pragmatic approach and a change of attitude are needed. This is emphasized by D'Souza when she says,

> The dangers involved in setting standards are very real but to refuse to do so is to indulge in ostrich-like behaviour. Standards whether they are recognised or not, do exist.... All one needs to avoid the dangers that inhere in standardisation is a spirit of tolerance and the realisation that English is not the exclusive property of any one nation or any one social class. What is needed is a change of attitude, not a denial of standards. (D'Souza 1993: 43)

As David Crystal says,

> A world Standard English exists, but is still at a fairly primitive stage of development in a similar position to that of British SE at the beginning of the fifteenth century (and actually with a less predictable future, for there are now several centres of gravity pulling the language in different directions. (Crystal 1994: 114)

In a study on standards (Gill 1993: 222) which involved 400 university students, there was an overwhelming acceptance of the educated Malaysian speaker as the standard to aspire to compared to the British speaker of Received Pronunciation. This was the speaker who spoke English with almost no grammatical mistakes and with an unmarked to slightly marked ethnic accent (Gill 1993: 234).

When we investigate the issue of standards, should we support one focal point (endonormative model) for all situations or should we investigate levels of acceptability of the sub-varieties for different situations? These are executives who speak sub-varieties of Malaysian English. Do we tell them that what they speak does not meet the standard, the focal point – or do we investigate to see what the reality of the situation is – that there may be acceptance for the varying manifestations depending on who they are speaking to? We may find that decision-makers in the workplace who have to face the reality of the situation may practise greater linguistic tolerance and flexibility and are more accommodating to change.

Therefore, is there developing in the formal variety, sub-varieties of the formal variety – are there layers of usage – some more appropriate and acceptable than others depending on the function to which they are applied? After all, 'English has a wide spectrum of domains in which it is used with varying degrees of competence by members of society, both as an intranational and an international language' (Kachru 1985: 13). It would be useful to examine the varying levels of competence of the sub-varieties of Malaysian English and whether they are found acceptable and appropriate for the different situations in the workplace.

Context of research

For Malaysians to be effective global communicators, the variety of the language that they use must be acceptable and appropriate for the particular function to which it is applied and the context in which it is used. Given the importance of English as an international language (EIL) in the professional domain, it is in this context that this study is placed. More specifically, it is the area of the language used for the delivery of oral presentations that this research is focused on. This is because one of the critical skills for executives in organizations is the ability to deliver effective oral presentations to different audiences in the professional context.

In discussing standards of language used for the delivery of presentations to varying audiences, there are a number of sociolinguistic factors that need to be considered. First, there is the classification of the language used by the executives along the modified lectal range of sub-varieties of Malaysian English. Second, there are the opinions of the gatekeepers as to the acceptability of the sub-varieties of Malaysian English used by the various speakers for different audiences. Another factor that is important is the attitude of the speakers themselves towards the language that they use, but this study will not deal with this.

The dynamics of the perspectives of both the linguists and the gatekeepers will throw essential light on what is acceptable and what is not acceptable in relation to standards and the emerging realities related to the delivery of oral presentations in the workplace.

In investigating the speakers delivering oral presentations, the focus is not on content in terms of clarity or logic of argument, which is obviously an important and related issue, but rather on the quality/nature of English used. We acknowledge that in terms of effectiveness, the non-verbal plays an important role as well but the quality of the language is focused on in this research because the quality of the language can get in the way of the message. In oral presentations, the quality of language – the phonological and syntactical quality – is a crucial component for its effectiveness.

Parallels can be drawn between business presenters in the workplace and news presenters on television. Bettina Chua Abdullah, a former anchor at CNBC Asia, informs us of the importance of the basics of the language for those who appear on television. From this, we can extrapolate the importance of these factors for presenters in the workplace. She says,

> Frequently, during my years as an anchor with a Malaysian TV station, I have had to field numerous complaints about the standard and quality of spoken English on the air. It was rare to find a viewer that wanted to share his thoughts about the actual programming content. Viewers griped about pronunciation, grammar, accents...

> The real tragedy of it all is that, when one has trouble understanding the language, the story, the news fades into the background... Oddly enough, English, (albeit, poorly communicated) was getting in the way of the news... The basics missing in TV English are grammar and pronunciation. The fact is that there are rules for spoken and written English that give it quality and make it easier to comprehend. And if yours is a TV station worth its salt, you'll know that unless you play by the rules, you'll alienate and lose your viewers... On the network news and in business reporting, we need an internationally accepted level of English. It has to be grammatically correct and pronounced properly. (Chua-Abdullah 1997)

Therefore, it will be important for this research to investigate the acceptability of the sub-varieties of Malaysian English, with a focus on the phonological and syntactical variation used in oral presentations to different audiences in the workplace.

The lexis will not be dealt with because the acculturation of lexis is a phenomenon that is widely accepted as a natural development. Research on lexis has depicted acceptable variation especially when it is contextualized within socio-cultural environments (see Anthonysamy 1997).

Lectal range of sub-varieties of Malaysian English

We need, in our moves towards standardization, a set of categories manifested as the lectal classification. At the same time, research can be carried out on the use of English in dynamic interactions in the workplace. The interactional dynamic approach can be used to examine the nature of language, discourse and creativity of English used with different participants, contexts and functions. As a result, a symbiotic relationship can be worked out with each feeding into the other – the data from the dynamic interactions feeding into the lectal classification and vice versa. Which aspect will be focused on largely depends on the purpose of the research – the context, the function of the communication and who the players are in the communicative event.

This research, since it deals with the acceptability of the sub-varieties of Malaysian English, will use as its base the lectal classification (Platt and Weber 1980; Baskaran 1987). Baskaran's (1987) work on the lectal range classified Malaysian English varieties based on the components of the phonology, syntax and lexis, into three categories – the acrolectal, mesolectal and the basilectal categories.

In this research, since it is the executives in the workplace that we are dealing with, all of whom have had a university education, the lectal range will spread across the acrolectal to the mesolectal range.

The basilectal category, whose phonological features are defined as possessing 'extreme variation – both segmental and prosodic, with intonation so stigmatized – almost unintelligible internationally' and syntax features as 'substantial variation/deviation – for national intelligibility only', will not be considered. This is because even though the executives have phonological and syntactical variation in their language, it is not so extreme as to be considered basilectal, as defined above.

In Baskaran's work, the acrolectal variety is defined as standard ME. It has phonological features where 'slight variation is tolerated so long as it is internationally intelligible' and syntax where 'no deviation is tolerated at all'.

Baskaran (1987) further defines the mesolectal variety as dialectal ME, of informal use and of national intelligibility. It has phonological features where 'more variation is tolerated, including prosodic features especially stress and intonation' and syntax where 'some deviation is acceptable although it is not as stigmatized as broken English (intelligibility is still there)'.

When a preliminary study was carried out, it was found that there were a number of speakers who fell in the mid-range; there was a need to classify them midway and there was no category. Even though the lectal range is a continuum, there is a need for the sake of clarity for certain categories to be formulated. Therefore, it was found, for the purposes of educated speakers in the workplace, that there was a need to include in its upper range a new category – the acro-mesolectal category. This is for speakers who have a marked Malay accent and a medium variation of syntactical features.

This resulted in the following modification (see Table 9.1):

Table 9.1 Lectal range of sub-varieties of formal Malaysian English

	Formal sociolinguistic range			
	Acrolect		**Acro-mesolect**	**Mesolect**
Phonology	Unmarked – accent	Mild Malay accent	Marked Malay accent	Markedly thick Malay accent
Syntax	No variation	Marginal variation	Medium variation	Greater variation

Educated Malay speakers of sub-varieties of formal Malaysian English

For this research, the six speakers are all executives who work in a major bank in the private sector. They range between those who have had a minimum of four and those with a maximum of seven years of working experience.

The samples of language were taken when these executives were delivering business presentations during a training programme, which covered 'Techniques in Delivering Effective Business Presentations'. They delivered their presentations to their colleagues in a formal environment. This is representative of their natural speech which is also used in formal workplace situations. Therefore, the recordings covered a wide enough spectrum of phonological and syntactical variation to represent the speakers' phonological and syntactical competence of language used in formal situations.

Ten linguists assessed the language, based on the audio-recordings of the six speakers, and categorized them along the modified lectal range.

Table 9.2 Linguists' phonological categorization of sub-varieties of formal Malaysian English

	Acrolect		Acro-mesolect	Mesolect
Phonology	**Unmarked accent**	**Mild Malay accent**	**Marked Malay accent**	**Markedly thick Malay accent**
Speaker 1		/// (3)	/////// (7)	
Speaker 2		// (2)	/ (1)	/////// (7)
Speaker 3		//// (4)	///// (5)	/ (1)
Speaker 4		///////// (9)	/ (1)	
Speaker 5			/// (3)	/////// (7)
Speaker 6		////// / (7)	/// (3)	

Table 9.3 Linguists' syntactical categorization of sub-varieties of formal Malaysian English

Syntax	**No variation**	**Marginal variation**	**Medium variation**	**Greater variation**
Speaker 1		/ (1)	//////// (8)	/ (1)
Speaker 2		// (2)	////// (6)	// (2)
Speaker 3		//// (4)	//// (4)	// (2)
Speaker 4	//// (4)	//// (4)	// (2)	
Speaker 5			/ (1)	///////// (9)
Speaker 6		/ / (2)	//////// (8)	

Their categorizations are marked by strokes (/). Even though there was no clear linguistic demarcation between the various sociolects, the linguists, based on their background and experience, were able to classify the various speakers along the continuum. In fact, their responses reflect a general consensus in the classification of the various speakers into the acrolect, acro-mesolect and mesolectal categories (see Tables 9.2 and 9.3).

Linguists' categorization of speakers

Speaker 1	Marked Malay accent	Acro-mesolectal speaker
	Medium syntactical variation	Acro-mesolectal speaker

Today, it is an honour for me to be able to stand here and present something to you. But, before I start, I would like to tell you a story. This story is actually happen somewhere in Johore last year. One fine day the rumours start flying, that Datuk Lau, the chairman and the founder of MBF is dying. By the afternoon, another set of stories came in. People were saying that, 'No, he is not dying, he's dead already.' And then by evening another set of rumours came in which said, 'Actually, it is not Datuk Lau who is dying, it is the company, MBF Finance is dying.' And then, you know whats happen next...It is not into any trouble and that they have more than enough money to pay the creditors and also the borrowers.

Speaker 2	Markedly thick Malay accent	Mesolectal speaker
	Medium – Greater syntactical variation	Mesolectal speaker

So, today I will...My topic will discuss strategic positioning where we should now analyse what is our strategy, how do we not to fall to the fate that have been eh...experienced by our friends...Why you need strategic positioning and the second one professional effectiveness. My statement here is important but not sufficient. I will answer this eh...two questions because eh...I think I have short of time to answer in one round. Before that, I will go to the meaning of the jargons – first one is operational effectiveness.

Speaker 3	Mild – Marked Malay accent	Acro-mesolectal speaker
	Marginal – Medium syntactical variation	Acro-mesolectal speaker

A very good morning to every one of you. First of all, I wish to thank for your willingness to share your very busy time listening and in fact...in fact to give your critiques and your opinions towards what I am going to present to you today. The issues that I am going to raise or highlight to you here is regarding our bilateral or trade balance that Malaysia has been suffering or enjoying for the couple of years ... we have been enjoying a trade surplus figure since way back in 19, way back in ... excuse me, ... we have been enjoying a trade surplus since end of 80s. But, however, this has not last long.

Speaker 4	Mild Malay accent	Acrolectal speaker
	Marginal syntactical variation	Acrolectal speaker

Good morning ladies and gentlemen. With multi-super corridor and cyber-path slowly creeping into our lives, there is one definite thing that we must do – we must change. We, as individuals have to change and our institution has to change. Why? If we don't change, we will become obsolete in the dynamic industry out there. We will become staff of a white elephant.

DRP is about changing. It is about changing the work processes in all departments, the way we do work, how we carry out our daily work. DRP affects all departments, every staff in the whole bank.

Speaker 5	Markedly thick Malay accent	Mesolectal speaker
	Greater syntactical variation	Mesolectal speaker

Good morning ladies and gentlemens. Welcome and thank you for comings today. Before I start this sessions I hope you will be enjoy, relax and get some benefit from my presentations today. Before, I start, I would like to ask you ones question – am I right to say that the function of the statistics departments just to collect or compile the data only – yes or no? OK the answer is no. We are not just to collect and compile the data only but we have to come up or produce the report for the users. ... So, come back to my topic, my topic today, I would like to brief you on the what type of the report that we have and who is our users and what are the benefit that you can gain from our reports.

Speaker 6	Mild Malay accent	Acrolectal speaker
	Medium syntactical variation	Acro-mesolectal speaker

Let me awaken all of you to the very crucial topic of market risk exposure and the concept of value at risk. All of you are aware, I'm sure that our country is facing an economic crisis, but looking back one year ago,

I'm also sure that all of us did not anticipate the condition that we are facing today. Ladies and gentlemen, if banks, corporations or even a simple businessman were to anticipate or even measure, control and monitor these form of market risk exposure, they would be in a better position today. ...

Today, I will be describing to you a simple definition of market risk and the concept of value at risk. This concept will be benefit to you and to the future generations .... Let me walk through to you eh to enlighten you before I proceed to the objective of market risk management.

Gatekeepers' responses to the acceptability of the various presenters for different audiences

Gatekeepers are defined as 'actors with control over key resources and avenues of opportunity. Such gatekeepers exercise control at and during key phases of the youngster's (executive's) status passage(s)' (Hammersley and Atkinson 1983: 38). The gatekeepers (those who hold positions of power and authority) play a crucial role in the workplace – they are the ones who have control over the workplace opportunities that these executives have. Therefore it is pertinent to focus on their viewpoints because employees who deliver oral presentations do so not only as individuals but more importantly as representatives of the organizations. Therefore, it would be necessary to find out what the opinions of senior executives are of the employees who use the range of the mesolectal to the acrolectal variety of Malaysian English when making oral presentations. After all, it is these members of management who function as the gatekeepers of the organization as they are the ones who not only determine the avenues of opportunity available to these executives but also safeguard the company's image while implementing company policy.

In contrast, it is sometimes said that, 'Surely it is what the users of the language do, not what a small elite would like them to do which counts in the end' (Kennedy 1985: 7). What counts in the end depends on the context in which the language is used and who decides on the acceptability of who speaks what to whom. If it depends totally on the speaker irrespective of the dialect/variety that he speaks, then the above quotation applies. But if it depends on the decision-maker, who is in a position of authority that influences the career track of the executives, then the speaker's variety (if the speaker is concerned about professional opportunities and advancement) will have to converge with the expectations/norms of appropriateness regarded as acceptable by decision-makers.

The ten gatekeepers in this study are managers or senior executives who possess decision-making authority in their various organizations. They are all Malays. This is to eliminate the ethnic variable which may play a part in the opinions of the senior executives as gatekeepers. They have a minimum of seven years of managerial experience in their companies.

These gatekeepers listened to the audio recordings of the speakers from the syntactical and phonological perspectives to decide if they would select the respective executives to deliver presentations to different audiences as stated in the questionnaire. The questions in the questionnaire that the respondents were asked were based on the audiences to whom the executives deliver oral presentations in the course of their work. There were five questions in all, one for each type of audience. Each question was expressed as follows.

Would this speaker be suitable to deliver presentations on behalf of the organization:

i. internally, within the organization to his colleagues?
ii. internally, within the organization to his superiors?
iii. externally, to other Malaysians working for other organizations?
iv. externally to foreigners – e.g. British, Canadian, Australian?
v. externally to foreigners – e.g. Koreans, Japanese?

Implications and recommendations

This study shows a clear result for Speakers 2 and 5 (Table 9.4). The linguists have classified these speakers in the mesolectal category of the sub-variety of Malaysian English. This is the category with a markedly thick Malay accent and greater syntactical variation. The gatekeepers have found these speakers suitable for presentations internally only at the level of colleagues. There is a clear message from the gatekeepers that these speakers will not be found acceptable to deliver business presentations to the senior management and to those external to the organization. During the feedback session to obtain further information from the gatekeepers as to why they have responded thus, the main reason given by one of the respondents was that, 'these speakers represent the organisation and not themselves individually, therefore the way they speak will affect the professional image of the organisation negatively. This cannot be allowed.'

Speaker 1 is classified by the linguists as an acro-mesolectal speaker, characterized with features of a marked Malay accent and a medium

Table 9.4 Responses of gatekeepers to the acceptability of oral presenters for different audiences in the formal workplace

Different audiences	Colleagues	Superiors	External Malaysians	External foreigners (British, Australians, Canadians)	External foreigners (Japanese, Koreans)
Speaker 1	Y = 9 N = 1	Y = 3 N = 7	Y = 1 N = 9	Y = 1 N = 9	Y = 1 N = 9
Speaker 2	Y = 7 N = 3	Y = 1 N = 9	Y = 0 N = 10	Y = 0 N = 10	Y = 0 N = 10
Speaker 3	**Y = 10** **N = 0**	**Y = 8** **N = 2**	**Y = 8** **N = 2**	**Y = 6** **N = 4**	**Y = 8** **N = 2**
Speaker 4	**Y = 10** **N = 0**	**Y = 8** **N = 2**	**Y = 8** **N = 2**	**Y = 8** **N = 2**	**Y = 8** **N = 2**
Speaker 5	Y = 8 N = 2	Y = 2 N = 8	Y = 0 N = 10	Y = 0 N = 10	Y = 3 N = 7
Speaker 6	**Y = 10** **N = 0**	**Y = 10** **N = 0**	**Y = 10** **N = 0**	**Y = 10** **N = 0**	**Y = 10** **N = 0**

Note: Y = YES, N = NO.

degree of syntactical variation. Speaker 3 is similarly classified by the majority of the linguists in the acro-mesolectal category. This category has features of mild to marked Malay accent with a marginal–medium degree of syntactical variation.

The gatekeepers have responded differently to these two speakers. Speaker 1 is found acceptable to deliver business presentations only internally to colleagues. She is not found suitable for superiors within the company and to audiences external to the company.

On the other hand, Speaker 3 is found suitable as a presenter to all the audiences. On further inquiry, it was found that most of the gatekeepers found his voice to be confident. Speaker 3 is louder and this leads to a stronger presentation of self. He is therefore acceptable for presentations where he needs to represent the organization. In contrast, Speaker 1 was found to be lacking in confidence. This was manifested through a reduced volume in the voice which gave the impression of lacking confidence.

This raised the question of whether confidence projection through the voice compensates for variation in the syntax of the language. The majority of the gatekeepers said it depended on the degree of variation. If it was in the medium range, as in Speaker 3, yes, then the ability to project one's voice through clear articulation and volume is an asset.

But this is not so if the degree of syntactical variation is great, as in Speaker 5. Then the confident projection of the voice does not compensate for the strong syntactical variation.

Speaker 4 is classified by the linguists as one who has a mild Malay accent and who speaks with a marginal syntactical variation – the features of the acrolectal speaker. This speaker is accepted by the gatekeepers as someone who is acceptable as a business presenter to all the varying audiences, both internal and external to the company.

Speaker 6 is classified by the linguists as one who has a mild Malay accent with medium syntactical variation. The phonological classification labels him as an acrolectal speaker but the syntactical classification would label him as an acro-mesolectal speaker.

Yet, of all the presenters, the gatekeepers found this speaker to be the one person they would, without hesitation, use to deliver business presentations to all the varying audiences, both internal and external to the organization.

Even though he has been classified by the linguists to possess medium syntactical variation, when the linguists' analysis of the variations were evaluated, it was found that there was one main variation, which is when he said, 'Let me walk through to you eh let me enlighten you…' which being in the field of English language education, they have found to be unacceptable, therefore, the classification in the medium syntactical variation. But, otherwise there were no major, consistent syntactical variations. His greatest advantage is that he possessed a clear and confident phonological style and projected his voice well. Therefore, he was regarded as acceptable for delivery of presentations to all the various audiences, both internal and external to the company.

This study shows a clear trend as to how all the speakers are regarded as acceptable for internal presentations, especially to colleagues. But when the audience is that of senior management within the company, only Speakers 3, 4 and 6 are found suitable. The trend progresses similarly for the audiences external to the company; only Speakers 3, 4 and 6 are regarded as acceptable to deliver business presentations to clients or customers external to the company.

What this shows is that any discussion on the above results has to be guided by linguistic reality and pragmatism (Kachru 1985). The linguistic reality is that in organizations in Malaysia there are executives who speak English with varying degrees of variation. The pragmatism is that there are varying norms of acceptability/appropriateness for different audiences – there is a place under the sun for all types of linguistic realities. It is not just one norm of reference that influences everything; there is acceptance of sub-varieties of Malaysian English in the workplace, but these are context and participant dependent.

It is important that the speakers in the workplace who are only able to speak one sub-variety of the language (the mesolectal variety) and are not able to switch to the higher level varieties (the acro-mesolectal and the acrolectal) need to be made aware that they can be disadvantaged in the professional domain.

As Widdowson stresses, 'nose picking and bad grammar are social markers' and 'human beings are free to behave as they choose as long as they are kept in place and do not threaten to gatecrash the party' (Widdowson cited in Tickoo 1991: 134). Therefore, if an executive speaks a sub-variety of English that is not acceptable, the gates will be firmly closed to deny entrance. This has a strong note of hopelessness. It might be more encouraging to stress that gates are flexible and can always be open if one is able to meet the criteria required by the gatekeepers. As Tickoo says, 'in each case before they seek membership in one or another important domain of public life, aspirants must learn the linguistic etiquette and behaviour that characterise it' (Tickoo 1991: 134). Therefore, one can work at one's mastery of language and reduce the degree of variation, and work at cultivating a more confident tone of voice to keep gates open and hope alive. As Alexander Graham Bell said, 'When one door closes, another opens; but we often look so long and so regretfully upon the closed door (gate) that we do not see the one which has opened for us.'

We have to help Malaysian executives open more gates and thus increase the opportunities for professional advancement. One way in which we can do this is working at a standard so that they have a realistic benchmark that they can relate to. There needs to be a standard which by general consent can function as a basis of comparison, an approved model. In the case of this study it is Speaker 4 and Speaker 6 who can potentially qualify for this role. They have the qualities of a speaker of Standard Malaysian English along the following lines: Phonology – 'variation tolerated as long as it is internationally intelligible'; Syntax – 'minimal variation tolerated'.

For future research, there needs to be a corpus of formal Malaysian English speakers that fall within the acrolectal and the acro-mesolectal range. Then gatekeepers and other executives would be asked which of these speakers they would accept as role models – models of spoken English that they would aspire to. This would then be followed up by detailed phonological and syntactical analysis of the corpus to enable codification of the standard that Malaysians are able to identify with, relate to and that they can call their own – one that is intranationally and internationally accepted.

Through dynamic research, where we involve not only linguists but also the gatekeepers, the decision-makers in industry, we can come up with recommendations that will help Malaysians achieve a standard that will be both intranationally and internationally acceptable in the formal workplace and that will open more gates for professional advancement. In our efforts to work towards this locally and internationally acceptable standard, it is essential that we obtain the viewpoints of those in the workplace, particularly the decision-makers. Only then can the variety that is recommended as the model be acceptable by all and achieve the status that it requires. As Kachru says, 'a variety may exist but unless it is recognized and accepted as a model it does not acquire a status' (Kachru 1992b: 56).

With globalization and all its inherent challenges, it is necessary for our executives to be aware of the implications of the type of English that they use in the workplace, especially for business presentations. Whether one likes it or not, those in managerial positions are those who make decisions. When one works for a company or an organization, it is those in managerial positions who implement the policies of the organization and safeguard its image – it is they who decide on the acceptable standards of the emerging linguistic realities for Malaysians in the formal workplace.

Note

*This chapter is based on publication in Symposium on 'Standards, Codification and World Englishes.' Edited by Saran Kaur Gill and Anne Pakir. In *World Englishes*, Vol. 18: 2, 215–31, July 1999. The author would like to thank Blackwell Publishing Ltd. for allowing her to reprint part of the article in this chapter.

References

Anthonysamy, J. 1997. 'Lexico-Semantic Variation in Malaysian English.' Master's Dissertation, Department of English, Faculty of Languages and Linguistics, University of Malaya.

Baskaran, L. 1987. 'Aspects of Malaysian English Syntax.' Ph.D Dissertation, Department of Linguistics, University of London.

Chua-Abdullah, B. 1997. 'Live and in English.' Paper presented at the International Symposium on *English is an Asian Language: The Malaysian*

Context. 18–19 August. Association of Modern Languages, Malaysia and the Macquarie Library Ltd. Australia.

Crystal, D. 1994. 'Which English or English Which?' In M. Hayhoe and S. Parker (eds) *Who Owns English?* Buckingham, Philadelphia: Open University Press, pp. 109–16.

D'Souza, J. 1993. 'Varieties of English Old and New: A Matter of Standards.' In A. Pakir (ed.) *The English Language in Singapore: Standards and Norms*, Singapore: Singapore University Press, pp. 32–46.

Fernando, L. 1986. *Cultures in Conflict: Essays in Literature and the English Language in South East Asia*. Singapore: Graham Brash.

Gill, S. K. 1993. 'Standards and Pedagogical Norms for Teaching English in Malaysia.' *World Englishes*, 12 (2), 223–38.

——. 2005. 'Language policy in Malaysia: Reversing direction.' *Language Policy, 4*(3), 241–60.

Graddol, D. 1997. *The Future of English?* London: British Council.

Hammersley, M. and P. Atkinson. 1983. *Ethnography – Principles in Practice*. London: Tavistock Publications.

Kachru, B. B. 1985. 'Standards, Codification and Sociolinguistic Realism: the English Language in the Outer Circle.' In R. Quirk and H. G. Widdowson (eds) *English in the World: Teaching and Learning the Language and Literatures*, Cambridge: Cambridge University Press. pp. 7–30.

——. 1992a. 'The Second Diaspora of English.' In T. W. Machan and C. T. Scott (eds) *English in its Social Contexts: Essays in Historical Sociolinguistics*, New York: Oxford University Press. pp. 230–52.

——. 1992b. 'Models for Non-Native Englishes.' In B. B. Kachru (ed.) *The Other Tongue: English Across Cultures*, 2nd ed. Urbana and Chicago: University of Illinois Press, pp. 48–74.

——. 1994. 'Teaching World Englishes without Myths.' In S. K. Gill et al. (eds) *Proceedings of the International English Language Education Conference – National and International Challenges and Responses*, Bangi: Language Centre, Universiti Kebangsaan Malaysia, pp. 1–19.

Kennedy, G. 1985. 'Commentator 1.' In R. Quirk and H. G. Widdowson (eds) *English in the World: Teaching and Learning in the Language and Literatures*, Cambridge: Cambridge University Press, pp. 7–8.

Quirk, R. 1985. 'The English Language in a Global Context.' In R. Quirk and H. G. Widdowson (eds) *English in the World: Teaching and Learning the Language and Literatures*, Cambridge: Cambridge University Press, pp. 1–6.

Platt, J. and H. Weber, 1980. *English in Singapore and Malaysia*. Kuala Lumpur: Oxford University Press.

Tickoo, M. L. 1991. 'Stakeholders and Standards: English for Tomorrow's India.' In M. L. Tickoo (ed.) *Languages and Standards: Issues, Attitudes and Case Studies*, Singapore: SEAMEO Regional Language Centre, pp. 131–52.

Venugopal, S. N. 1994. 'Standard English and English Language Education: Of Anachronistic Definitions and Current Relevance.' In S. K. Gill et al. (eds) *Proceedings of the International English Language Education Conference – National and International Challenges and Responses*, Bangi: Language Centre, Universiti Kebangsaan Malaysia, pp. 322–30.

Wong, I. 1983. 'Simplification Features in the Structure of Colloquial Malaysian English.' In R. B. Noss (ed.) *Varieties of English in Southeast Asia*. Anthology Series, No. 11, 125–49. Singapore: Singapore University Press.

Wong, I. 1991. Models for Written English in Malaysia. In M. L. Tickoo (ed.) *Languages and Standards: Issues, Attitudes, Case Studies*. Anthology Series No. 26, 97–108. Singapore: SEAMEO Regional Language Centre.

Newspaper reports

King, Alistair, 'English: Certain Standards Must Be Observed.' *The Star*, 28 July 1990: 16.

Pro Bono Publico, 'Let's Appreciate Our Own Style of Speaking English.' *The Star*, 4 September 1990: 17.

New Straits Times, July 10 2008. Talks to Review Programme, p. 8.

10
English in Asian Advertising and the Teaching of World Englishes

Tej K. Bhatia

Introduction

Imagine the Taj Mahal, regarded as one of the most beautiful monuments in the world and the symbol of love, running the risk of losing its status as one of the Seven Wonders of the World! With its undisputed place in global history books and the honour bestowed upon it by UNESCO in 1983 as the symbol of world heritage, the media and advertising companies seduced Indians and non-Indians worldwide into believing that the Taj's age-old glory was in danger when the fierce New7Wonders (N7W) campaign took off some 18 months ago. The campaign was the brainchild of Bernard Webber, a Swiss businessman, and was actually waged by his for-profit corporation – New Open World Corporation (NOWC). The campaign stressed the need for recognizing the N7W by public opinion poll around the world. The first phase of global pooling brought bad news to Indians – the Taj was about to lose its old glory and was languishing far below with a rank of twenty-one. Alarmed by this sluggish performance, Indian print and electronic media went into a frenzy, and some marketing firms got into the act as well and urged Indians worldwide to vote. Advertising gimmicks like slick radio, TV, print and Internet campaigns involving hot air balloons, even a blind child saying, 'I have heard it (i.e. the Taj) is beautiful', implored Indians of all ages, particularly youths, into voting through telephones, Internet and cell phone SMS (or text messages), the product of India's new telecom revolution. Of course, every vote in turn became the beneficiary of slick advertising campaigns for products and services (See Sarkar 2007 for more details). The 18-month campaign, sugar-coated with deception, primarily through English, turned out to be a money-making bonanza for Webber and his partners such as the Indian representative of NOWC, I Media Corporation Limited (IMCL) and telephone companies. What is even more interesting is that the announcement of the good news and a coverage of glitzy Lisbon ceremony announcing the verdict made headlines on 8 July 2007 throughout Indian media, with the NOWC foundation still being labelled as 'a Swiss non-profit group' even in the top ranked English language Indian daily newspaper, *The Times of India* (see the news report, 'Taj makes it to new seven wonder list'). This exemplifies the mushrooming of new and complex mix of advertising and the emergence of an era of interactive advertising in Asia, particularly in India.

The aim of this paper is to examine the distinct context and varied facets of language use in conventional advertising in Asia. For the purpose of comparing and contrasting, conventional and new media (Internet) are also referred to. In addition to isolating its salient features, the issue of globalization vs. localization which is central to international advertising is also addressed. Finally, the implications for the teaching of Asian English/world Englishes are presented. The scope of the paper is restricted to English language advertising in Asia.

Asian English-advertising: Context and typology

Asian advertising marks a point of departure from advertising in the West in a number of ways: First, in terms of context: advertising in the Western Anglophone countries – the United States, Canada and the UK – is largely monolingual in nature, as is evident by the large body of research on this topic (see Martin 2006; Bhatia 2006). Even the advertising aimed at linguistic minorities rarely goes beyond the cosmetic character of minority languages and/or scripts. Second, in terms the typology of English users and usage, B. Kachru's (1992) Three Concentric Circle model of English users worldwide shed further light on the distinct nature of linguistic form and function witnessed in advertising in Asia. Asian advertising, unlike Western advertising, is essentially grounded in the Outer Circle and Expanding Circle of English which lends it a very complex mosaic of English mixing with Asian languages, scripts and accents among others (see Hsu 2001; Hermeren 1999; Myers 1999; McKeldin 1994). Third, for a number of reasons including law and regulation, media reach, etc. the range of media forms accessible in Asia is richer than and their reach is different from Anglophone countries. A case in point is the widespread use of wall advertising in countries such as India and China and the limited reach of television in the rural areas in these two countries. Finally, the mixing of literary forms (primarily poetry) and the use of popular media such as cartoons (Japan) and films (e.g. Bollywood) also renders a distinct flavour to Asian advertising.

Key issues

Although there are number of key issues (e.g. media buying, ad placement, etc.), which confront Asian as well as global advertisers, the following are the most pertinent from the viewpoint of the topic at hand.

Standardization vs. adaptation

Theodore Levitt, the Business Guru from Harvard, made a stunning prediction in the 1980s that 'The era of mulitinational companies customizing their products and advertising... is over.' The claim was based on the premise that in the age of rapid globalization or even hyper-globalization, customizing messages was counterproductive. Therefore, the new mantra of globalization meant homogenization in terms of the language use, product name, logos and even the content of the message. In technical terms, it is called the 'standardization' view of the ad. Of course, there is a dissenting view to this 'standardization' which mirrors the 'one-size-fits-all' approach and in that process undermines the importance of the diversity – of tastes, sensitivities, identities and cultural norms – witnessed in human societies. The 'Adaptation' view, on the other hand, calls for the customization of global ads in order to court a particular group and it is slowly but steadily making its mark in international advertising in the age of diversity marketing (see Chandra, Griffith and Ryans 2002; Heileman 1997; Hite and Fraser 1988; Kanso 1991; Kujala and Lehtinen 1989; Mueller 1992; Onkvisit and Shaw 1987; Ryans and Ratz 1987, among others). How to resolve the dilemma or paradox of 'standardization' vs. 'adaptation' in international advertising still remains a central concern for advertisers and marketers. A middle-ground approach (glocalization) offers a reasonable solution to this debate which finds its validity in the growing phenomenon of language mixing in Asia and to some extent in the world. (For the linguistic mechanism of the glocalization approach, see Bhatia 2000: 168.)

Language attitude and choice

The question of language choice and attitudes figure prominently in the 'standardization' vs. 'adaptation' debate. English and the Roman script is the overwhelming choice of global advertisers and marketers. English has effectively dethroned its competitor languages such as French and Russian, and continues to do so with such dynamism and vigour that it has become the single most important and favourite linguistic tool of globalization.

While the question of language choice is practically settled, the question of the variety of English is still far from being settled in international advertising. Asian advertising further underscores this point. A cursory examination of Asian advertising reveals that the Inner Circle varieties coexist with the Outer Circle and Expanding Circle varieties of English, thus highlighting that the Inner Circle English is not the only choice accessible to international advertisers.

Audience reach and modality choice

The differential nature of the accessibility of media forms and their reach to consumers also contribute to the distinct character of advertising in Asia. For instance, the two Asian giants India and China, which have large rural populations, can be reached most economically and effectively through non-conventional media form called 'wall advertising'. This media form is practically inaccessible in the West and in some Asian countries due to government regulation and association with graffiti. The choice of such a modality not only makes an economic sense, but is imperative for the limited reach of TV in rural areas. (For more details about the non-conventional media such as wall advertising and video van (dubbed 'magic media'), see Bhatia 2000, Chapter 3.)

Outer and expanding circle advertising

As pointed out earlier, in order to come to grips with the distinct character of Asian advertising, Kachru's Three Concentric Circle typology of English users is instructive. According to this typology, Asian Englishes belong either to the Outer Circle (e.g. India) or to the Expanding Circle (as in China and Japan). In the Outer Circle, English evolved in the multilingual, multicultural and multiethnic environment and is the by-product of the colonialism and socio-political environment of those countries. In multilingual countries such as India, where 22 official languages exist along with scores of dialects, English serves as a link language and enjoys an official status, particularly in domains such as education and regulation. Therefore, unlike the Inner Circle where English is spoken either as the first or the more dominant language, in the Outer Circle, on the other hand, English is acquired as an additional language, i.e. second, third or even fourth language. In the Expanding Circle countries, however, English serves primarily as a foreign language, as in the case of Japan and China.

As the single most important source of global bilingualism and through its (English) contact with Asian languages, there has been an emergence of mixed varieties of Asian Englishes such as Japlish, Chinglish, Konglish, Hinglish, and Singlish, to name a few.[1] With forces of globalization, marketization and media working furiously, together with the positive attitude towards English in Asia, English usage in day-to-day interaction and particularly in Asian advertising and media has achieved a distinct state of fusion and hybridization of linguistic forms, which is unprecedented in the history of global English. In addition, the creative requirements of advertisers and marketers have further added such a complexity to the dynamics of English in Asia that it defies conventional wisdom and offers a lot of surprises. For instance, consider the case of Expanding Circle English. With very low incidence of bilingualism with English, one would think that incidences of mixing English with native languages would be very low. However, any cursory examination of advertising exhibits just the opposite pattern. Overt and covert (by means of non-Western scripts) English-mixing in Japanese, Chinese and Korean ads competes with the incidence of mixing witnessed in the Outer Circle countries. Furthermore, as Bhatia (2006: 605) points out, the influence of American and British English is so significant particularly in some modalities such as conventional advertising (television and radio) that the Inner Circle seems to be exercising a 'melting pot' effect in global Englishes. The bi-directional accommodation and mutually feeding relationship between the three circles of English lends further support to Yano's claim that the distinction between Inner Circle and Outer Circle will eventually disappear (Yano 2001: 122). If the present trend continues, advertising in Asia is ready to make yet another leap leading to the fuzzy boundaries of the three circles in an effort to respond to the global as well as local tastes of Asian consumers at the same time.

Nature and mode of language mixing

As is self-evident from the earlier discussion, one of the hallmarks of Asian advertising is its mixed character. Even the Inner Circle, advertisers show openness to the mixing and sprinkling of foreign words and scripts in an ad. A few diacritics and slight adaptation of syntactic and phonological forms lend monolingual ads the flavour of French, German or other European languages (*l'eggs, el cheapo, nueva, esta*). This effect is often termed 'mock' effective in linguistic literature. However, this type of mixing can best be characterized as the 'low-level' mixing which is motivated by cosmetic factors (see Bhatia and Ritchie 2004). The nature of mixing in Asian advertising, on the other hand, is qualitatively distinct from Inner Circle mixing. In terms of formal properties, the high-level mixing has achieved such a level of fusion and complexity that it poses a challenge for the theoreticians of code-mixing and code-switching.

Consider the case of the Domino Pizza ad's slogan in India – *Hungry kya*? 'Are you hungry?' The question word *kya* means 'what' when it is placed in the middle of a sentence (e.g. *aapkaa nam kyaa hai* 'What is your name?'). However, when placed in the sentence-initial position (i.e. unmarked position) of a declarative sentence, it performs a function of a yes–no question. The mixing witnessed in the slogan of Domino's Pizza is syntactically and psycholinguistically complex for the following three reasons: (1) the question word *kya* is actually processed as *kyaa*; (2) the question word is placed in the marked position (i.e. sentence/phrase-final position) giving rise to potential ambiguity between the information-question word 'what' and the yes–no marker; (3) a competent English-Hindi bilingual rules out the information-question interpretation and settles for a yes–no question interpretation. In addition to structural and psycholinguistic factors, the slogan poses a challenge for the theoretical concept of determining the 'matrix' vs. 'embedded' language in code-mixing/switching. In short, the Hindi word *kyaa* is not a borrowing, but performs a very complex formal and functional role. Also, in terms of its rendition of function, it lends the air of informality to the mixed slogan. This best exemplifies the high-level fusion which mixing is capable of rendering in Asian advertising.

The fusion manifests itself in the following four ways:

- mixing of English with other languages
- mixing of English with non-Roman scripts
- mixing of world English accents
- mixing of world Englishes.

Mixing of English with Asian languages: Bilingual to multiple-language mixing

The mixing sites of English with native languages ranges from attention-getters, product naming, slogans, labels and the body of ads. Consider the following slogans of the global brands:

English-*Hindi*

(1)	*ThanDaa*	*matab*	Coca-Cola		
	cold/cool	meaning	Coca-Cola		
	'Coca-Cola – meaning cool.'				
(2)	Coca-Cola	*piyo*	*ThanDaa,*	*jiyo*	*ThanDaa*
	Coca-Cola	drink	cold	live	cold
	'Coca-Cola – drink cold and live cool.'				

English-*Japanese*

(3) *hontoo no aji na no ni shaapu na toobun zero*. Coca-Cola Zero.
real of taste even though sharp sweetness zero. Coca-Cola Zero.
'It's the) real taste but zero the sharp sweetness. (That's) Coca-Cola Zero.'

English-*Chinese*

(4) Heineken, *jiushiyao hainigen*
'I just want Heineken.'
(*hainigen* is a adapted transliterated form of Heineken)

Consider the attention-getter of an ad for a renowned national fast food chain in India – Nirula's (Figure 10.1).
English-*Hindi*

(5) Nirula's – *in* pizzas *ko* resist *karnaa mushkil hii nahii namumkin hai.*
'Nirula's – it is not only difficult to resist these pizzas but it is impossible as well.'

Nirula's one-page ad is only in English; at least that is the impression one gets at the first sight. The ad is not only psycholinguistically intriguing but also underscores the unmarked pattern of Indian advertising akin to language mixing. The product being advertised is a variety of pizzas and the target consumers are primarily urban Indians. The first word *in* prepares Hindi-English bilinguals to turn on the English-language in order to process the sentence, the second word *pizzas* further supports such a language onset procedure. However, the third word calls for a repair strategy when it becomes obvious to a competent bilingual that the English-sounding prepositional phrase is in fact a postpositional phrase in which *in* 'these' turns out to be a Hindi

Figure 10.1 Nirula's advertisement

modifier. The fourth word is the English verb *resist* which undergoes yet another process of verb formation (i.e. the Hindi complex verb formation) by means of a Hindi verb anchored by *karnaa* 'to do' (similar to the Japanese *suru* construction), ultimately rendering the Hindi-code mixed equivalent of English verb 'to resist'. Similarly, the product types in the left and the right column (a variety of pizzas) also reveal a close partnership between English and Hindi and thus expanding the scope of the fusion and hybridization of linguistic forms on one hand and creating new product types on the other. This pattern is not exclusive to India, but also representative of Asian advertising with varying functions.

The phenomenon of mixing with English is not restricted to the two languages, that is English + dominant or majority language of the region as exemplified by the Hinglish, Chinglish and Japlish ads given earlier. The discussion in the following sections will reveal yet another dimension of mixing which can be best characterized as multiple mixing – a type of fusion which is the by-product of either actual or perceived multilingualism on the part of advertisers and marketers and the users of English. What is astonishing is that multiple language mixing in South Asian countries is the norm and not the exception in Asia. At least it is true of Japan. While mixing with English and other languages is motivated by cosmetic factors (i.e. the precedence

Table 10.1 Language and domain distribution in Indian advertising

Language	Audience	Appeal	Value/aim	Product/ discourse domain
English	Male/female	Outworldly	Modern, Western	Fashion, science, sports, entertainment
Hindi	Female	Emotional	Utility, pragmatic	Domestic, household
Sanskrit	Male/female	Deep-rooted cultural	Reliability	Alternative medicine (Ayurvedic)
Persian	Male	Luxury (royal)	Utility (physical)	Cigarettes

of attention-catching over intelligibility; mock westernization effects) in Japanese, Indian advertising involves a complex array of functions summarized in Table 10.1 above.

As if the triple or quadruple language mixing was not dynamic or colourful enough, the latest trend is to woo the rural consumers by means of mixing English with rural or regional varieties of Hindi, particularly with Bhojpuri. Multiple language mixing shows some striking parallelism with multiple script mixing in Japan. It appears finally that the Indian advertising industry is heeding the call issued by Bhatia (2000: 299) advising multinational companies to incorporate themes that reflect rural Indian cultural tradition as well as multiple language and script mixing to maximize intelligibility.

The success of the Maggi Noodle campaign is a case in point, having created Maggi Mania in India with the punch line, *maggi kaa mania hui gavaa re!* ('Hey, has Maggi mania possessed you?'). In this ad, the head noun (*Mania*), the possessed/genitive phrase (*Maggi kaa* 'Maggi's') and the verb phrase (*huii gavaa re* 'lit. has happened, hey') is drawn from English, Hindi and Bhojpuri, respectively. Similarly, the Hutch mobile ad *waat naan-sense* 'what nonsense' is grounded in non-standard Indian English pronunciation and culture (pun: naan = English *non-* and Hindi *naan* 'bread'). Similarly, both written and spoken indigenous varieties of English are often mixed with native varieties of English to provide a distinct Asian flavour.

Product naming and company naming is another important domain that English occupies in Asian advertising. Bhatia (1987: 35) shows English performs an overwhelming function in product naming in India. The analysis of more than 1,200 advertisements, primarily in

Hindi, that were printed between 1975 and 1985 revealed that more than 90 per cent of the advertisements carried a product name in English. This was also true for rural products. The forces of globalization and marketization have further strengthened the role of English in this domain. Power or super brands further provide impetus to English use.

Let us examine the language choice of the ten 'most trusted brands' of 2007, an annual survey conducted by *Brand Equity*, a prestigious business magazine: 1. Colgate; 2. Vicks; 3. Lux; 4. Nokia; 5. Britannia; 6. Dettol; 7. Lifebouy; 8. Pepsodent; 9. Pond's; and 10. TATA Tea. The absence of any brand names in Hindi or other Indic languages is striking. Only the number 10 brand has Indic influence (i.e. TATA). An analysis of the top 100 most trusted brands reveal only 11 per cent of brand names are from either Hindi or Indic languages (e.g. *Amul, Rasna, Ujala, Nirma, Limca, Hamam, Suffola, Lahar Kurkure, Dabur, Godrej, Amritanjan*). This finding has been consistent with the findings of Bhatia's study of product names (1987).

Product names such as Nokia underscore the contribution of non-English speaking countries to global product naming. Nokia, which jumped from 71 to 4 in the rankings in the past three years, is drawn from Finnish. Global product names such as Walkman (Japan), Nike (Greek) and Samsara (Sanskrit) are other success stories. These product names are the outcome of English-external sources, and yet reveal an interesting three-dimensional aspect of fusion at the underlying level: (1) *Phonotactic aspect* – cases in which non-English items are perceived as 'actual' English due to meeting the phonotactic condition of English phonology. In other words, they sound like an English word; and (2) *Transcreational aspect* – English names are reinterpreted (or transcreated) as non-English names on structural grounds. The product name *Suffola* illustrate this point. Suffola is not an Indic name to begin with. However, it is perceived as such. It has an Indic reality in mind of Indian consumers since the *suff* is a close approximation of Hindi *saaf* 'clean' and *-ola* is interpreted as an agentive suffix, thus interpreting the product name as 'one which cleans'; (3) *Product name development aspect* – product names which are perceived as unmixed items turn out to be mixed in nature, when one probes further into the process of product name development. Take the case of the multinational Indian company Dabur, a leader in Indian medical and cosmetic products. There is no doubt in the mind of a Hindi/Indian speaker that the name is drawn from Indic sources. In the Devanagari rendition of Dabur the word-initial consonant is written in the retroflex letter, thus further highlighting its Indic character. However, the product and/or the company name came about as a result of mixing. Dabur is the clipped form of 'Doctor Burman' in which essentially the second syllable of each word is clipped. What makes this name even more interesting is that the Indian pronunciation of English word, *DaakTar* was chosen before the process of clipping was carried (the final consonant 'k' of the first syllable was also clipped). English alveolar sounds become retroflex in Indian English. These three aspects of fusion represent yet another deeper facet of creativity through actual and perceived mixing on one hand, and overt and covert mixing on the other.

Mixing of accents

The power and ideology of accent is alive and kicking in Asian advertising. Mixing of accents in electronic media (radio, TV) is the pattern which is gaining prominence throughout Asia. The use of Western models and Inner Circle English accents are no longer confined to Japan. In India, where the use of foreign models was despised at least in the rural areas about a decade ago (see Bhatia 2000: 244), one witnesses a shift towards the use of foreign models, artefacts, locations, and thus, Indian advertising is now showing more openness to absorb British and American accents. Such a shift is motivated more by indexing primarily the global identity and association of the product, as opposed to asserting exclusive American or British identity. This finding is credited to Pillar (2001, 2003) and is also valid for Asian advertising. Of course, for some product categories such as English music and American popular culture, an American or British accent is required, as are other national accents associated with national stereotypes, and thus with national products, e.g. Chinese with noodles, Japanese with sushi and Indian with curry.

The appeal of the non-standard accents is a near-universal phenomenon which is naturally exploited in Asia not only to signal regional identities and local stereotypes but also to render socio-psychological effects such as the trustworthiness of the product advertised and sincerity on the part of the advertiser or actor. It is hard to imagine the Maggi commercial with a sprinkle of Bhojpuri but in the ad the words pronounced without a Bhojpuri accent.

The forces of marketization and outsourcing (such as call centres in India and the Philippines) have added yet another dimension to the mixing of accents. A 'put-on accent' is another recent addition to the inventory of accents, used in Indian high-end products.

Mixing of scripts

A prominent Hindi newspaper titles its business page with a prominent header: Business & Brands. Except for the symbol &, the two English words are written in the Devanagari script. Another page entitled Youth Trends shows equal partnership between the Devanagari (youth) and the Roman (trends). It is not that English words from technical and global business are written in the Devanagari script, even the special supplement devoted to day-to-day family affairs bear the signature line of English in the Devanagari script. A case in point is a story devoted to general remedies for the rainy or monsoon season: the title is drawn from Indian English – Rainy Remedy – but is scripted in the Devanagari script. The use of English in non-Western scripts (Hangul in Korea; Katakana in Japanese; scores of Indic scripts such as Devanagari and Gurmukhi; and Arabic in India and Pakistan) in advertising is yet another colourful feature of Asian advertising. At the surface, such a mixing seems absurd because the target consumers of these ads or newspaper readership are not bilinguals. However, a deeper analysis of such a mixing reflects what can best be termed as conscious or unconscious linguistic planning on the part of national and international advertisers or newspaper editors who expect English-based bilingualism as being a part of the global citizen. Such cases exemplify the type of script mixing motivated by 'covert' bilingualism. The overt effect of such ads or captions is cosmetic, leading to the 'mock' effect of globalization and Westernization. Japanese advertising is notable for multiple script mixing and for its mock effects. The Japanese pattern shows striking parallelism to the Hindi newspapers' pattern motivated by covert bilingualism.

Another type of script mixing performs the function of introducing 'overt' bilingualism. Unlike 'covert' bilingualism, advertisers do not

Table 10.2 Script mixing in global advertising: Functions

Covert	Overt
Bilingualism through English	Mixing of native and non-native Englishes
Positive linguistic attitudes toward English	Paraphrasing, reiteration, pun, other stylistic functions
Globalization and Westernization	Structural Linguistic accommodation Marketing multiple identities Globalization and Westernization

deprive their readers the pronunciation and meaning of the English lexical item. This pattern is witnessed quite widely in South-East Asia and Japan. Not only does the mixing of English in non-Roman scripts set the stage of bilingualism, the instances of overt bilingualism often become the contact point for the cross-fertilization of native and new Englishes (for more details, see Bhatia 2006: 609–10). Table 10.2 summarizes the function of script mixing in Asian advertising. Regardless of whether mixing is motivated by the consideration of covert or overt bilingualism, it carries overtones of globalization and Westernization.

Resolving globalization (standardizaton) vs. localization (adaptation) paradox

What is intriguing to observe is that advertisers, either unconsciously or by design, have developed two distinct models of globalization/standardization and their relation to localization/adaptation, which in turn govern their linguistic representational strategies and linguistic choices. These views can be characterized as 'competitive' and 'cooperative' views. The two divergent views are encoded employing two distinct underlying linguistic strategies in global advertising: the competitive view leads to language segregation, whereas the integrative view yields language mixing. The language segregation is the natural outcome of the perception of globalization and localization as oppositions, while the language integration is the consequence of the perceived accommodation between the two. The perceived models of globalization and its linguistic renderings are summarized in Table 10.3.

Although both patterns are attested in Asian advertising, language mixing strategies offer a midway approach to resolving a paradox, the most favoured approach of Asian advertisers. Not only does such an accommodative approach serve as a conflict resolution device but it also yields optimal results in terms of socio-psychological features which pure linguistic systems are incapable of rendering.

Table 10.3 Models of globalization: competitive and cooperative

Model	Approach	Language/script	Text
Competitive	either/or (linguistic segregation)	one	monolingual
Cooperative	mixed	two or more	bilingual or multilingual

Implications for the teaching of world Englishes

If language mixing in the media and advertising is the barometer of the pattern of language use in a society, the use of the mixed linguistic system is not just an Asian reality, but is a growing global phenomenon. Either unconsciously or by design, global media has given further impetus to this growing trend in order to meet their creative needs. Growing recognition that bilingualism/multilingualism, particularly English-based bilingualism/multilingualism, is a natural phenomenon, is self-evident from the growing body of sociolinguistic research on code-mixing and code-switching, as it poses a new challenge for English pedagogy not just in Asia but worldwide. A recent report issued by Devos, an influential 'think tank' in the UK, calls for the recognition of the new linguistic reality and a shift from the outmoded practice of teaching of 'Imperial' English. The report entitled 'As you like it: Catching up in an age of Global English' by Samuel Jones and Peter Broadwell favours the teaching of Hinglish or Chinglish to new immigrants over the traditional practice of teaching standard British English. The report goes on to argue that mixed systems reflect new reality of the global marketplace. 'If UK wants to be the part of this new world, it needs to get involved with the bazaar and not keep trying to impose its creed.' (For more details about Devos' recommendations, see Chapter 9: 90–101; www.demos.co.uk/files/As%20%20You%20like%20it%20-%20 web.pdf.) In addition to a wide array of functions rendered by language mixing worldwide, sociolinguistic research also underscores the accommodative function of code-mixing and switching. Language mixing not only accommodates multiple identities but also promotes the intelligibility of the message (see Bhatia 2006 for details). Code-mixed English is critical for the teaching of world Englishes, global cultural literacy and global business, and cross-cultural intelligibility.

Asian attitudes toward English are very positive overall. English is no longer viewed as a 'colonial' or 'oppressor' language but has become the integral part of the Asian linguistic heritage. Survey after survey come to the same conclusion that Asia desires to learn English. But what variety of English would an Asian like to learn? Although there is no unanimous agreement over this issue, the preference for learning a 'variety specific to my country' over Inner Circle varieties is very strong in Asia, particularly in the Outer Circle countries of Asia such as South Asia and Singapore (see Smith and Nelson 2006; Abbi et al. 2000; Agnihotri and Khanna 1997; Bansal 1969). This preference is also gaining strength in countries such as Japan and China. This shows that there is a shift in the learners' choice from the 'native speaker' model of learning and emulating English by the second language learners to the alternative model, termed the Competent Bilingual Model. This model is best summed up by Graddol – 'a fluent bilingual speaker, who retains a national identity in terms of accents, and who also has the special skills required to negotiate understanding with another non-native speaker' (Graddol 2006: 7; also for details see Bhatia and Ritchie (1996) concerning bilingual language mixing and second language acquisition).

Interestingly, the native-speaker model is still alive and kicking. The forces of globalization and particularly global business have added a new context and urgency to the teaching of English particularly in countries such as India and the Philippines which serves a hub of business process outsourcings (BPOs) and knowledge process outsourcings (KPOs). Notable among the new agents of English language teaching are the business-operated call centres in Asian and African countries adding a totally new measure to approaches such as the teaching of English as a second dialect (ESD) and the language immersion approach. The call centres in India, for instance, teach native varieties of English (e.g. varieties spoken in the USA and the UK) by practices which can best be characterized as the absolute immersion approach (AIA). The AIA approach requires learners not only to emulate the speech pattern of the speakers of the target variety but also to impersonate their identity. The two goals are achieved by requiring learners to take English names (thus prohibiting the use of real names at work and outside work), to imitate their accent (by eradicating their own accent), and by imposing English on the family members of the learners in their family setting (by prohibiting the use of native languages). These learners are asked to watch popular TV shows and to keep track of weather on a particular day in a particular city to carry out an effective conversation with the calling client. In some countries, such as China and Korea, the desire to learn English has been exploited to such an absurd extent that plastic surgeons have begun to perform a linguistic version of cosmetic surgery, claiming to improve the pronunciation of learners almost overnight (see Markus 2002). The time has come for language teaching professionals to act as watchdogs against unethical and unhealthy practices of language teaching.

The Devos report calls for revisiting the monolithic or prescriptivist model of language teaching – one language, one nation and one standard – which is at the heart of the native speaker model approach. It stresses the need of a new holistic communicative competence approach which treats language mixing as its natural aspect. The call is out; the question remains how seriously the profession of English language teaching will respond to this call.

Conclusion

Language mixing is one of the unifying features of Asian English-advertising which manifests itself in a wide variety of linguistic forms and functions. In terms of form, it is not restricted to the mixing of two languages and scripts but also exhibits openness to multiple language, accents and script mixing. This pattern marks a point of departure from the inner-circle English advertising. On functional grounds, it offers a rich array of meaning ranging from creating a mock-effect to rendering socio-psychological meanings motivated by the deeper creative needs of advertisers and marketers. Needless to say, the teaching of English in Asia and worldwide need to incorporate this reality as rightly stressed by the Devos report.

Note

1. There are qualitative and quantitative differences between these varieties. However, I am using these terms in a wider sense as used by the media. For more on the issue of the legitimacy, first language and second language varieties of such mixed systems, see Bhatia and Ritchie (forthcoming).

References

Abbi, A., R. S.Gupta and R. Gargesh. 2000. 'A sociolinguistic inquiry into the acceptance level of Hindi as a pan Indian language.' New Delhi: ICSSR project report.

Agnithotri, R. and A. L. Khanna. 1997. *Problematizing English in India*. New Delhi: Sage.

Bansal, R. K. 1969. *The Intelligibility of Indian English: Measurements of the intelligibility of connected speech, sentence and word material, presented to listeners of different nationalities*. Hyderabad: Central Institute of English and Foreign Languages.

Bhatia, T. K. 1987. 'English in advertising: Multiple mixing and media.' *World Englishes* 6(1), 33–48.

——. 1992. 'Discourse functions and pragmatics of mixing: Advertising across cultures.' *World Englishes* 11(2–3), 195–215.

——. 2000. *Advertising in Rural India: Language, Marketing Communication, and Consumerism*. Tokyo: Tokyo Press.

——. 2001. Language mixing in global advertising. In Edwin Thumboo (ed.) *The Three Circles of English*, pp. 195–215. Singapore: Singapore University Press.

Bhatia, T. K.. 2006. 'World Englishes in global advertising.' *The Handbook of World Englishes.* In Kachru, Kachru and Nelson (eds), Chapter 33.

Bhatia, T. K. and C. R. William. 2004. 'Bilingualism in global media and advertising.' In T. K. Bhatia and W. C. Ritchie (eds), *Handbook of Bilingualism*, pp. 513–46. Oxford: Blackwell.

——. 1996. 'Bilingual Language Mixing, Universal Grammar, and Second Language Acquisition.' In W. C. Ritchie and T. K. Bhatia (eds) *Handbook of Second Language Acquisition*, [Chapter 19], pp. 627–82. San Diego: Academic Press.

——. Forthcoming. 'Language mixing, universal grammar and second language acquisition.' In W. C. Ritchie and T. K. Bhatia (eds). *A New Handbook of Second Language Acquisition*. Oxford: Elsevier. Chapter 26.

Chandra, A., D. A. Griffith and J. K. Ryans. 2002. 'Advertising standards in India: US multinational experience.' *International Journal of Advertising, The Quarterly Review of Marketing Communications* 21:1. Internet version, page numbers not given.

Graddol, D. 2006. *English Next.* London: British Council.

Heileman, J. 1997. 'Annals of advertising: All Europeans are not alike.' *The New Yorker* (28 April/5 May), 174–81.

Hermerén, L. 1999. *English for Sale: A Study of the Language of Advertising.* Lund, Sweden: Lund University Press.

Hite, R. E. and C. Fraser. 1988. 'International advertising strategies.' *Journal of Advertising Research* 28 (5), 9–17.

Hsu, J. 2001. 'The sources, adapted functions, and the public's subjective evaluation of the Englishization of Mandarin Chinese in Taiwan.' In E. Thumboo (ed.) *The Three Circles of English*, pp. 241–56. Singapore: Singapore University Press.

Kachru, B. B. 1992. 'The second diaspora of English.' In R. W. Machan and C. T. Scott (eds) *English in Its Social Contexts: Essays in Historical Sociolinguistics*, pp. 230–52. New York: Oxford University Press.

Kachru, B. B, Y. Kachru and C. L. Nelson (eds). 2006. *The Handbook of World Englishes.* Oxford: Blackwell.

Kanso, A. 1991. 'The use of advertising agencies from foreign markets: Decentralized decisions and localized approaches?' *International Journal of Advertising* 10: 129–36.

Kujala, A. and U. Lehtinen. 1989. 'A new structural method for analyzing linguistic significance in market communications.' *International Journal of Advertising* 8: 219–36.

Markus, F. 2002. 'Chinese find learning English a snip.' *BBC News World Edition.* Accessed on 26 February 2004.

Martin, E. 2006. 'Marketing identities through language: English and global imagery in French advertising.' New York: Palgrave Macmillan.

McKeldin, C. 1994. *Japanese Jive: Wacky and Wonderful Products from Japan.* New York: Tengu Books.

Mueller, B. 1992. 'Standardization vs. specialization: An examination of westernization in Japanese advertising.' *Journal of Advertising Research* 1, 15–24.

Myers, G. 1999. *Ad Worlds: Brands, Media, Audiences.* London: Edward Arnold.

Onkvisit, S. and J. Shaw. 1987. 'Standardized international advertising: A review and critical evaluation of theoretical and empirical evidence.' *Columbia Journal of World Business* (Fall), 43–55.

Pillar, I. 2001. 'Identity constructions in multilingual advertising.' *Language in Society* 30: 153–86.
——. 2003. Advertising as a site of language contact. *Annual Review of Applied Linguistics* 23, 170–83.
Ryans, J.and D. Ratz. 1987. 'Advertising standardization: A re-examination.' *International Journal of Advertising* 6, 145–58.
Sarkar, P. 2007. 'Milking phony patriotism.' *Times of India* 13 July, p. 8.
Smith, L. E. and C. L. Nelson. 2006. 'World Englishes and intelligibility.' In *Handbook of World Englishes*, 428–45.
'Taj makes it to new seven wonder list.' *Times of India*. 2007. 8 July, front page.
Yano, Y. 2001 'World Englishes in 2000 and beyond.' *World Englishes*, 20(2), 191–231.

Part IV

The Future of Englishes: A Paradigm Shift?

11

Asian Englishes in the Asian Age: Contexts and Challenges

Braj B. Kachru

Introduction[1]

The dynamics of Asian Englishes in 'the Asian Age' with 'Asian Values', 'Asian Creativity' and 'Asian Constructs' have altered the profile of world Englishes in challenging ways. The English language now comprises the largest number of English bilinguals: Just the two countries, China and India, have over 533 million users of English, almost equal to the total population of the Inner Circle of English (e.g. the USA, UK, Australia and Canada). The current, hotly debated avatars of globalization in technology, education and in a variety of cultural shifts continue to manifest in 'globalization' of Asian Englishes, too.

The study of multi-canons in English and its pluralism entails that we begin with the distinction between English as a medium and English as a repertoire of cultural pluralism: one referring to the form of language (*mādhyama*), and the other to its function (*mantra*), its content. It is the medium that is designed and organized for multiple cultural conventions. It is in this sense that one can explain the concepts 'global', 'pluralistic' and 'multi-canons' with reference to the users and uses of English across cultures and languages. What we share as members of the international English-using speech community is the medium, that is, the vehicle for the transmission of the English language. We use the phonetic medium when we speak to each other. We use the graphic medium when we write to each other. The medium *per se*, however, has no constraints on what message – cultural or social – we transmit through it.

When we call English a global medium, it indicates that those who use English across cultures in Africa, Asia and Europe have in some degree a shared code of communication. We share in our use of English a large inventory of the sound system, the vocabulary and the syntax. And the result of this shared competence is that, in spite of various types of differences, we believe that we communicate with each other – one user of English with the other, a Nigerian with an Indian, a Japanese with a German, a Kashmiri with a Tamil, a Bengali with a Singhalese, and a Singaporean with an American. It is in this broad sense of interlocutors that we have *one* language and *many* voices.

It is this cross-cultural function in education, in business, in tourism, in personal interaction and in literary creativity that has given English an unprecedented status as a global and cross-cultural code of communication. And the evidence for such unparalleled roles acquired by one language has been constructed by linguists and educators in multiple ways. We see this in the hegemony of English across cultures, power of English in the domains of administration, education, literary creativity and business. English is presented as Aladdin's lamp for opening the doors to cultural and religious 'enlightenment', as the 'language for all seasons', a 'universal language', a language with no national or regional frontiers and the language on which the sun never sets.

Medium vs. message

The globalization of English has, however, come at a price. How high the price is depends on whom one talks to. The English language and literature have ceased to be exclusively Eurocentric, Judeo-Christian and Western. There is, as it were, a gradual opening up of the language beyond the traditionally accepted canons: it is not that other Asian and African canons are necessarily accepted or recognized – far from that. However, there is an articulate debate about such issues. Henry Louis Gates, Jr optimistically warns us,

> cultural pluralism is not, of course, everyone's cup of tea. Vulgar cultural nationalists – like Allan Bloom or Leonard Jeffries – correctly identify it as the enemy. These polemicists thrive on absolute partitions: between 'civilization' and 'barbarism', between 'black' and 'white', between a thousand versions of Us and Them. But they are whistling in the wind. (Gates 1992: xvi)

The language and literary creativity in English have acquired many faces, of many colours, regions and competencies. And Gates appropriately characterizes these as 'loose canons' which have resulted in 'the Culture Wars'.

The resultant pluralism has introduced dimensions which are unparalleled, not to be found in a natural language or in an artificial language. And now, at least in some circles, the use of the term 'English literature' is considered rather restricted and monocultural. Instead, the term 'English literatures' is steadily gaining acceptance (see Quirk and Widdowson 1985), and the term 'Englishes' or 'world Englishes' does not raise eyebrows in every circle. This terminological feud is not innocent; it is loaded with ideologies, economic interests and the strategies for power. And now, rightly, a serious question is being asked about English: 'Whose language is it anyway?'

When we study English as a pluralistic language, we are actually focusing on its layer after layer of extended processes of convergence with other languages and cultures. And this convergence and contact is unique since it has altered the traditional resources for contact, for example, French, German, Italian and Scandinavian. A variety of functional and pragmatic contexts have led the English language to open itself up, as it were, to convergence with the non-Western world: that part of the world which was traditionally not a resource for English. It is here that, for example, West Africa, East Africa, South Asia, West Asia and the Philippines become relevant and have become contributors to the pluralism, and in return share the pluralism of the language. The opening up of the language, and the multiculturalism in the language, does not mean that these multi-strands, from the Inner Circle or the Outer Circle, have been accepted by the linguistic vigilantes or the power elite. That has yet to happen. The canons in the Outer Circle, the African American, the Chicano and the Asian American continue to be 'loose canons'.

By pluralism, then, we mean the multiple identities which constitute a repertoire of cultures, linguistic experimentation and innovations, and literary traditions. And they come from a variety of sources. It is in this sense that English embodies multiculturalism. And it is in this sense that English is a global language. The input to this multiculturalism represented in the language comes from three types of users who constitute three Concentric Circles – the Inner Circle, the Outer Circle and the Expanding Circle. These three circles have historical, sociolinguistic, ideological and pedagogical significance which I have discussed in several earlier studies (B. Kachru 1985; see also B. Kachru, 2005: 211–20). As I have emphasized earlier, the Circles do not indicate any ranking but historical development and evolving functional contexts.

Exponents of multiculturalism

The strands of multiculturalism in world Englishes are of several types, but all have one thing in common: they manifest the multilinguals' creativity. This creativity is not necessarily consistent with the traditionally accepted norms by the pundits of the English language in the Inner Circle. I shall briefly discuss the exponents of the fusion of multiculturalism in world Englishes. The multilinguals' creativity has brought to English a variety of multiple cultural identities – Nigerian, Indian, Singaporean, Japanese and Chinese – which are distinct from the Judeo-Christian identity of the language. An example is *The Serpent and the Rope* (1960) by Raja Rao of India which essentially follows India's Sanskritic tradition. The Sanskritized style of the novel has an ideological and metaphysical context, e.g. 'God is, and goodness is part of that is-ness.' In reading G. V. Desani's *All About H. Hatter* (1951), the textural competence demands knowledge of Sanskrit compounding (*samasa*) for interpreting, e.g. 'Ruler of the firmament; Son of the mighty-bird', '... Thy sister my darling, thy name?' V. S. Naipaul believes that R. K. Narayan's novels are '... religious books...and intensely Hindu' (Naipaul 1977: 13). Yet, another attempt in this direction is Shashi Tharoor's *The Great Indian Novel* (1989), a contemporary story woven around the *Mahabharata*, an epic of ancient India, and the longest poem in the world, dating back to the fourth century BC. An often-quoted passage from Chinua Achebe, the Nigerian writer, provides an example to show how he approaches 'the use of English' (Africanized English) in the choice of style in *Arrow of God* (1964). In 1965, demonstrating the effectiveness of his stylistic shifts, Achebe contrasts the following two passages where the Chief Priest is telling one of his sons why it is necessary to send him to church. The Africanized version is:

> I want one of my sons to join these people and be my eyes there. If there is nothing in it you will come back. But if there is something then you will bring back my share. The world is like a mask, dancing. If you want to see it well, you do not stand in one place. My spirit tells me that those who do not befriend the white man today will be saying, 'had we known', tomorrow. (p. 29)

And, Achebe rightly asks, 'supposing I had put it another way. Like this for instance':

> I am sending you as my representative among those people – just to be on the safe side in case the new religion develops. One has to

> move with the times or else one is left behind. I have a hunch that those who fail to come to terms with the white man may well regret their lack of foresight. (p. 29)

Achebe concludes: 'The material is the same. But the form of one is in character and the other is not. It is largely a matter of instinct but judgment comes into it too.' Achebe's observation combines culture, creativity and innovation, within African literary tradition. What Achebe says is one facet of style choice in creativity. The other is, following the convention and tradition. The rhetorical style in Indian English, for example, is based on '... the tradition of writing in Indian languages basically derived from the Sanskritic tradition'. (See, for details, Y. Kachru 1992, especially p. 347.)

The Africanization or Asianization of English itself manifests in other ways too. The medium is appropriately localized to function in the socio-cultural, religious and interactional contexts of Africa and Asia. It is evident in culture specific personal interactions, in the news media, in matrimonial advertisements, in obituaries and in letters of invitation. The matrimonial columns reflect African or Asian sensitivity to colour, caste hierarchy, regional attitudes and family structure. In matrimonial columns in India the advertiser wants a *fair graduate of Bhardwaja gotram, Astasastram girl, subsect no bar, preferably convent-educated, average complexion,* and sometimes prefer *mutual alliance.* Indians invite a *cousin-brother,* or a *cousin-sister* to a *military hotel* with a *compound wall* situated on a *kutcha road* where they do not eat on a *dining-leaf.* A Brahmin in the South of India normally has *forehead-marking* or a *caste mark* and a *nine-stranded thread.* Indians may have an *England or America returned co-brother-in-law who* has an *issue-less* sister, and they believe, or do not believe in, *intermarriage* or *interdining* due to various *communal considerations.* They use a *tiffin-carrier* to carry their *coconut paysam* when they go *out of station.* When they are not ready to take a *head bath,* they may take just a *body bath.* They do not die, but they *leave for heavenly abode,* or they have a *sad demise.* And they arrange *kirtan and ardasa* for the *peace of the departed soul.* The South Asian lexicon of English, including such Indianisms, was originally published under the title *Hobson-Jobson* in 1886, and reprinted both in India and the UK in 1985.

The same is, of course, true of African English, or varieties of Pacific English. What is *English-returned* in South Asia becomes *been-to* in African English; one has to have *long legs* (influence) to secure service. To say a person *has no chest,* or has *no shadow* is equivalent to saying that a person is timid, and *may we live to see ourselves tomorrow* replaces *good night*. Okara comments that,

> Now a person without a chest in the physical sense can only mean a human that does not exist. The idea becomes clearer in the second translation [one has no shadow]. A person who does not cast a shadow of course does not exist. (Okara, 1963: 15)

What we see, then, is that the processes of acculturation are identical in India or Nigeria, though their lexical realization may not be identical.

We see identical linguistic devices used in discourse strategies and speech acts: These are transcreated into English to approximate the Asian and African cultural contexts, religious subgroups, and interactional strategies of a variety of African and Asian languages. These include culture-specific patterns of apologies, compliments, condolences, persuasion, politeness and requests. These contextualized strategies are skilfully exploited by, for example, Mulk Raj Anand, Raja Rao, Anita Desai and Salman Rushdie in India, and by Chinua Achebe, Wole Soyinka and Nuruddin Farah in Africa. It is this acculturation of English which rightly raises the question: My language, your culture: Whose communicative competence? (see Nelson 1992).[2]

This very significant question has yet to be answered. The reason is that our current paradigms of constructs and teaching of English continue to be based on monolingual and monocultural – and essentially Western – traditions of creativity and canon formation.

Canon expansion

This, then, takes us to a complex question of what is meant by the concepts 'canon' and 'multi-canon'. This, of course, is an elusive question, like defining the terms 'standard' or 'norm' for a language – English or any other. 'Standard', as Abercrombie (1951: 15) has warned us, provides 'an accent bar', and 'the accent bar is a little like color-bars to many people, on the right side of the bar, it appears eminently reasonable'. And this is true of canon formation. As for norms and standards, one has to recognize '... the politics and ironies of canon formation', as Gates (1992: 32) convincingly does, in defining the canon of African-American literature.

In connection with canon formation, several questions come to mind. One might ask: What are the defining characteristics of a canon? Now, keeping in mind what I said about the notion 'standard' and 'norm', canon is both a symbol of self-identification and an indicator of power. It is also a highly planned strategy for exclusion. However, canon does presuppose a cultural identity and tradition, a linguistic experimentation and innovation, and an extended period of creativity which makes it possible to compare creativity within a canon and across canons, in spite of what the gate-keepers of canons tell us. It is in this sense, then, one talks of the 'masterpieces', the 'classics' and the 'standard works'.

I used the words 'self-identification' and 'power'. A good example of this is provided by Edward W. Said when he refers to a rather acrimonious debate on the curriculum changes at Stanford University. Bernard Lewis, a senior Orientalist working in the United States, entered the debate on changing the 'Western canon'. In Said's view, Lewis 'took the extreme position' when he said 'if Western culture does indeed go a number of things would go with it and others would come in their place'. Said's response to Lewis is:

> No one had said anything so ludicrous as 'Western culture must go', but Lewis's argument, focused on much grander matters than strict accuracy, lumbered forward with the remarkable proposition that since modifications in the reading list would be equivalent to the demise of Western culture, such subjects (he named them specifically) as the restoration of slavery, polygamy, and child marriage would ensue. To this amazing thesis, Lewis added that 'curiosity about other cultures', which he believes is unique to the West, would also come to an end. (Said 1993: 37)

This position of a distinguished Orientalist is not much different from William Bennett's (1992) call for 'reclaiming our heritage', or Indian-American Dinesh D'Souza's (1991) alarm about multiculturalism.

The question, however, becomes more complex when other dimensions are added to what is believed to be one medium representing one canon. What is generally not recognized is:

(a) that English as a medium is used by two distinct types of speech communities: those that perceive themselves as monolingual and monocultural, and those that are traditionally multilingual and multicultural;
(b) that these speech communities represent distinct literary and or oral traditions and mythologies; and
(c) that the norms of literary creativity and contextually appropriate linguistic experimentation are not shared.

This obviously raises the question concerning *intelligibility, comprehensibility* and *interpretability* of texts across users of the medium, and what one would like to consider the same language, English (see Smith 1981 and later; Y. Kachru 1985, 1987; see also Y. Kachru and Smith 2008).

A number of creative writers from Africa and Asia, and Chicano writers in the USA, have addressed this complex question. One often-quoted observation of Chinua Achebe, in 1965, comes to mind: Can an African ever learn English well enough to be able to use it effectively in creative writing? His answer is 'certainly yes' but then, he adds: 'if on the other hand you ask: "Can he [an African] ever learn to use it like a native speaker?" I should say, *"I hope not. It is neither necessary, nor desirable for him to be able to do so"'* (emphasis added). At another place answering a question, Achebe most aptly says:

> Most African writers write out of an African experience and of commitment to an African destiny. For them, that destiny does not include a future European identity for which the present is but an apprenticeship. (Jussawala and Dasenbrock 1992: 16)

One might ask: what are the implications of canon expansion? Canon expansion is an indicator of two processes: divergence and convergence. Divergence marks the differences between two or more varieties of English, and convergence indicates shared *Englishness* in the world Englishes. It is the shared features which mark, for example, Nigerian English, Kenyan English or Indian English as varieties of what we know as English. In the Outer Circle, the divergence is conscious, as in, for example, Achebe, Rao, Anand and also a result of a multilingual's creativity. Ngũgĩ refers to this multilingual context when he says that in Kenya, there is Swahili as the lingua franca, and there are 'nationality languages' such as Gikuyu and Luo. And 'by playing with this language situation, you can get another level of meaning through the interaction of all three languages' (see Jussawala and Dasenbrock 1992: 34).

Multi-canons as symbols and substance

Multi-canons in English have symbolic and substantive meaning: symbolic in the sense that one's identity is symbolic, and substantive in the way the identity is expressed, articulated, negotiated and preserved in language.

It is believed that a member of the English-speaking speech community is one who considers English her/his mother tongue, and thus becomes a speaker of English as 'mother tongue'. This assumption, passed on from one generation to another, is flawed. The idealization of terms such as 'speech community' and 'mother tongue' may, at one level, have theoretical justification, but pragmatically, functionally and pedagogically, one must ask several questions. We know, for example, that African-American, or Chicano speakers of English are members of the *English-speaking* speech community; they are native speakers of two distinct varieties of English. However, pedagogically and attitudinally – more attitudinally – the society, the educational system, the gate-keepers of the 'norms' have assigned few, if any, socially vital domains to such varieties.

It is not just an issue of attitude toward another variety: more than that, it also becomes an issue of ideology and that of power. And it is the ideological issues which reflect in the selection of paradigms of enquiry, and models for research. These issues determine how one conceptualizes a speech community, how one constructs the barriers between US and THEM for INSIDERS and OUTSIDERS. The issue has more serious implications when monolingualism, knowing only one language, is considered the norm for generalizations about the English-knowing speech community, for pedagogical models, for discussing literary creativity, and of course, for theory construction. This digression is, I believe, directly related to our understanding of the global uses of English.

And if we look at the global language use, the norms of language interaction, the literary creativity across societies – Asian, African and European – it is evident that the majority of world's population is either bi- or multilingual, or at least, diglossic. The diglossic users of a language choose between a formal and colloquial variety of language, as do, for example, Arabic, Tamil and Greek speakers.

And from a multilingual's perspective, even the concept *second* language learning is in reality somewhat restrictive and misleading. The concept *second* language learning and teaching does not have pragmatic validity in West Africa, East Africa, South East Asia and South Asia. In these regions, as in many other regions, bilingualism or trilingualism is a part of daily interaction. It is in such interactional contexts that English has emerged as yet another linguistic code interfacing in Nigeria with Yoruba, Hausa and Igbo, in Singapore with Chinese, Malay, Tamil and Panjabi, and in Kenya with Swahili and several 'nationality languages', and in India with over twenty languages recognized by the Indian Constitution. It is in such culturally and linguistically pluralistic contexts that African English, South Asian English and Philippine English have developed. I purposely used the modifiers *African, South*

Asian and *Philippine* with English. The modifiers are markers of change and adoption: change due to contact with languages, and adoption in terms of acculturation.

In what I have said so far, I have tried to unfold a paradigm and a dimension of English which looks at language variation, linguistic creativity and linguistic identity within a pluralistic perspective. This approach to the study of English is rewarding in several ways, particularly if adopted in the classroom and in the curriculum. Let me elaborate on this point with reference to the mythology that has been cultivated about English in world contexts.

Myths about world Englishes

These myths, discussed earlier in B. Kachru (1994), are the result of half-baked and partially valid hypotheses, a lack of empirical and sociolinguistic insights, or are motivated by economic and power-related intentions. I shall consider some of these myths below:

1. THE INTERLOCUTOR MYTH: That across cultures English is functionally learnt to interact with the native speakers of English, American, Australian or British. Actually, most of the interaction in English takes place among and between its 'non-native' speakers: Indians with Sri Lankans, Germans with Singaporeans, Japanese with Malaysians, and so on.
2. THE MONOCULTURAL MYTH: That English is learnt essentially as a vehicle to study American or British culture, or what has been labelled the Judeo-Christian literary tradition. This is only partially true. Actually, in the Outer Circle, English is increasingly used to impart native cultural values and historical traditions. An analysis of the textbooks, print media and creative writing in India, Nigeria, Kenya, Pakistan and Singapore provide convincing evidence for this claim. The roles English is assigned are primarily national and integrative.
3. THE EXOCENTRIC NORM MYTH: That the exocentric models of American or British varieties of English are actually taught and learnt in the global context. In reality the endocentric models provide overwhelming input. However, there is a serious confusion between what is believed to be the norm and the actual linguistic behaviour.
4. THE INTERLANGUAGE MYTH: That the non-native varieties are essentially 'interlanguages' or 'fossilized' varieties striving to achieve 'native-like' character. It has already been shown that this conceptualization is of very limited merit (see e.g. Sridhar and Sridhar 1992; Nelson 1992).

5. THE INTELLIGIBILITY MYTH: That the varieties used in the Inner Circle have intelligibility across varieties. The empirical studies do not support this view.
6. THE CASSANDRA MYTH: That the diversification and variation in English is an indicator of linguistic decay, that restricting the decay is the job of 'native speakers' as teachers of English literature and language, and that of the ESL professionals.

This is, of course, a partial list of the myths (see also B. Kachru 1987 for theoretical, methodological, formal, functional and attitudinal fallacies).

Grammar wars and standards

In all major languages, historical issues related to ideology, attitudes and standardization have been at the centre of the cross-cultural grammar wars. In the case of English, this is reflected, for example, in the anthology of 'readings in language, history and cultural identity' entitled *Proper English?* (edited by Tony Crowley, 1991). The readings include papers by John Locke (1690), Jonathan Swift (1712), Samuel Johnson (1747), Thomas Sheridan (1762), James Buchanan (1764), Noah Webster (1789), John Walker (1791), John Pickering (1816), T. Watts (1850), Archbishop R. C. Trench (1851), G. F. Graham (1869), Henry Alfrod (1864), Henry James (1905), Henry Newbolt (1921), Henry Wyld (1934), A. S. C. Ross (1954), Alison Assiter (1983) and John Marenbon (1987). This debate, spread over centuries in the Inner Circle, has still not abated, and yet new constructs and perspectives – ideological, theoretical and methodological – continue to be brought into it (see e.g. B. Kachru, Y. Kachru and C. L Nelson (eds) 2006, pp. 446–71, 545–66).

As an aside, one might add here that earlier examples of such grammar textbooks, with loaded ideological, political and social agendas, have a long history. One such example, now from the Outer Circle, is provided by Frances B. Singh (1987) which I could not resist quoting several times in my earlier papers. In her pioneering study on pre-Raj and post-Raj South Asia (India), Singh 'examines the various connections for four grammar books [...] posit between the English language and Indian society'. The grammars are by J. Nesfield (1895), L. Tipping (1933), P. C. Wren and H. Martin (1954), and C. D. Sidhu (1976). In her perceptive analysis, Singh first presents Nesfield's agenda in construction of the grammar text:

> The sentences of Nesfield's text propagate the notion of the British supremacy and impose a view of history which justifies colonial rule.

> It is a view which corresponds to the contemporary conception of English as an imposed foreign language, the language of political domination and synonym for it. (1987: 253)

Second comes the construct of Tipping; his position is:

> ... that English is to be assimilated to the Indian context. The revised edition of Wren and Martin's grammar follows in the Tipping tradition. English is no longer seen as something imposed, but as something in the process of being Indianized. (1987: 253)

Finally, comes the grammar of Sidhu which, says Singh, 'is radically different from the others':

> It reveals a familiarity with the way life is experienced in India. Sidhu's grammar proves that English language teaching can be taught through and express Indian experiences. (1987: 253)

And Singh rightly concludes that:

> In so doing, the English language becomes the opposite of its historical role: a mode of communication which expresses Indians' consciousness of themselves as citizens of an independent country. (1987: 253)

World Englishes in the classroom

In the USA, multiculturalism as a societal or as a pedagogical concept has been perceived both as a divisive practice and also as an enriching experience. It has been seen as a step toward national Balkanization, and as a laboratory for mutual understanding. In literature and language the variationist approaches have been applauded for social realism and attacked as 'liberation linguistics', an offshoot of 'liberation theology' (see B. Kachru 1988; Quirk 1988). However, we must agree with Robert Hughes, the author of *Culture of Complaint: The Fraying of America*, who says that

> In society as in farming monoculture works poorly. It exhausts the soil. The social richness of America, so striking to the foreigner,

> comes from the diversity of its tribes. Its capacity for cohesion, for some spirit of common agreement on what is to be done, comes from the willingness of those tribes not to elevate their cultural differences into impassable barriers and ramparts. (cited in H. Gates Jr, *New Yorker*, 19 April 1993: 115)

And commenting on this, Henry Gates Jr is right when he says that Hughes '... provide[s] some of the most gruffly appealing defenses of genuine multiculturalism that we have' (*New Yorker*, 19 April 1993: 115).

And now, let us take this vision of America beyond America, and bring in Europe, the Middle East, South and East Asia, West, East and Southern Africa, the Philippines and South America. That is almost the globe; that is the global vision. That abstract global vision with its linguistic diversity, cultural interfaces, societal hierarchies and conflicts are captured in various strands of world Englishes. The vision is Indian, Vedantic and metaphysical in Raja Rao; It is Nigerian in Wole Soyinka and Chinua Achebe; It is East African in Ngũgĩ and it is a Singaporean blend of Chinese and Malay in Catherine Lim's creativity. The architects of each tradition, each strand and each construct have used the linguistic raw material of what is considered a Western medium, moulded it, reshaped it and redesigned it. And the resultant creativity reflects vitality, innovation and cultural and linguistic fusion. It is not the creativity of a monolingual and monocultural; it has redeemed the medium from, as it were, 'exhaustion'.

That this literature is a product of multilingualism, and of multiculturalism, has yet to be seriously realized. The use of such literature(s) as a resource in the classroom has yet to be fully explored. The difficulties in doing so are not only that appropriate pedagogical resources are limited. That may be true. But the more serious difficulty is that there is a need of paradigm shift in the teaching of English, in addition to a shift in the attitude toward world Englishes. The attitudes about English are partially the result of the myths about the global users and functions of Englishes.

A position on the periphery

What is more frustrating, we have marginalized such creativity and multicultural dimensions of English by using terms such as 'Commonwealth literature' or 'Third World literature'. I will not elaborate on this point, but will present an often-quoted illuminating observation by Salman Rushdie. Rushdie appropriately comments on his own experience:

> When I was invited to speak at the 1983 English Studies Seminar in Cambridge, the lady from the British Council offered me a few words of reassurance. 'It's all right,' I was told, 'for the purposes of our seminar, English studies are taken to include Commonwealth literature.' At all other times, one was forced to conclude, these two would be kept strictly apart, like squabbling children, or sexually incompatible pandas, or, perhaps, like unstable, fissile materials whose union might cause explosions. (Rushdie 1991: 61)

And Rushdie continues,

> A few weeks later, I was talking to a literature don – a specialist, I ought to say, in *English* literature – a friendly and perceptive man, 'As a Commonwealth writer,' he suggested, 'you probably find, don't you, that there's a kind of liberty, certain advantages, in occupying, as you do, a position on the periphery?' (ibid.)

In reality, one doesn't have to quote Rushdie here; one sees this attitude about the African American canon, and the Chicano canon. And not many years ago – just over half a century ago – the same attitude was expressed about the American literature in Britain. The great pundit of the American language, H. L. Mencken, summarizes well the British attitude to American English when he writes: 'This occasional tolerance for things American was never extended to the American language' (Mencken 1936: 23). This was in 1936!

Literature in world Englishes and linguistic innovations from diverse cultural contexts provide refreshing texts for interdisciplinary debate and research on topics such as the following:

> Cross-cultural discourse; The bilingual's creativity; Language contact and convergence; Language acquisition; Intelligibility; Lexicography; and Language, Ideology and Power.

Toward a paradigm shift

In teaching world Englishes, it seems a new perspective can be presented in three academic areas: the diffusion of the English language; multicultural literary creativity; and methodology of teaching. The teaching

Table 11.1 Labels used to symbolize the power of English

Positive	Negative
National identity	Anti-nationalism
Literary renaissance	Anti-native culture
Cultural mirror (for native cultures)	Materialism
Modernization	Westernization
Liberalism	Rootlessness
Universalism	Ethnocentricism
Technology	Permissiveness
Science	Divisiveness
Mobility	Alienation
Access code	

of world Englishes, then, entails a paradigm shift in several ways. The following points deserve special attention for training professionals, and for teaching advanced students:

(a) sociolinguistic profile of the forms and functions of English;
(b) variety exposure and sensitivity;
(c) functional validity of varieties within a variety (e.g. Nigerian Pidgin, Basilect, Bazaar English);
(d) range and depth of uses and users;
(e) contrastive pragmatics; and
(f) multiculturalism in content and creativity.

There is also a provocative ideological facet to English teaching: Why is English considered a language of power? What ideology does English represent? Why do, for example, Ngũgĩ – and some others – consider English a 'culture-bomb', and '[...] probably the most racist of all human languages' (1981: 14). Why does English evoke – or symbolize – positive or negative labels such as the one seen in Table 11.1.

Conclusion

These are some of the provocative and challenging questions for discussion, around one language in its various global incarnations and in its multi-canons. I believe that we are depriving ourselves – as teachers and students – of an immense source of cross-cultural resources, and strategies of multilinguals' creativity, if world Englishes are viewed exclusively from Judeo-Christian – and monolingual – perspectives.

By marginalizing the global uses of English we are constructing a wall around an important world vision. And this reminds me of what an Indian pragmatist and political leader, Mohandas K. Gandhi (1864–1948), said so well in another context: 'I do not want my house to be walled in on all sides and my windows to be stuffed. I want cultures of all lands to be blown about my house as freely as possible. But I refuse to be blown off my feet anyway' (cited in B. Kachru 1992: 11).

The medium of English now provides that cross-cultural house in the form of pluralistic world Englishes. What is needed is a pluralistic vision to use this resource with sensitivity and cross-cultural understanding. The consequences of not facing the pragmatic contexts of world Englishes are serious: The issues involved are linguistic, socio-cultural, psychological and indeed educational.

It was in 1973, when concerns such as these were generally swept under the carpet by the agencies that controlled and directed English language teaching across cultures, that Dwight Bolinger, in his Presidential address at the Linguistic Society of America reminded us that 'truth is a linguistic question'. And we must pay heed to Bolinger's warning that 'a taste of truth is like a taste of blood'[3] (see Bolinger 1973).

Notes

1. This paper incorporates several points that I have discussed in more detail in my recent published papers and presentations at various conferences.
2. For such culturally and context-determined examples in Japanese English, see e.g. McCeary 1990, pp. 61–9; and B. Kachru 'Past imperfect: The Japanese agony', Kachru 2005, pp. 73–95.
3. For a detailed discussion for various perspectives – and critiques – of world Englishes, and origin and development of Asian Englishes, see e.g. Bolton, Kingsley and B. Kachru (2006a); Bolton, Kingsley and B. Kachru (2006b); and Kachru, Yamuna and Nelson (2006). For references until the 1990s see B. Kachru (1998) 'World Englishes 2000: Resources for research and teaching', in *World Englishes 2000*. L. E. Smith and M. L. Foreman (eds). pp. 209–51. See also B. Kachru 1981, 1983, 1985, see also 2008; see also Phillipson 1992; Tollefson 1991.

References

Abercrombie, D. 1951. 'R.P. and local accent.' *The Listener*, 6 September 1951. [Reprinted in Abercrombie, David (1965) *Studies in Phonetics and Linguistics*. London: Oxford University Press.]

Achebe, C. 1964. *Arrow of God*. London: Heinemann.

——. 1965. 'English and the African writer.' *Transition*. 4(18), 27–30. Also in *The Political Sociology of the English Language: An African Perspective* (1975). Edited by Ali A. Mazrui. The Hague: Mouton.

Bennett, W. J. 1992. *The De-valuing of America: The Fight for Our Culture and Our Children*. New York: Summit Books.

Bolinger, D. 1973. 'Truth is a linguistic question.' *Language*, 49, 539–50.

Bolton, K. and B. B. Kachru. 2006a. *World Englishes: Critical Concepts in Linguistics*, 6 Vols. London: Routledge.

——. 2006b. *Origin and Development of Asian Englishes*, 5 Vols. London: Routledge.

Crowley, T. (ed.) 1991. *Proper English*. New York: Routledge.

Desani, G. V. 1951. *All about H. Hatter*. New York: Farrar, Straus and Young.

D'Souza, D. 1991 *Illiberal Education: The Politics of Race and Sex on Campus*. New York: The Free Press.

Gates, H. L. 1992. *Loose Canons: Notes on the Culture Wars*. New York: Oxford University Press.

——. 1993. 'Review of *Culture of Complaint: The Fraying of American* by Robert Hughes (New York and Oxford: Oxford University Press, 1993).' *New Yorker*. 19 April, p. 15.

Hughes, R. 1993. *Culture of Complaint: The Fraying of American*. Oxford: Oxford University Press.

Jussawala, F. and R. W. Dasenbrock. 1992. *Interviews with Writers of the Post-Colonial World*. Jackson: University Press of Mississippi.

Kachru, B. B. 1981. 'The pragmatics of nonnative varieties of English.' In L. E. Smith (ed.) *English for Cross-cultural Communication*. London: Macmillan, pp. 15–39.

——. 1983. *The Indianization of English: The English Language in India*. New Delhi: Oxford University Press.

——. 1985. 'Standards, codification and sociolinguistic realism: The English language in the Outer Circle.' In Quirk and Widdowson (eds), Cambridge: Cambridge University Press, pp. 11–30.

——. 1986. 'The bilingual's creativity and contact literatures.' In *The Alchemy of English: The Spread, Functions, and Models of Non-native Englishes*. Oxford: Pergamon Press, pp. 159–73.

——. 1987. 'The bilingual's creativity: Discoursal and stylistic strategies in contact literature.' In L. E. Smith (ed.) *Discourse across Cultures: Strategies in World Englishes*. New York: Prentice-Hall, pp. 125–40.

——. 1988. 'The spread of English and sacred linguistic cows.' In P. H. Lowenberg (ed.) *Language Spread and Language Policy: Issues, Implications and Case Studies. Georgetown Round Table on Language and Linguistics 1987*. Washington DC: Georgetown University Press, pp. 207–28.

——. 1994. 'Teaching World Englishes without Myths.' In S. K. Gill, et al. (eds) *INTELEC '94: International English Language Education Conference, National and International Challenges and Responses*. Bangi, Malaysia: Pusat Bahasa Universiti Kebangsaan Malaysia, pp. 1–19.

——. 1998. 'World Englishes 2000: Resources and teaching.' In L. E. Smith and M. L. Foreman (eds) *World Englishes 2000*. Hawaii: University of Hawaii Press, pp. 209–51.

Kachru, B. B. 2005. *Asian Englishes: Beyond the Canon*. Hong Kong: Hong Kong University Press (also Oxford University Press, New Delhi, India).

——. 2008. 'World Englishes in world contexts.' In H. Momma and M. Matto (eds) *A Companion to The History of The English Language*. Oxford: Wiley-Blackwell, pp. 567–80.

——. (ed.) 1992. *The Other Tongue: English across Cultures*. 2nd ed. Urbana, IL: University of Illinois Press.

Kachru, B. B., Y. Kachru and C. L. Nelson. (eds) 2006. *The Handbook of World Englishes*. Oxford: Blackwell Publishing.

Kachru, Y. 1985. 'Discourse strategies, pragmatics and ESL: Where are we going?' *RELC Journal*, 16(2), 1–30.

——. 1987. 'Cross-cultural texts, discourse strategies and discourse interpretation.' In L. E. Smith (ed.) *Discourse across Cultures: Strategies in World Englishes*. New York: Prentice Hall, pp. 87–100.

——. 1992. 'Culture, style and discourse: Expanding noetics of English.' In B. B. Kachru (ed.) *The Other Tongue: English across Cultures*. 2nd ed. Urbana, IL: University of Illinois Press, pp. 340–52.

Kachru, Y. and C. L. Nelson. 2006. *World Englishes in Asian Contexts*. Hong Kong: Hong Kong University Press.

Kachru, Y. and L. E. Smith. 2008. *Cultures, Contexts, and World Englishes*. London: Routledge.

McCreary, D. R. 1990. 'Loan words in Japanese.' *Journal of Asian Pacific Communication*, 1(1), 61–9.

Mencken, H. L. 1936. *The American Language*. 4th ed. New York: Alfred A. Knopf.

Naipaul, V. S. 1977. *India: A Wounded Civilization*. New York: Vintage.

Nelson, C. L. 1992. 'My language, your culture: Whose communicative competence?' In B. B. Kachru (ed.). *The Other Tongue: English across Cultures*. 2nd ed. Urbana, IL: University of Illinois Press, pp. 327–39.

Nesfield, J. 1895. *English Grammar Series, Book IV: Idiom, Grammar and Synthesis for High Schools*. Calcutta: Macmillan.

Ngũgĩ wa Thiong'o. 1981. *Writers in Politics*. London: Heinemann.

Okara, G. 1963. African speech... 'English words.' *Transition*, 10(3), 13–8.

Phillipson, R. 1992. *Linguistic Imperialism*. Oxford: Oxford University Press.

Quirk, R. 1988. 'The question of standards in the international use of English.' In P. H. Lowenberg (ed.) *Language Spread and Language Policy: Issues, Implications and Case Studies. Georgetown Round Table on Language and Linguistics 1987*. Washington DC: Georgetown University Press, pp. 229–41.

Quirk, R. and H. G. Widdowson (eds) 1985. *English in the World: Teaching and Learning the Language and Literatures*. Cambridge: Cambridge University Press.

Rao, R. 1960. *The Serpent and the Rope*. London: John Murray.

Rushdie, S. 1991. 'Hobson-Jobson.' In *Imaginary Homelands: Essays and Criticism 1981–1991*. London: Viking, pp. 81–3.

Said, E. W. 1993. *Culture and Imperialism*. New York: Alfred A. Knopf.

Sidhu, C. D. 1976. *An Intensive Course in English*. New Delhi: Orient Longman.

Singh, F. B. 1987. 'Power and politics in the content of grammar books: The example of India.' *World Englishes*, 6(3), 195–9.

Smith, L. E. (ed.) 1981. *English for Cross-cultural Communication*. London: Macmillan.

——. (ed.) 1987. *Discourse across Cultures: Strategies in World Englishes.* New York: Prentice Hall.

Smith, L. E. and C. L. Nelson. 1985. 'International intelligibility of English: Directions and resources.' *World Englishes,* 4(3), 333–42.

Sridhar, K. K. and S. N. Sridhar. 1992. 'Bridging the paradigm gap: Second language acquisition theory and indigenized varieties of English.' In B. B. Kachru (ed.) *The Other Tongue: English across Cultures.* 2nd ed. Urbana, IL: University of Illinois Press, pp. 91–107.

Tharoor, S. 1989. *The Great India Novel.* Delhi: Penguin.

Tipping, L. 1933. *Matriculation English Grammar of Modern English Usage.* London: Macmillan.

Tollefson, J. W. 1991 *Planning Language, Planning Inequality: Language Policy in the Community.* London: Longman.

Wren, P. C. and H. Martin. 1954. *High School English Grammar and Composition.* Revised ed. New Delhi: S. Chand.

12
Plurilithic Englishes: Towards a 3D Model

Alastair Pennycook

With the growth of the Asia manufacturing and service industries, the prediction that China and India will have the first and third largest global economies within 30 years, a population that comprises over 50 per cent of the world's people, and massive English language programmes throughout the region, it is no surprise that the role of English in Asia has become a major concern. Notwithstanding the difficulties in defining what Asia comprises – either in terms of geo-political scope (are Australia and New Zealand, Iran and Israel, Papua New Guinea and New Caledonia part of the region?[1]) or in terms of cultural continuity (does it really make sense to talk about shared culture and knowledge across this region?) – it seems that it is nevertheless possible to talk at some level of 'the Asianness in Asian Englishes and their gradual, yet marked, distinctiveness' (Kachru 2005: xv). With increasing collaboration across the region, and the eventual possibility of an Asian economic and political entity that parallels the European Union, a comparison with Europe is intriguing. While Europe has sought to make its national languages the working languages of the EU (while also supporting some of the minority languages of the region), Asia has embedded English as the working language of many of its international organizations, such as ASEAN.

English has nevertheless come to play a dominant role in Europe, described either in negative terms as 'a simplified, pidginized but unstable "Euro-English" that inhibits creativity and expressiveness, whether English is used as a mother tongue or as a foreign language, a language that is spoken with so much imprecision that communication difficulties and breakdowns multiply' (Phillipson 2003: 176), or in a more positive light as the European lingua franca (Jenkins 2000; Seidlhofer 2001). Looking at the growing role of English in Asia, it is important to establish whether the focus is on the role of the language(s) within the social, cultural and political contexts of the region (English in Asia), a pan-Asian variety of English as a lingua franca (Asian English), or the development of regional varieties of English that may reflect the diversity rather than the commonality of Asia (Asian Englishes). Indeed it is the tension between these orientations – the centripetal pull of the interest in English as an Asian lingua franca, and the centrifugal pull of a pluralist model of Asian Englishes – that is a central issue of contention in recent debates.

Sorting out the circles

Putting aside centrist claims that take a pragmatic, triumphalist or reactionary stance on the need for central models of English, as well as more critical stances that emphasize the homogenizing effects of the spread of English (for further discussion, see Pennycook 2007), current discussion focuses around two divergent accounts. On the one hand the resolutely pluralist camp of the world Englishes framework, which seeks to show how English becomes localized in different regions of the world; on the other hand the English as a lingua franca (ELF) research which seeks to show how English is always under negotiation. A plausible case can in fact be made that the ELF focus is trying to address precisely that gap left by the holes in the WE model: How to come to grips with a non-centrist understanding of English as an international language that is dependent neither on hegemonic versions of central English nor on nationally defined new Englishes, but rather attempts to account for the ever-changing negotiated spaces of current language use? The ELF model, it is argued 'liberates L2 speakers from the imposition of native speaker norms as well as the cultural baggage of World Englishes models' (Rubdy and Saraceni 2006: 8).

Locating the study of global English firmly within an understanding of globalization, Yano draws attention to the need, as he puts it with the typical delicacy and subtlety of phrase for which he is renowned, 'to slightly modify the Kachruvian circles in the course of this century' (2001: 122). The first issue he draws attention to is the increased establishment of varieties of English in the Outer Circle, so much so that the numbers of native speakers of these varieties have now reached quite significant proportions. At the very least, Yano suggests, this raises questions concerning the separability of Inner and Outer Circles. Here he takes up the distinction made by Braj Kachru between 'genetic' and 'functional' nativeness, arguing that 'these functionally native ESL speakers in the outer circle are expected to far exceed those genetically native English speakers in the inner circle not only by their numbers but by their economic and technological power' (ibid.). Here, then, Yano opens up an issue of great significance, though the use of Kachru's genetic/functional distinction perhaps obscures the point.

This distinction, as Kachru explains, refers on the one hand to 'the historical relationship' between languages (for example Hindi, Kashmiri and Bengali or Tamil, Telugu and Malayalam) and on the other the 'RANGE and DEPTH of a language in a society' (emphasis in original) (where range refers to 'the domains of function' and depth to 'the degree of social penetration of the language') (2005: 12). This distinction has led to a considerable amount of confusion for several reasons: First, there is confusion among speakers, languages and contexts. The distinction refers to languages, not to speakers, so the nativeness here is not that of people having a particular first language, but rather has to do with the relationship between languages on the one hand, and social contexts on the other. One may or may not be a native speaker of a language that is genetically or functionally native in a particular context. Second, the notion that English is 'genetically native' in the Inner Circle problematically overlooks the languages it supplanted (many Indigenous languages in Australia, for example) and also seems to suggest that a speaker of a related language (say, German) might share genetic nativeness with English speakers. Thus while this distinction appears to be aimed at showing that languages can become transplanted from one place to another, so that English in Singapore, or indeed Spanish in Argentina or French in La Martinique, have become indigenized, the notion of 'genetic nativeness' remains problematic. And this issue of how a language may function in different contexts needs to be carefully separated from the question of whether people grow up speaking the language.

Yano's useful point, therefore, that the distinction between Inner and Outer Circles is a fragile one could rest on firmer ground than this problematic genetic/functional distinction. He then goes on to suggest that 'the inner circle itself may become questionable because of continued inflow of immigrants and increase of foreign residents' (2001: 122). While Yano is again absolutely right that the notion of the Inner Circle should be subjected to far more critical scrutiny than has often been the case, the issue he raises here needs to be pursued further. One of the many problems with the circles model of world Englishes is the conflation of countries, people and languages (Bruthiaux 2003). If we take Yano's point seriously that increased migration threatens the status of Inner Circle English, we also have to raise further questions: Is the point here that the proportion of native speakers in Inner Circle countries is decreasing, thus undermining the status of these countries as Inner Circle users of NS varieties? Or is the point that increased migration is changing the nature of Inner Circle English? In the first case, we also need to consider whether historically the Inner Circle has not always been a place of diversity. If we are dealing with the second case, where the English itself is changing, we need to ask whether Inner Circle English has not always been influenced by other languages. Certainly, however, the changing demographies of all so-called Inner Circle countries, is indeed challenging the notion that some unsullied form of native-speaker English is their dominant code.

To discuss Australia, for example, only in terms of an Inner Circle, norm-providing model – in Kachru (2005) and Kachru and Nelson (2006) Australia appears quirkily to provide the Inner Circle norms for the rest of Asia – and to ignore the diversity of what English means for Australians is to avoid the more complex and interesting questions around, for example, Aboriginal English and its relation to Kriol (see Malcolm 2001). English for Indigenous Australians can be a creole, a foreign language, a second language or a first language. English for other Australians may be a community lingua franca, a second language or a foreign language. Among other things, it depends crucially on issues of access. None of this work on models of English makes much sense without a good grasp of the political contexts in which English operates. Too much of the discussion here of negotiation, appropriation or nativization occurs in a social, economic and political vacuum. As Ruanni Tupas warns, while WE and ELF models 'may have legitimized different cultures and local users of English around the world, ... the issue of who among the speakers and/or learners of English in their respective localities have access to any of these Standard Englishes in the first place is still not adequately addressed' (2006: 169).

Certainly, by raising this issue, by suggesting that 'the demarcation between the inner circle and the outer circle in the Kachruvian concentric circles will become more obscure and therefore less meaningful' (2001: 122), Yano has raised a key concern about the status of these circles. It is a shame, therefore, that having questioned the permeability of one division, he does not go on to question the other, namely the line between Outer and Expanding Circles, arguing instead that speakers of English as a native language, whether in the Inner or Outer Circles, 'will remain distinctly separated' from speakers of English as a foreign language in the Expanding Circle. Here, it seems to me, Yano is in fact in two minds since while on the one hand he insists on this division, he also suggests that 'it is possible that some EFL speakers can also become functionally ESL speakers ... through the intensive and extensive exposure to and use of English, although Kachru did not refer to these EFL speakers' (2001: 123). Yano's telling insights here suggest that in spite of his apparent unwillingness to concede that English has started to play a significant internal role in Japan, the distinctions between the circles is fragile indeed.

Towards a real 3D model

The new model of world Englishes that Yano presents is a 'three-dimensional sociolinguistic perspective rather than the two-dimensional Kachruvian three-circle model perspective' (2001: 122). First, and highly significantly, this new model proposes that 'the concentricity of the three circles which indicates the idea of the native-speaker-centredness can be removed and all the varieties of English ... will be on a parallel with each other' (2001: 123). This is in fact a radical departure from the oft-criticized normativity of the concentric circles that has always placed NS norms in the centre while paradoxically claiming to counter NS normativity. The second element that Yano introduces is a vertical element based on the acro-/basilect distinction more common in creole studies. Here he suggests that the use of English for international communication tends towards the acrolectal while domestic and private use may tend towards the basilectal. The model Yano develops based on these insights portrays each variety of English as an 'equal-sized cylinder with no distinction between ENL, ESL and EFL. Seen from above, the varieties appear to be a bundle of circles of equal size indicated by dotted lines to show the looseness of the boundaries among varieties. Seen from the side, the upper portion is the acrolectal use of variety as EGL (English as a Global Language) ... while the lower part is for basilectal use for domestic communication' (2001: 123–4).

Once again, Yano (2001) opens up some key perspectives on English that can help us expand our thinking on English in many useful directions. I would like to push these insights further in the following ways: First, by questioning the arguments that exclude Japanese speakers on the grounds that they only use acrolectal English, and which by extension suggest that all Expanding Circle English is acrolectal. Japanese speakers of English, he argues, only use acrolectal English for international communication and do not have any basilectal domestic forms. While it may be tempting to assume that English for global communication (EIL/ ELF/ EFL) may always be acrolectal since this is generally learned exonormative English dependent on mutual comprehension, this is surely not always the case. It may be so in particular business and what we might call elite communicational settings, but it is surely not always so. Japanese use English within Japan for a range of purposes – different, admittedly, from countries such as Singapore or Malaysia – and English has to be seen as a major semiotic resource in Japan (see for example, Backhaus 2006; Seargeant, in press). They also use it outside Japan and in a very wide range of circumstances, from a business meeting in Hanoi, to catching a wave off the Gold Coast in Australia, from a hip-hop group collaborating with artists from Korea, Hong Kong and Malaysia to military engineers in Southern Iraq. We need to be cautious, therefore, not to assume that when English is used as a lingua franca, or as an international language, or as a foreign language, it is necessarily acrolectal. While this may be the case for the business meeting in Hanoi, it may not so clearly be so in the context of military engineering, and it is much more likely to be meso- or basilectal in the case of surfing or popular music. In short, learning English as an international language may involve the learning of a range of styles and registers.

Indeed, this is precisely the domain of English as a lingua franca, which is why, as I suggested earlier, an understanding of ELF may fill that gap left by the concentric circles model with respect to the Expanding Circle. The problem here has been the attempt to limit the purview of world Englishes to nation-based models. Yet, once we open up an understanding of English as it is used across multiple domains, it is evident that there are very good grounds to move away from nations as the basis for our descriptions of English. From a WE perspective it is common to chide other views of English for not accommodating sufficient accounts of diversity in their models. Y. Kachru and Nelson, for example, contrast a world Englishes approach with terms such as 'world English' (Brutt Griffler 2002), 'English as an International Language' (Jenkins 2000), and 'English as a Lingua Franca' (Seidlhofer 2001), since all of these 'idealize a monolithic entity called "English" and neglect the inclusive and plural character of the world-wide phenomenon' (2006: 2).

While it may appear, however, that there is an important distinction between a WE approach, with its apparently centrifugal focus on local variation, and an ELF approach with its supposedly centripetal focus on the development of regional varieties (European and Asian English), at another level, this is a matter only of relative scale. While studies of

Indian English, for example, would fall into the first camp, it is also clear that Indian English is more chimerical than this terminology allows. As Krishnaswamy and Burde observe, 'Like Indian nationalism, "Indian English" is "fundamentally insecure" since the notion "nation-India" is insecure' (1998: 63). Given the diversity of Indian languages and regions and the need to see India not so much as an imagined community but rather as an unimaginable community, it is unclear why Indian English itself should not be viewed as a lingua franca. To discuss an entity called South Asian English, which comprises varieties across India, Sri Lanka, Pakistan and Bangladesh, is to talk in terms of a monolithic lingua franca English. Thus, when Braj Kachru focuses on 'educated South Asian English' rather than 'Broken English' (2005: 39) he is surely open to the same critiques that he and others level at the purveyors of monolithic English rather than world Englishes. Thus, as Parakrama (1995: 25–6) argues, 'The smoothing out of struggle within and without language is replicated in the homogenizing of the varieties of English on the basis of "upper-class" forms. Kachru is thus able to theorize on the nature of a monolithic Indian English.' Similarly, Canagarajah (1999: 180) observes that in Kachru's 'attempt to systematize the periphery variants, he has to standardize the language himself, leaving out many eccentric, hybrid forms of local Englishes as too unsystematic. In this, the Kachruvian paradigm follows the logic of the prescriptive and elitist tendencies of the center linguists.'

In order to address such questions we need to get beyond questions only of pluralization (English versus Englishes), since they leave unexamined questions of scale and ideology. This raises the question as to whether diversity in fact can be sought in the countability of world Englishes rather than the non-countability of ELF, or whether we need a more complex understanding here. By characterizing and dismissing work that falls under the ELF rubric, critics fail therefore on the one hand to see that it depends very much what one is trying to do with ELF (whether this is an attempt to capture a core to international English communication and teach it, or whether it is an attempt to account for the amorphous, ongoing, moment-by-moment negotiation of English that is actually its daily reality), and on the other that work that falls under apparently different frameworks, such as WE, may in fact only vary along a narrow line of scope. If an ELF approach is concerned only with devising an alternative NNS rather than NS standard, even if it is doing this as a pedagogical response to the need for something other than NS and WE models, it is certainly open to criticism for being potentially reductive and prescriptive. If, on the other hand, it is trying to capture the pluricentricity of ongoing negotiated English – or, as we might call it, the *plurilithic* as opposed to monolithic character of English, since an ELF approach may posit no centres at all – it may be more pluricentric than WE. As Rani Rubdy and Mario Saraceni put it, 'In the end, the validity of the EIL/ELF proposal will probably depend upon whether or not it chooses to embrace a polymodel approach to the teaching of English or a monolithic one, whether it leads to the establishing and promoting of a single (or a limited form of) Lingua Franca Core for common use among speakers in the Outer and Expanding Circles, possibly stripped of any cultural influences, or whether it will be flexible enough to manifest the cultural norms of all those who use it along with the rich tapestry of linguistic variation in which they are embedded' (2006: 13).

The problem for both frameworks, of course, is the impossibility of describing in any comprehensive fashion the ongoing negotiation of language. Descriptions of language, in this sense, have always been impossible, and have always relied on abstractions. The heart of the question therefore is this: Once we get beyond the accusations of monocentric and pluricentric models, in what ways is the research committed to a vision of diversity and in what ways to an attempt to systematize? While some proposals for ELF do indeed appear to have systematization as their goal, others seem more interested in capturing the momentary negotiations of English. Kirkpatrick argues that an ELF model is preferable to native or nativized (Inner or Outer Circle) models on the grounds that it becomes 'the property of all, and it will be flexible enough to reflect the cultural norms of those who use it. In this it differs markedly from both native and nativized varieties of English, as native and nativized varieties must by definition reflect the cultural norms of their speakers' (2006: 79). While for some this variety may need to be described and taught, for others, it is more a question of how 'postcolonial speakers of English creatively negotiate the place of English in their lives' (Canagarajah 2006: 200).

Returning again to the development of Yano's (2001) model, I am suggesting that rather than considering the Expanding Circle along national lines (Japanese English, Chinese English and so forth), it makes much more sense to incorporate the work on ELF into this model. Once we take on board these insights, furthermore, the problematic nation-oriented framework of WE also becomes more questionable. In developing Yano's model further, therefore, I shall maintain the three-dimensionality, the equality between varieties, and the use of acro- and basilectal concepts, while adding further dimensions. If some would argue that three dimensions are enough, I would like to suggest that we do not in fact yet have three dimensions to this model. Kachru's model is in fact one-dimensional: It only presents lists of languages moving in one direction that might as easily be placed along a line; Yano's is in fact two-dimensional: It presents varieties one way and depth (acrolects to basilects) the other, but is missing the third, lateral dimension: users and contexts. What we in fact need is an understanding of the relationship among language varieties or resources as used by certain communities (the linguistic resources users draw on); contextual uses of language (the use of these language resources in specific contexts); and language users' relationship to language varieties (the social, economic and cultural positioning of the speakers).

This is, therefore an attempt to move away from nation-based models of English and to take on board current understandings of language as used transidiomatically and within communities other than those defined along national criteria. This view is more closely linked to what Jacquemet calls transidiomatic practices: 'the communicative practices of transnational groups that interact using different languages and communicative codes simultaneously present in a range of communicative channels, both local and distant'. Transidiomatic practices, Jacquemet explains, 'are the results of the co-presence of multilingual talk (exercised by de/reterritorialized speakers) and electronic media, in contexts heavily structured by social indexicalities and semiotic codes'. For Jacquemet, such practices are dependent on 'transnational environments', the mediation of 'deterritorialized technologies', and interaction 'with both present and distant people' (2005: 265). Here too we can start to incorporate the idea of communicative repertoires: Individual language knowledge should be defined 'not in terms of abstract system components but as communicative repertoires – conventionalized constellations of semiotic resources for taking action – that are shaped by the particular practices in which individuals engage' (Hall et al. 2006: 232). From this point of view, language knowledge is 'grounded in and emergent from language use in concrete social activity for specific purposes that are tied to specific communities of practice' (Hall et al. 2006: 235).

Canagarajah makes a related point in his discussion of lingua franca English (LFE). This distinction between English as a lingua franca and lingua franca English is important since the former tends towards an understanding of a pre-given language that is then used by different speakers, while the latter suggests that LFE emerges from its contexts of use. According to Canagarajah, 'LFE does not exist as a system out there.

It is constantly brought into being in each context of communication' (2007: 91). From this point of view, 'there is no meaning for form, grammar or language ability outside the realm of practice. LFE is not a product located in the mind of the speaker; it is a social process constantly reconstructed in sensitivity to environmental factors' (2007: 94).

This is consistent with the argument I have been making for the need to escape the predefinition of a language user by geographical location or variety and instead to deal with the contextual use of language. As Bruthiaux (2003) reminds us, the concentric circles conflate varieties, speakers, geographical locations and history; we need instead to focus on sociolinguistic contexts of language use: Who is using what in what way where? Yano's 3D model opens up the space for us to do this: Instead of considering each variety to exist independently and then asking whether so-called Expanding Circle varieties also exist, we need to understand variety not as object but as fluidity: variety exists across the spectrum. This is Yano's horizontal plane, with variety across regions of the world. Second, we need to understand vertical variety in terms of contextual use of language; and third, we can now see the third dimension in terms of users. Put another way, if we adapt a *transtextual* model of language (cf. Pennycook 2007) to look at English use, we can look at this in terms of interlingual variety on one plane (inter/linguistic resources), colingual (who says what to whom where) and the ideolingual (what gets taken from what language use with what investments, ideologies, discourses and beliefs) on the other (see Figure 12.1).

This allows us to bring far more than just variety from central English norms into the 3D model. This is no longer about whether count nouns get pluralized, local language terminology enters English, tag questions become fixed or verb tense and aspect are realized differently. By starting with the possibility of transidiomatic practices rather than language norms, we can incorporate variety as well as speaker locality, and thus raise questions about access to varieties 'which will still be largely determined by one's proximity to education and, for that matter, all other related symbolic goods in the social market' (Tupas 2006: 180); the contextual linguistic capital of language users, which as Lorente (in press) shows in the context of domestic workers in Singapore is not just about varieties of English but rather is a far more complex struggle over linguistic capital and ideology; and the ways in which our language desires are produced in the global marketplaces of English, where 'English emerges as a powerful tool to construct a gendered identity and to gain access to the romanticized West' (Piller and Takahashi 2006: 69). Instead of treating difference as epiphenomenal variegation, with

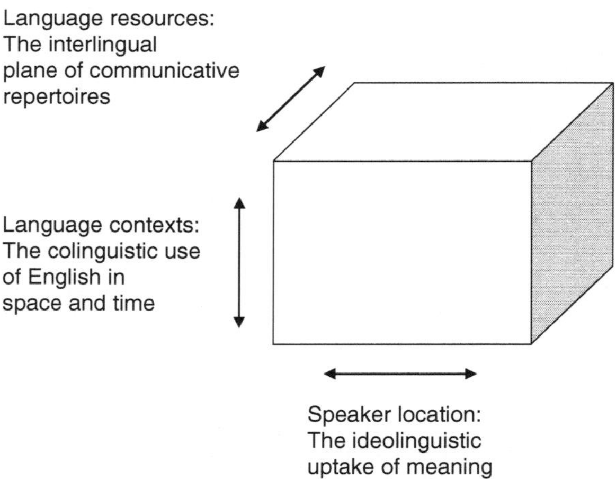

Figure 12.1 A 3D transtextual model of English use

language users, culture and history peripheral to the similarity at the heart of English, instead of 'the inability of linguists to give primacy to language speakers and to the history of a language that remains a fundamental limitation to this day' (Nakata 2007: 39), we can make all this central.

On the top surface we have, as in Yano's model, language varieties, though these are not separated into linguistic tubes defined by national boundaries but are a more open field of choice. We need to escape from the circles, tubes and boxes based on nations that have so bedevilled world Englishes and linguistics more generally. My proposal here is that the top plane is English as a lingua franca (or lingua franca English), which is taken to include *all* uses of English. That is to say, English as a lingua franca is not limited here to Expanding Circle use or NNS–NNS interactions but rather is a term to acknowledge the interconnectedness of all English use. In this field, English users all over the world draw on various resources in English. And in this sense, 'in its emerging role as a world language, English has no native speakers' (Rajagopalan 2004: 112).

The vertical plane takes up Yano's (2001) interest in registers, though here these are no longer tied to cylindrical national varieties and their supposed ranges (only acrolects for the Expanding Circle; acrolect to basilect for other varieties) but rather to the actual contextual use of language: the Japanese dive instructor in the Philippines, for example, describing the afternoon dive sites, assisted by her Danish co-instructor and Philippine dive master, to a group of divers from different parts of the world. The language is English, though it is also mixed with others; the register comes from the diving community ('at 100 bar give me a sign, OK?'); the non-verbal communication (the sign for 'low on air'), the use of other props (a chart of the dive site), all contribute to the contextual use and understanding of translingual English. And, along the third dimension, the listeners come with language histories, and means of interpretation – the ideolinguistic dimension where English is one of many languages, a code useful for certain activities, a language connected to certain desires and ideologies. As Canagarajah (2007) reminds us, lingua franca English does not exist outside the realm of practice; it is not a product but a social process that is constantly being remade from the semiotic resources available to speakers, who are always embedded in contexts and who are always interacting with other speakers.

Conclusion

I have been arguing in this paper for a dynamic model of global Englishes based on Yano's (2001) thought-provoking discussion. Unlike Schneider's Dynamic Model which suggests that 'the evolution of language follows principles of its own' (2007: 19) and that there is therefore a 'common core' behind the processes of localization (2007: 29), however, I have been trying to explore a model that seeks neither universal nor national framings of English but instead incorporates the local, agency and context in their complex interactions. Drawing on Yano's (2001) 'three-dimensional sociolinguistic' development of the concentric circle model of world Englishes (WE), I have argued in this paper for several perspectives that enable us to develop our thinking about English in the world. To the extent that the WE framework has been very useful in dealing with Outer Circle Englishes, but much less sure of what to do with the Expanding Circle, a case can be made for an approach that combines both WE and English as a lingua franca (ELF) approaches. The crucial question is not one of pluralization – English or Englishes – but rather what language ideologies underlie the visions of plurality. To argue for a monolithic version of English is clearly both an empirical and a political absurdity, but we need to choose carefully between the available models of pluricentric Englishes, and might be better off thinking in terms of plurilithic Englishes. This notion can avoid the pitfall of states-centric pluralities that reproduce the very linguistics they need to escape in order to deal with globalized linguascapes. From this perspective, we can start to address Yano's questions as to whether English can ever represent Japanese culture: We do not need to think of Japanese English in terms of a national variety, and instead can deal with a transtextual version of cultural and linguistic diversity.

Note

1. According to the map in both Kachru (2005) and Kachru and Nelson (2006), Australia, New Zealand and Papua new Guinea are part of Asia. According to the Asia TEFL organization, Iran and Israel are in Asia (Australia and New Zealand's memberships are under discussion).

References

Backhaus, P. 2006. 'Multilingualism in Tokyo: A look into the linguistic landscape.' In D Gorter (ed.) *Linguistic Landscape: A new approach to multilingualism.* Clevedon: Multilingual Matters, pp. 52–66.

Bruthiaux, P. 2003. 'Squaring the circles: issues in modeling English worldwide.' *International Journal of Applied Linguistics*, 13(2), 159–77.

Brutt-Griffler, J. 2002. *World English: A study of its development.* Clevedon: Multilingual Matters.

Canagarajah, S. 1999. *Resisting Linguistic Imperialism in English Teaching.* Oxford: Oxford University Press.

——. 2006. 'Interview.' In Rubdy, R. and M. Saraceni (eds) (2006) *English in the World: Global rules, global roles.* London: Continuum, pp. 200–12.

——. 2007. 'The ecology of global English.' *International Multilingual Research Journal*, 1(2), 89–100.

Hall, J. K., A. Cheng and M. Carlson. 2006. 'Reconceptualizing multicompetence as a theory of language knowledge.' *Applied Linguistics*, 27(2), 220–40.

Jacquemet, M. 2005. 'Transidiomatic practices, language and power in the age of globalization.' *Language & Communication*, 25, 257–77.

Jenkins, J. 2000. *The Phonology of English as an International Language.* Oxford: Oxford University Press.

Kachru, B. 2005. *Asian Englishes: Beyond the Canon.* Hong Kong: Hong Kong University Press.

Kachru, Y. and C. Nelson. 2006. *World Englishes in Asian Contexts.* Hong Kong: Hong Kong University Press.

Kirkpatrick, A. 2006. 'Which model of English: Native-speaker, nativized or lingua franca?' In R. Rubdy and M. Saraceni (eds) *English in the World: Global rules, global roles.* London: Continuum, pp. 71–83.

Krishnaswamy, N. and A. Burde. 1998. *The Politics of Indians' English: Linguistic colonialism and the expanding English empire.* Delhi: Oxford University Press.

Lorente, B. P. (in press). 'In the grip of English: linguistic instrumentalism and the "competitiveness" of overseas Filipino workers.' In K. Bolton and M. L. S. Bautista (eds). *Philippine English: Issues in Language and Literature.* Hong Kong: Hong Kong University Press.

Malcolm, I. 2001. 'Aboriginal English: adopted code of a surviving culture.' In D. Blair and P. Collins (eds) *English in Australia*. Amsterdam: John Benjamins, pp. 201–22.

Nakata, M. 2007. *Disciplining the Savages: Savaging the Disciplines*. Canberra: Aboriginal Studies Press.

Parakrama, A. 1995. *De-hegemonizing Language Standards: Learning from (post) colonial Englishes about 'English'*. Basingstoke: MacMillan.

Pennycook, A. 2007. *Global Englishes and Transcultural Flows*. London: Routledge.

Phillipson, R. 2003. *English Only Europe? Challenging language policy*. London: Routledge.

Piller, I. and K. Takahashi. 2006. 'A passion for English: Desire and the language market.' In A. Pavlenko (ed.) *Bilingual Minds: Emotional experience, expression and respresentation*, Clevedon: Multilingual Matters, pp. 59–83.

Rajagopalan, K. 2004. 'The concept of "World English" and its implications for ELT.' *ELT Journal* 58(2), 111–17.

Rubdy, R. and M. Saraceni. 2006. 'Introduction' In R. Rubdy and M. Saraceni (eds) *English in the World: Global rules, global roles*. London: Continuum, pp. 5–16.

Schneider, E. 2007. *Postcolonial English: Varieties around the world*. Cambridge: Cambridge University Press.

Seargeant, P. (in press) *The Idea of English in Japan: Ideology and the Evolution of a Global Language*. Clevedon: Multilingual Matters.

Seidlhofer, B. 2001. 'Closing a conceptual gap: The case for a description of English as a lingua franca.' *International Review of Applied Linguistics*, 11(2), 133–58.

Tupas, R. 2006. 'Standard Englishes, pedagogical paradigms and conditions of (im)possibility.' In R. Rubdy and M. Saraceni (eds) *English in the World: Global rules, global roles*. London: Continuum, pp. 169–85.

Yano, Y. 2001. 'World Englishes in 2000 and beyond.' *World Englishes* 20(2), 119–31.

13
The Future of English: Beyond the Kachruvian Three Circle Model?*

Yasukata Yano

Introduction

English has spread throughout the world and has developed into many local varieties for intra-national use as a second language. Economic globalization has also made English one of the most powerful means of international communication. The more people use English, the more people learn the language; many countries have introduced English into the primary school curriculum and young learners are rapidly increasing. The European Union primary schools teach English from Grade 1 as part of the 'mother tongue plus two foreign languages' policy (Kawahara and Yamamoto 2004: 95). In Malaysia, Singpore and other ESL countries English is also taught from Grade 1. EFL countries such as China and Korea teach English from Grade 3 onwards, and Japan will start teaching English at Grades 5 and 6 in 2011 (Honna et al. 2008). As Graddol (2006: 72) predicts, English might be a basic skill for all in the future. From the need to use English frequently and intensely within wider regions such as Europe and Asia rather than globally, however, English would be converged to major regional varieties such as Euro-English and Asian English in the near future (Yano 2001: 126). When and if English becomes a basic skill for all, the roles that native speakers provide norms, second language users develop norms, and foreign language users depend on norms provided by native speakers will be changed.

English to Englishes

Language changes with time, as dictionaries tell us when we leaf through their pages. Who can imagine today that the word 'nice' originally, or at least until 700 years ago, meant 'stupid'? The word 'gay' meant 'cheerful and enjoyable to be with' until the 1960s when it began to mean 'homosexual'. The word 'salon' was an elegant social scene among eighteenth-century French aristocrats, but now it is where hairdressers or beauticians carry out their business.

Language changes with space as well. As Widdowson (2003: 45–6) writes, a disease spreads from one country to another and, wherever it is, it is the same disease, but language is not transmitted without being transformed. When English is brought to new environments, it takes in indigenous languages, beliefs, views, values, traditions, attitudes and ideologies (see Morizumi, Park, this volume). It transforms itself to meet and accommodate the local needs of expressions and identities. English has been transformed to many varieties of Englishes, in North America, the South Pacific and further in Asia and Africa. As B. Kachru (this volume) describes, 'we have *one* language and *many* voices'.

Why is 'potato chips' in British English 'French fries' in American English? Why is 'lift' 'elevator'? Why is the 'underground' the 'subway', a 'flat' an 'apartment' and 'the ground floor' 'the first floor'? Professor Higgins might shout, 'Pants, pants, pants! Why can't Americans say "trousers, trousers"!' Why is a sheep called 'jumbuck' in Australian English? Why is a stone a 'gibber'? Why is the pavement the 'footpath'? Even within the Inner Circle, there are such varieties. Nevertheless, native speakers have been 'norm providers' and have been keepers of the language's standards, judges of its pedagogic norms, and models for learners to follow.

English has spread to the Outer Circle such as South and Southeast Asia as an intra-national lingua franca. As English increasingly penetrates into these domains, users have transferred phonological and lexical elements from indigenous languages, code-switched and created new expressions. They develop the norms on their own endonormative standards in order to accommodate the local needs of expression, communication and identity.

In South Asian English, idioms and metaphors are transferred from the native languages. 'In olden times, woman just *worked like a bullock*'; 'You are a big man and we are but *small radishes from an unknown garden*.' Duplication is used for emphasis, such as, 'Cut it into *small small* pieces'; *Yes? No?* and *Isn't it?* are used as general tags as in 'You are coming, *yes*?' 'He was angry, *isn't it*?' (Y. Kachru and Nelson 2006: 157–8).

In Southeast Asia, being sensitive is 'onion-skinned' and what makes your body hot is 'heaty', for example: 'Don't tease my daughter. She is an *onion-skinned* girl'; 'Durian is *heaty*, so don't eat too much.' They create 'prepone' from 'postpone' and gender is added to the word 'cousin' and 'cousin-brother' and 'cousin-sister' are commonly used (Honna ed. 2002). When they are nervous, they might say 'I have a mouse in my chest.' When I asked why they don't use native speakers' idioms, a fellow Filipino linguist replied, 'If Americans can say, "I have butterflies in my stomach," why can't we say, "I have a mouse in my chest"'? Indeed, for those in the Philippines, English is theirs to express themselves, their society and their culture.

In Africa, English is used mostly in ex-British colonies in the east, west and southern parts of the sub-Saharan continent. Y. Kachru and Nelson (2006: 199–202) report that, under the influence of local languages: articles are omitted, as in 'Let strong ... team be organized' and 'I am going to cinema'; mass nouns are used as countable as in 'all my furniture*s*', 'all his propert*ies*' and 'noise*s* of laughter'; redundant pronouns are inserted to echo the subject, as in 'My daughter *she* is a college student'; and to the question 'Hasn't the President left?' the answer is 'Yes (he hasn't left yet)' or 'No (he has left)'. Semantic extension also occurs, and 'some amount' means money or cash, 'a benchman' is an intimate friend, a 'machine' is a sewing machine, 'minerals' are soft drinks and a 'steer' is a steering wheel.

In the Expanding Circle (EFL regions) such as China, Egypt and Thailand, speakers are norm-dependent. Yet local cultural traditions are inevitably reflected in their language use because of the need to express their own ideas, opinions and feelings, which are often foreign to the Judeo-Christian tradition of the West. Chinese speakers of English, for example, use plenty of 'face' collocations because *mien zu* or face is an important concept for them. In business negotiations, they say: 'You haven't showed us the least amount of *face*'; 'You are simply losing my *face*'; and 'Please stand my *face*.' The Japanese tend to use passive sentences, reflecting the Japanese way of thinking, which sometimes gives the impression that the speakers are deliberately hiding the agent. 'We decided to close down the factory' tends to be 'It was decided to close down the factory.' In the Arabic world, religious faith is reflected in English usage. The following is the first part of an e-mail request for a donation.

> Assalamualaikum,
> In the name of Allah the Beneficent; the Merciful, the Master of the day of Judgments, I greet you in the Name of Allah, the Beneficent, the Merci-ful. To whom All the Praise (HQ; 31:26; 17:111); and the most Beautiful Names (HQ: 7:180; 17:110; 20:8; 59:24) belongs. I am from ... (An e-mail message from Al Ahli Usman, 27 May 2005)

If the English language spreads and continues to change into locally acculturated and institutionalized varieties, will the language develop into separate languages? It might, as Latin once did. However, we also have a converging force.

Towards regional standard Englishes

In the globalized world of today, people, capital, commodities, information and services move constantly and massively across national boundaries. The technology of the air transportation system allows people to travel around the globe. The technology of the computer-assisted communication system makes it possible for people to have daily contacts on a global scale. As people's global interactions become closer and more frequent, they are brought together, form relationships of interdependency and communicate more closely, which in turn requires knowledge and competence of a common language, English. The more English is used internationally, the more its varieties converge for higher mutual intelligibility. Therefore, will we have one single, international standard type of English which is higher in terms of prestige and functionality than the existing British and American standard Englishes? I do not think it will be desirable, necessary or feasible to have one variety of English for international use.

Today English is used for both intra- and inter-national communication, with two opposing forces at work: that for divergence (institutionalization of local varieties for intra-national use) and that for convergence (standardization of varieties for higher international intelligibility). The interface between the two will be the standardizing force within wider regions such as Asia and Europe. Intensity as well as frequency of interaction in English within respective regions rather than across regions; I conjectured in Yano (2001: 126) that English would be converged to six major regional standard Englishes in the near future – Anglo-American English, Euro-English, Asian English, Latin English, Arab English and African English.

These varieties function as a pan-regional communication tool such as pan-European English and a pan-Asian English just like standard Englishes have been formed over local varieties for wider use. Asian English, for example, is not a single, codified English, but a league of acrolectal varieties such as standard Indian English, Malaysian English, Philippine English and Singaporean English. Jenkins (2003: 18) and Pennycook (this volume) rightly point out that my argument in Yano (2001) missed the fact that EFL speakers also use basilect in international interactions. They

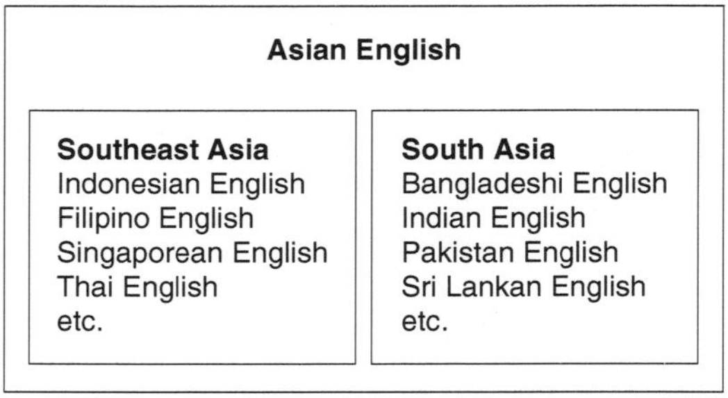

Asian English	
Southeast Asia Indonesian English Filipino English Singaporean English Thai English etc.	**South Asia** Bangladeshi English Indian English Pakistan English Sri Lankan English etc.

Figure 13.1 Regional standard Englishes

share intra-regional intelligibility by sharing Asian cultural traditions and identities while keeping respective local lingua-cultural features and identities rather than conforming to Anglo-American standards as is shown in Figure 13.1. Their use of Englishes does not necessarily follow that of Anglo-American, which is based on the Judeo-Christina cultural tradition.

They have been used for communication within the region in business, political and social activities. ASEAN's only official language is English and the language has been used in education as in the RELC (Regional Language Centre), where ELT professionals for ASEAN member nations are trained by Asian ELT professionals. In a sense, this is a way of 'Asianizing' English and its use to make it fit the Asian contexts; it is also a way of standardizing it to be Asian English, the pan-Asian means of communication.

From the geography-based model to the person-based model of English speakers

Economic, technological and demographic globalization brings political, cultural, social and linguistic changes to our societies on a global scale. It encourages the spread of English. English learners, especially young learners, are on the increase as many countries have introduced English into the primary school curriculum. Graddol (2006: 72, 120, 122) expects that in the foreseeable future English becomes a basic skill, and no longer a special talent. It may then be worth re-examining whether the presently dominant geography-based descriptions of English use in the world continue to be valid. The best known and most influential is the Kachruvian model of the three concentric circles, the Inner Circle, the Outer Circle and the Expanding Circle

(B. Kachru, 1992: 356). As B. Kachru (this volume) mentions that three circles indicate evolving *functional contexts* [emphasis added], I may be wrong to connect the circles to geographical locations, but Pennycook (this volume) illustrates the obscurity of the three circle distinction with multilingual Australian situations. Accordingly, we have described English speakers in terms of native speakers, second language speakers and foreign language speakers. But who are native speakers of English?

Traditionally, native speakers of English are defined (as in Cook 2003: 28) as 'people who acquired the language naturally and effortlessly in childhood ... *in the community which uses the language*' [emphasis added]. However, Crystal (2003: 6) referred to a couple in the Emirates, a German oil industrialist and a Malaysian, who communicate with each other through English learned as a foreign language and whose children learned 'English as a foreign language' as their mother tongue. Crystal maintains that such children are rapidly increasing the world over. In these times of global mobility, there are also increasing numbers of children who have native speaker parents who grew up in non-English speaking communities. Native speakers of English will not necessarily be those who are born and raised in the English-speaking community. When those children whose parents are non-native speakers or who grew up in non-English-speaking societies become omnipresent, the idea of connecting native English speakers and the geographical location, the Inner Circle, may be challenged. The idea of 'native speaker versus non-native speaker' itself also needs to be re-examined. B. Kachru (2005: 213) maintains that 'the attitudinally loaded dichotomy of *natives* versus *non-natives* is now pragmatically of doubtful validity'.

Second, demographic changes have taken place in the Inner Circle due to the constant and massive influx of immigrants, permanent and temporal residents such as businesspeople, engineers, researchers and students. In some cities in the south-western states in America such as Arizona, California, New Mexico and Texas, Spanish speakers have already outnumbered English speakers and Hispanification is bringing new linguistic realities (U.S. Census Bureau 2005). J. Jenkins (personal communication, 11 July 2003) observes that young Londoners of age 25 or under use the invariable tag, 'in it?', as in sentences such as 'You are happy, in it?' It might be the result of the influence of immigrants from South Asia, for whom the invariable 'isn't it?' is an institutionalized usage. This demographic change might also challenge the Kachruvian model which connects native speakers and the Inner Circle.

Third, B. Kachru (2005: 12, 25) recognized second-language speakers in the Outer Circle as 'functional native speakers'. Through my own association with linguists, ELT professionals and businesspeople in Asia I feel that increasing numbers of second-language speakers are getting native speakers' intuition on grammatical correctness and acceptability as well as generative ability. Presently, only the educated seem to be 'functional native speakers', but in Singapore, from Grade 1 onwards, the medium of instruction for all subjects is English except that of the learner's mother tongue, and children have started using English on the street and even at home. Schools in many Asian countries use English as an instruction medium at the primary, secondary and tertiary levels. When second language varieties such as Indian English, Malaysian English and Singapore English are firmly institutionalized, and these 'functional native speakers' start to use the language on their own endonormative standard, they no longer will seek the native speaker norm. Then, the time might come when we need to reconsider the geographical demarcation between the Inner Circle and Outer Circle.

Fourth, in the Expanding Circle, there are people who speak new varieties of English, which are acquired in adulthood in the Expanding Circle. They are lingua-culturally de-Anglo-Americanized but possess functional clarity and international intelligibility. Euro-English as a pan-EU lingua franca is one such example, where the language functions as a communication means between and among multi-ethnic, multicultural and multilingual non-native EU citizens. If these foreign-language users stop being norm-dependent and turn to 'norm-developers' after second language speakers, the distinction between the Outer and Expanding Circles might be questioned. More than 20 years ago, B. Kachru (1985: 13–14) described the obscure nature of the circles:

> The outer and expanding circles cannot be viewed as clearly demarcated from each other; they have several shared characteristics, and the status of English in the language policies of such countries changes from time to time. What is an ESL region at one time may become an EFL region at another time or vice versa.

If English teaching becomes a basic part of the primary school curriculum on the global scale, and English becomes a basic skill for everyone in the distant future, then a time might come when it no longer matters whether or not you have naturally acquired English in a community where the language is used as a mother tongue. What will matter is how proficient you have become, not where you have learned the language. It follows that the communal or geographical factor fades away and the educational factor looms up. Then the status of the English speaker will possibly be judged by his or her level of cross-cultural communicative competence as an English-knowing bi- or multilingual individual, not by whether he or she is a native speaker. In the future, therefore, the geography-based models might need to be reconsidered if and when native speakers' norm-providing role, second language speakers' norm-developing trend and foreign-language users' norm-dependent nature no longer hold.

The three-dimensional cylindrical model

The Kachruvian and other geography-based models rightly depict the spread of English in terms of history and the present state. To delineate a transitional model from the geography-based ones to the future individual person-based one, I proposed the three-dimensional cylindrical model shown below in Figure 13.2, from Yano (2007: 38). (See Pennycook, this volume, for the 3-dimensional transidiomatic model he proposed.)

The upward arrow in the centre shows the proficiency level. To begin with, foreign language users in the Expanding Circle must reach the proficiency level of adult native speakers in the Inner Circle who have acquired the language naturally through socialization in the English-speaking communities. So must second language speakers in the Outer Circle, but being 'functional native speakers' they have much less – or for some, no – gap of the proficiency level with native speakers. Beyond that level, it is up to the individual speakers. Native speakers as well as non-native speakers need to learn pragmatic strategies of communication across cultures. Therefore, the targeted proficiency level of EGP (English for General Purposes) is set a bit above that of the adult native speaker's proficiency level.

To acquire ESP (English for Specific Purposes) proficiency, English speakers in the three circles equally must make an effort to gain professional and linguistic knowledge in respective disciplines, which have much less to do with being a native speaker. You can be engaged in international business dealings wherever you learned business English and the ABC of international business – Brazil, Russia, and China. But native speakers without such knowledge and training can not.

Intra-Regional Standard English (intra-RSE) is placed below English as an International Language (EIL). It is because intra-RSE represents communication within wider regions such as Europe and Asia, whereas Regional Standard Englishes serve as a pan-European or pan-Asian means of communication within respective regions.

At the top of the scale is EIL, which is the ultimate level of proficiency for cross-regional or international communication. It is 'a loose league of regional standard Englishes' (Yano 2001: 126). These Englishes are varieties of English with multi-ethnic, multicultural and multilingual local identities and yet with high international intelligibility. Consequently they are more pluricentric and therefore more accommodating than the presently dominant Anglo-American native speaker Englishes. In the distant future, all the cylinders are erased from Figure 13.2 below, but the upward arrow in the centre, indicating just the English proficiency level of individuals, remains.

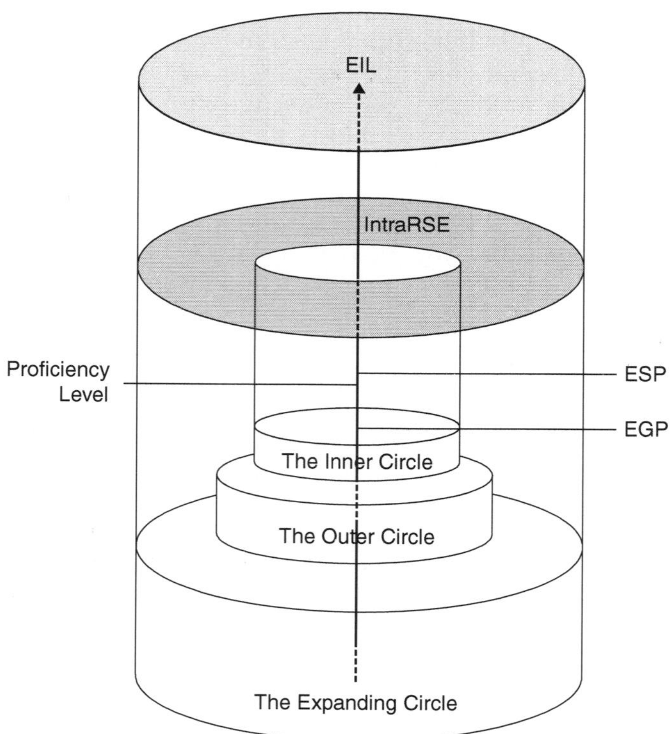

Figure 13.2 Three-dimensional model of English use (Yano 2007: 38)

English as an international language

What would be the function of English as an International Language? It will be a means to understand, interact with and express various cultures. In this point, the language policy of the EU is suggestive. In its *Common European Framework of Reference for Languages*, the Council of Europe states its principles as (2001: 2):

> ... that the rich heritage of diverse languages and cultures in Europe is a valuable common resource to be protected and developed, and that a major educational effort is needed to convert that diversity from a barrier to communication into a source of mutual enrichment and understanding;
>
> that it is only through a better knowledge of European modern languages that it will be possible to facilitate communication and interaction among Europeans of different mother tongues in order to promote European mobility, mutual understanding and co-operation, and overcome prejudice and discrimination;

The Council of Europe encourages all EU citizens to acquire a knowledge of the languages of other member states so that they can exchange information and ideas with speakers of different languages, communicate their thoughts and feelings to them, and achieve a wider and deeper understanding of the way of life and forms of thought of other peoples and of their cultural heritage. Accordingly, the EU has developed its' mother tongue plus two foreign languages' policy from Grade 1, and multilingual children are growing as is declared in the European Year of Languages 2001 (Kawahara and Yamamoto 2004: 98). However, the reality is that English is the *de facto* lingua franca in this multicultural and multilingual region (Marco Modiano, personal communication, 5 October 2007). It is a new variety of English transformed to a means of understanding, communicating and expressing European multi-cultures, not that of Anglo-American culture.

The 1998 survey conducted as part of a Eurobarometer study indicates that 47 per cent of the European Union population speaks English, although there are only 16 per cent native speakers. However, the percentage must be much higher by now. Phillipson (2007) grudgingly reports that continental European countries are transferring to the UK and Ireland about 16 to 17 billion Euro per annum in English learning (quoting Grin's (2005) research). However, I take it as a transitional phenomenon until they make English fit their own communicative situation. The making of Euro-English is under way, as you hear and read in radio and TV news, and newspapers and magazines, in business interactions, conferences and on the streets. Euro-English will be taught by European teachers, with their own materials and with their own methods. Europeanized English, or Euro-English, has a slight accent of European languages and artificial school-English-like tones, but is precise, clear and highly intelligible to international ears and eyes. In a sense, Euro-English speakers have an advantage over native speakers of mono-cultural English, who need to learn the strategies of cross-cultural communication. Whether Euro-English develops to be an institutionalized and codified variety remains speculative and can be confirmed in future generations of multilingual EU citizens.

Australia also presents an interesting model for the future use of English as an International Language. The country broke away from its traditional Britishism or 'White Australian policy' and took the post-war recruited immigration programme in order to populate the vast continent to defend, maintain and expand economic power. Lo Bianco (2003: 20–3) reports that the Adult Migrant English Program (AMEP) was the most successful language policy initiative and more than 40,000 new arrivals from nearly 90 language backgrounds from Europe, Asia, Latin America, the Middle East and Africa learned English under this programme in 2001, and more than 1.5 million since it commenced (Lo Bianco 2003: 7–8). In 2001, foreign-born Australians amount to 23.6 per cent of the total population and the English they learned functions as a language of many foreign cultures rather than that of Australian culture (Bunkacho 2003: 2).

What is going on in the European Union and Australia is that English is changing from the language of Anglo-American culture to that of a variety of cultures. In the process of the shift, English has come to be more regular, more pluricentric and more accommodating in order to attain high learnability and high useability for all learners. Phonologically, for example, pronunciation and spelling come closer as 'through' is increasingly spelled 'thru' as in the highway sign 'THRU TRAFFIC', 'GOOD THRU' on a credit card, and so on. This is good since spelling is supposed to reflect the pronunciation of the word. Jenkins (2000: 137–8, 2003: 126) argues that *th*-sounds need not be included in her phonological Lingua Franca Core, the basic sounds to learn in the English as a Lingua Franca (ELF), and has confirmed that communication is not blocked even if *th*-sounds are replaced by [s, z] or [t, d] among European speakers of English, based on her data collected from a wide range of contexts of several years. Morphologically, the irregular plural

Table 13.1 Regularization of irregular plural suffix

Singular	Plural (conventional)	Plural (new)
continuum	continua	continuums
corpus	corpora	corpuses
formula	formulae	formulas
spectrum	spectra	spectrums
syllabus	syllabi	syllabuses
symposium	symposia	symposiums

suffix of countable nouns of Greek/Latin origin is better replaced by the regular plural-s suffix. In some of the examples below (Table 13.1), new regularized plural forms are already in practice as we hear and read.

Syntactically, two-word verbs, idiomatic, metaphoric and proverbial expressions unique to Anglo-American culture have come to be used less and less. Tags of tag questions are becoming an invariant form, such as 'isn't it' in the Outer Circle. In standard English, tags take the opposite of positive or negative form of the verb in the main clause and agree with it in tense, number and person and that complexity causes difficulty for second and foreign language learners. This invariant form may become standard usage sooner than we expect as we find invariant forms in many languages such as *n'est-ce pas* in French, *nicht wahr* in German, *no* in Spanish and *ne* in Japanese. Whether [s, z, t, d] replace th-sounds and whether the invariant 'isn't it' comes to be the standard usage need to be confirmed in future users of English as an International Language.

In many parts of the English-speaking nations, people began pluralizing uncountable nouns such as advices, furnitures, luggages *and* properties, and omitting the third person singular present ending. The same linguistic phenomenon is going on among American youths. According to the survey undertaken by Nielsen/Net Rating, 60 per cent of the online population under the age of 17 use advices, furnitures and use the spelling, 'u, ur, r, wuz, cuz' for 'you, your, are, was, because' and 'b4 and 2' for 'before and two, too and to'. To the dismay of high school teachers, those teenagers began to use these 'conversational writing' spellings, which they use for instant messaging on mobile phones, web logs, and e-mail, in formal writing such as term papers ('US teenager's online lingua franca,' the *New York Times*, 21 September 2002).

Pluricentricity encourages us to change our perspective of English from the language of native speakers in their intra-national use to the language of speakers, native or not, in the international settings. This means to internationalize English and make it more accommodating for wider communication by de-Anglo-Americanizing and releasing the language and its use from the restriction of the Judeo-Christian tradition. For example, we can expand our greetings from 'How are you?' to 'Dressed up! Where are you going?' and 'Have you eaten yet?' depending on the given cultural settings, while the principle of showing 'the friendly concern' stays unchanged (see Morizumi, Park, this volume).

The 'written language' plays a crucial role to establish English as an International Language in that it standardizes vocabulary, word meaning and spelling as well as grammar. Through the written language, we can modify and standardize its linguistic features towards more general and more regular ones as a desirable EIL. The pronunciation–spelling agreement is desirable for English to grow to be a world language.

EIL will be socio-culturally more hybrid, more accommodating and more comprehensive in that it is a composite of elements drawn from other languages and cultures as it develops. English is no longer the sole property of native speakers. The language belongs to all those who learn it and use it. As English-knowing bi- or multilinguals (see also Jenkins 2003: 141–3), non-native speakers use the language as access to the wider world and as an added means of expression of themselves, their societies, their cultures and their identities. They keep equal distance from other cultures and communicate on an equal footing without discarding their national and cultural identities in order to assimilate themselves to Anglo-American culture. When the native-non-nativeness dichotomy is replaced by an individual person's proficiency, English language education will become extremely important.

English for general cultures vs. English for specific cultures?

Is it possible to think of English for Specific Cultures (ESC) as against English for General Cultures (EGC) by the analogy with EGP and ESP? From the pedagogic perspective, we may start teaching vocabulary items, expressions and grammatical rules which are what can be called culture-general and save idioms and other culture-specific expressions for later studies. As the candidate of EGC, for example, the following expressions have identical Japanese counterparts (Makino 2004):

> bitter experience, blood freezes, break the law/rules/promise, cold/warm colour, deep/shallow knowledge/sleep, can't believe one's eyes/

ears, close one's eyes to—, the flow of the time, be rotten to the core, sharp eyes/pain, will of iron, etc.

They are easy for the Japanese to understand and use because the same conceptualization is used in both languages. If we can classify words, phrases and sentences into EGC and ESC, we may teach expressions such as 'Do you have any valuables in your car?' and 'It's not fair' first and save such expressions as 'Have you any valuables in your car?' and 'It's not cricket' until the learners particularly need to learn British English. Or we teach 'I am nervous' as part of EGC, and later add 'I have butterflies in my stomach' or 'I have a mouse in my chest' when the learners are advanced enough to learn American and/or Asian English.

Will Chinese take over from English as an international language?

The more widely a language is used, the more powerful the language becomes. This is because more people use the language as access to more knowledge and information, as a means of communication with more people, and produce more cultural products using the language, and therefore, more people learn the language. However, Latin proved that it is not just the number of speakers that is important but also the power of those speakers. Romans did not outnumber the peoples they subjugated. It was their military, economic, technological and governing power that led other peoples to learn Latin, then the international language. Today, it is the power of English-speaking countries, especially the United States, which has led others to learn the language.

However, economists predict that the world's economic centre will shift from North America and Europe to Asia, especially China, India and ASEAN nations. They observe the rapid growth of the emerging economic superpowers called BRICs – Brazil, Russia, India and China. The 2003 analysis by Goldman Sachs estimates that 'If things go right, in less than 40 years, the BRICs economies together could be larger than the G6' (Graddol 2006: 32).

China, the world's factory, is the world's top exporter of products. Having vast cheap human resources, it has grown to a major international economic power and still its annual GDP growth rate is more than 10 per cent. With its $1 trillion foreign currency reserves, China's investment instantly influences the international financial world. And the popularity and power of a language follows the power of people who speak the language.

In 2002, China opened more than 200 Confucian Institutes overseas and dispatched teachers of the Chinese language. The Chinese government aims to bring up 100 million foreign speakers of Chinese overseas within the next five years (*Asahi Newspaper*, 26 April 2008). Since November 2006, the Chinese authorities require foreign top executives at securities firms to pass written and oral exams in Mandarin, the national tongue, so that they can communicate effectively with the Chinese staff, the government and investors (the *International Herald Tribune*, 24 August 2007). The government obviously intends to make Chinese a major international business language.

Will China's economy continue to grow at the present rate and allow Chinese to take over from English as an international language? I doubt it. China has to feed 1.3 billion people in order to keep its present productivity, and the country has already turned to the world's biggest food importer. Worse still, due to deforestation and desertification, the self-sufficiency ratio for food is rapidly going down. China also needs energy such as coal, oil and natural gas to maintain its productivity but its domestic supply is far from sufficient. There is a serious problem of income inequality between rural and urban areas as well. While 800 million peasants can hardly afford to keep food on their tables in rural areas, there are 25 million affluent city dwellers, younger and better-educated, with spending power of $117 billion in constant dollar terms (the *International Herald Tribune*, 14 August 2007). While President Hu Jintao emphasizes a 'harmonious society', the gap between China's rich and poor is widening. Filling the gap is an enormous task and it will slow down the economic growth. Another problem is that when a labourer's wages are raised, factories will move to Vietnam, Cambodia and other countries where labour cost is less. Still another issue is the government officials' scandals. The voice of China's growing middle class can no longer be ignored. Some also began raising questions about how state revenues were being spent, a subject that had scarcely ever entered public discussion. The Communist Party's hold on power may be under threat if they leave those scandals. And most importantly, China is urged to advance education for the entire nation, especially moral education to instil a sense of social responsibility in citizens and prevent exporting harmful products. When people are educated and become aware of social justice, they may threaten the present autocratic government. At any rate, it may take a long time for the Chinese language to be needed more than English as an international language.

India, the world's service centre, is another fast-rising economic power. According to *Asahi Newspaper* (11 February 2005), call centres in India assist US and European companies by filing their income tax return and taking care of legal matters. Outsourcing firms for the US and Europe in India have grown by 30 per cent annually for the past several years and has earned $17 billion. It is expected to grow at the same rate for years to come. With the rapid growth of the IT industry, India's GDP has continued to grow by 8 per cent a year. With its population of 1.1 billion, 70 per cent of which is extremely poor, however, India faces the same difficulties as China concerning food and energy supplies, income differences, infrastructure and education. Brazil and Russia have enormous natural and human resources and their potentiality may exceed the two top-running superpowers, China and India, in the long run. The ratio of younger people in the populations of Brazil and Russia seems to be higher than the other two and it promises secured human resources in these countries. If Chinese or other languages take over English as an international language, it will take decades or generations.

Conclusion

History proved that the spread of a language has always taken place when the users of the language grew to have 'power' – military, economic, technological, cultural or whatever. Whatever economists say, the Unites States still has power which leads other peoples to learn English. Today English is still the most widely used language and therefore the most taught foreign language. It has been incorporated into the primary school curriculum in many parts of the world. However, when and if the language becomes a basic skill for all, people will learn and use it not because the United States has power, but because it functions as a cross-cultural means of communication among English-knowing bi- and multilinguals of different ethnic, cultural and linguistic backgrounds, of different beliefs, worldviews, values, abilities, ideologies and of different educational backgrounds. The use of the language goes far beyond the function of communicating with its native speakers as is the case in learning most foreign languages other than English. It may not be pleasant for native speakers of English who feel English is their property, but the speakers of English as a lingua franca may not seek native speakers as a norm-provider any longer. That's the way English will be as an international language. In this sense what is going on in the EU, Australia and ASEAN nations is profoundly suggestive, the outcome of which may be the model of the future English as an International Language.

The nineteenth century was the century of military power. The twentieth century was that of economic power. Now the twenty-first century is the century of knowledge. We can never emphasize too much the importance of education, language education included.

Note

*This chapter is partly based on the author's presentation at the symposium of the 13th Conference of the International Association for World Englishes (IAWE) in Regensburg, Germany on 5 October 2007.

References

Asahi Newspaper, 26 April 2008.

Bunkacho (The Agency for Cultural Affairs). 2003, *Shogaikoku ni okeru Gaikokujin-ukeire-sisaku oyobi gaikokujin ni taisuru gengokyouiu-sisaku ni kansuru chosaken-shu-hokokusho (A report of investigation on foreign countries' policies of receiving foreigners and policies of language education for foreigners).* Tokyo: Bunkacho.

Cook, G. 2003. *Applied Linguistics*. Oxford: Oxford University Press.

Council of Europe. 2001. *Common European Framework of Reference for languages: Learning, teaching assessment.* Cambridge: Cambridge University Press.

Crystal, D. 2003. *English as a Global Language*, 2nd ed. Cambridge: Cambridge University Press.

Graddol, D. 2006. *English Next.* London: British Council. Foreign language skills in the European Union (Survey no. 50.0 – fieldwork Oct.–Nov. 1998 Standard Eurobarometer 50 – Fig. 6.11<http://europa.eu.int/comm/education/policies/lang/llanguages/index_en.html>

Grin, F. 2005. 'L'enseignement des langues étrangères comme politique publique.' *Rapport au Haut Conseil de l'évaluation de l'école* 19. (2005) 3 January 2006 <http://cisad.adc.education.fr/hcee/documents/rapport_Grin.pdf>

Honna, N. (ed.) 2002. *Sanseido Dictionary of Asian Englishes.* Tokyo: Sanseido.

Honna, N., Y. Takeshita, K. Higuchi and J. Saruhashi. 2008. Kokusai-hikaku de miru '"Eigo ga Tsukaeru Nihonjin" no Ikusei no tame no Kodo-keikaku' no Seika ni Kansuru Chosa-kenkyu Hokokusho*: (A Report on International Comparative Studies of 'Action Plan to Foster the Japanese with English Competene.'*). Tokyo: Aoyama Gakuin University.

International Herald Tribune, 11 February 2005; 14 and 24 August 2007.

Jenkins, J. 2000. *The Phonology of English as an International Language.* Oxford: Oxford University Press.

——. 2003. *World Englishes: A resource book for students.* London: Routledge.

Kachru, B. B. 1985. 'Standards, codification and sociolinguistic realism: the English language in the outer circle.' In R. Quirk and H. G. Widdowson (eds) *English in the World: Teaching and learning the language and literatures.* Cambridge: Cambridge University Press.

——. 2005. *Asian Englishes beyond the Canon.* Hong Kong: Hong Kong University Press.

Kachru, B. B. (ed.) 1992. *The Other Tongue: English across Cultures*, 2nd ed., Urbana, IL: University of Illinois Press.

Kachru, Y. and C. L. Nelson. 2006. *World Englishes in Asian Contexts*, Hong Kong: Hong Kong University Press.

Kawahara, T. and T. Yamamoto. 2004. *Tagengo-shakai ga yattekita (Multi-lingual Society Has Come)*. Tokyo: Kuroshio Shuppan.

Lo Bianco, J. 2003. 'A site for debate, negotiation and contest of national identity: language policy in Australia.' In *Guide for the development of language education policies in Europe: from linguistic diversity to plurilingual education*. Strasbourg: Council of Europe, 1–35.

Makino, S. 2004. 'Doo-bunka-shiron (On Pan-Culture).' Lecture at the Annual Symposium of the Japan Association of Teaching Language and Culture. (31 July, Waseda University, Tokyo.)

New York Times, 21 September 2002.

Phillipson, R. 2007. 'The new linguistic imperial order: lessons from Europe of worldwide relevance.' *5th Nitobe Symposium: European Languages and Asian nations: History, Politics, Possibilities*. Sophia University, Tokyo (2–3 August).

Seidlhofer, B. 2004. 'Research Perspectives on Teaching English as a Lingua Franca', *Annual Review of Applied Linguistics* 24, 209–39.

U.S. Department of Commerce Census Bureau. 2005. 'Annual Estimates of the Population by Sex, Race and Hispanic or Latino Origin for the United States: April 1, 2000 to July 1, 2004.'

Widdowson, H. G. 2003. *Defining Issues in English Language Teaching*. Oxford: Oxford University Press.

Yano, Y. 2001. 'World Englishes in 2000 and beyond.' *World Englishes*, 20(2), 119–31.

——. 2007. 'English as an International Language: Its Past, Present, and Future.' In M. Nakano (ed.) *On-Demand Internet Course Book: World Englishes and Miscommunications*. Tokyo: Waseda University International, 27–42.

Index